SUCH IS
MY LOVE

Joseph Pequigney

SUCH IS MY LOVE

A Study of Shakespeare's Sonnets

The University of Chicago Press

Chicago & London

JOSEPH PEQUIGNEY is professor of English
at the State University of New York at
Stony Brook.

THE UNIVERSITY OF CHICAGO PRESS, CHICAGO 60637
THE UNIVERSITY OF CHICAGO PRESS, LTD., LONDON

© 1985 by The University of Chicago

94 93 92 91 90 89 88 87 86   5432

Library of Congress Cataloging in Publication Data

Pequigney, Joseph.
  Such is my love.
  Includes index.
  1. Shakespeare, William, 1564–1616. Sonnets.
2. Sonnets, English—History and criticism.
3. Erotic poetry, English—History and criticism.
4. Homosexuality, Male in literature. I. Title.
PR2848.P46 1985   821'.3   85-984
ISBN 0-226-65563-6

For Steven Mays

"be most proud of that which I compile,
Whose influence is thine and born of thee."

Contents

Acknowledgments

When I consider those for whose help or encouragement in doing this book I owe the most gratitude, the following persons come first to mind: my departmental colleagues Thomas Maresca and Richard Levin; the students in honors and graduate courses in English at Stony Brook with whom I read the Sonnets; my late mother, Margaret Dugey Pequigney, and Cathy Cashion, my niece; and Audre Proctor, who rectified what she cheerfully typed. I benefited, besides, from the release-time program of the English Department at Stony Brook and from access, as a member of the Washington Square community, to the facilities of the Elmer Holmes Bobst Library of New York University.

Who will believe my verse in time to come?

—Sonnet 17

1

Introduction

To rank Shakespeare's Sonnets with his major achievements and to count some of them among the finest love poems in the language are unexceptionable evaluations, despite the curious fact that the foremost subject of the sequence is a love between men. This fact has always posed a problem for editors, critics, and scholars: the problem of protecting the work and its author from the embarrassment and scandal of homosexuality. The vast majority have found a solution in various stratagems designed to underpin a categorical denial of any perversity whatever in the sonneteer's friendship with the handsome youth. In recent decades, however, some bolder spirits have perceived an "erotic" quality in the friendship, but this quality proves vague and elusive; for it does not affect the poet's sexual conduct or even his desires, which remain, as do the friend's, wholly heterosexual. Moreover, the critical perception turns out, in every case, to have little or no effect on textual exegesis. This minority position, as I see it, essentially conforms with the one taken by the majority of the commentators.

The stand I take on the question of eroticism is hardly one of conformity, for I argue (1) that the friendship treated in Sonnets 1–126 is decidedly amorous—passionate to a degree and in ways not dreamed of in the published philology, the interaction between the friends being sexual in both orientation and practice; (2) that verbal data are clear and copious in detailing physical intimacies between them; (3) that the psychological dynamics of the poet's relations with the friend comply in large measure with those expounded in Freud's authoritative discussions of homosexuality; and (4) that Shakespeare produced not only extraordinary amatory verse but the grand masterpiece of homoerotic poetry.

These proposals do not exhaust my motive, which is to lead the reader to reexamine other aspects of the Sonnets as well. A second major thesis, of no less importance than the one described above and closely bound up with it, is that the received arrangement of the poems—received from the first edition—is accurate. The commentaries are rife with objections to this arrangement, and, even when it is sometimes countenanced, it is usually viewed with skepticism and is never demonstrably confirmed. I seek to demonstrate, mainly by scrutiny of evidence internal to the text, that the Sonnets are well and meaningfully organized in the originating Quarto and, on that basis, to maintain that Shakespeare, in addition to writing the great individual poems, incorporated them into the greatest of all love-sonnet sequences.

Shake-speares Sonnets, Never Before Imprinted was the title given the Quarto published by T. T. in 1609. The title does not rule out, but instead implies, their prior circulation in manuscript form. None of the manuscripts survives, however, and a mere thirteen copies of the first edition are extant. We are very much beholden to Thomas Thorpe, for without him the poems would have vanished, leaving hardly a trace behind.[1] One might expect him to be duly honored; he has instead been censured for putting out an unauthorized edition of the Sonnets and for muddling their authorial organization. Both charges are unprovable: the evidence for the first is inadequate and, for the second, arbitrary. While I do not plan specifically to essay a defense of Thorpe, a defense of him will be implicit throughout.

The Quarto (hereafter Q) did not have a true second edition for close to a hundred years. It was, some thirty years after it first appeared, subjected to treatment ironically similar to the treatment that Shakespeare's script supposedly suffered from Thorpe—that is, to piracy and derangement. John Benson published, in 1640, *Poems: Written by Wil. Shake-speare,* which included a corrupt version of the sonnet sequence. He used the text of Q but, apparently to conceal that fact, omitted eight of the sonnets, interspersed alien lyrics among them, and reshuffled them extensively.[2] He reprinted the remaining one hundred forty-six sonnets as seventy-two "poems," each furnished with a title and each consisting of a single sonnet or a combination of two, three, four, or five. If Benson is noteworthy, it is not for any merit his volume has but for its precocious and prophetic defects. He may be seen as the first of a long line, extending to the present day, of rearrangers of Q's disposition of the poems. He may also be seen as the first of those who attempt to safeguard the Sonnets from the imputation of sexual inversion. He was not above tampering with the diction by changing pronouns from masculine to feminine or the gender reference of nouns, as when "love" (in the sense of 'lady beloved') replaces "friend" at 104.1 and "boy" at 108.5, and certain of the titles he devised had the purpose of converting the object of address from a man to a woman; for example, the heading of Sonnets 113–15 is "Selfe flattery of *her* beauty," and that of 122 is "Upon . . . a Table Booke from his *Mistress*." Those who since have shared his goal, however, adopt less disingenuous means than altering words and obtruding misleading titles.

In 1711 the Quarto itself was finally, and faithfully, reprinted in a two-volume collection of Shakespeare's poems published by Bernard Lintot. The title page asserts that "The Second Volume contains One Hundred and Fifty Four Sonnets, all of them to his Mistress." This, though impossibly naive, once more bespeaks early anxiety about the cycle's probity. Further and improved editions appeared throughout the eighteenth century, culminating in 1780 and 1790 with those produced by Edmund Malone, who, Hyder Rollins tells us, "gave the first really important critical text of the sonnets . . . and (with the aid of Steevens and others) the first commentary."[3]

In the two centuries since then the editorial, scholarly, and critical commentary has swollen to massive proportions. Yet it readily lends itself to succinct recapitulation. This suggests the weighty influence the expositors exert on one another and the restricted scope of their disagreement. But that they are more in unison about what questions to raise than about how these questions should be resolved is apparent in the following composite account, which is derived from the mainstream of the commentary.

Sonnets 1–126 "seem to" concern the older poet's, or Shakespeare's, friendship with a young nobleman. These sonnets (a) deal solely with him or (b) they may not, since in some of them he may be tacitly displaced by another or others, male or female. The love for him is (a) decent, "natural," nonamorous, as Sonnet 20 patently affirms, the friendship being of a conscious, idealized, "platonic," and now archaic type that flourished in the Renaissance; or else the love is (b) tinged with some kind of inactive eroticism. While Sonnets 127–54 focus on the passion for the dark lady, and while she figures in Sonnets 40–42, she is taken to figure also in a number of other sonnets before 127; for a triangle that encompasses the three principals, and entails intercourse between her and the friend, is the salient occurrence of the sequence and is the chief or exclusive cause of the jealousy that periodically racks the poet. Again, the fair friend and the dark lady, along with the rival poet referred to in Sonnets 78–86, (a) are wholly fictitious, or (b) are depictions of real but unknown persons, or (c) admit of historical identifications.[4] In the case of (c), speculation centers mostly on the youth, who is surmised to be either the earl of Southampton or the earl of Pembroke or, occasionally, some other nobleman. Marlowe and Chapman are the leading candidates for the role of the literary rival; the lady has generally fared less well in generating a historical counterpart.[5] Regardless of whether the incidents and interpersonal transactions rendered are actual or imaginary, everything comes through as uncertain or indistinct because the Quarto, unauthorized and unsupervised by Shakespeare, (a) prints the Sonnets in a version to be understood as disarranged to a greater or lesser extent; or (b) the order of the poems in Q must be accepted in lieu of a more satisfactory alternative; or (c) the lost original order may be reconstructed by astute transpositions.

These stock postulations are, in my judgment, dubious for the most part, and few will go uncontested. I do agree that all of the first one hundred twenty-six sonnets deal with the poet's response to one and the same friend. I also agree that the friend, the rival poet, and the woman may well correspond to historical persons, but I think that none of the three has been, or is ever likely to be, identified. I also think that those commentators who allow for an erotic element in the poet's attachment to the young man and for the validity of the traditional order of the sonnets are on the right track, but their positions may still be criticizable, whether for conceptual and exegetical deficiencies or for adopting a merely conjectural approach to issues that are both crucial and capable of being resolved.

On other matters my findings will counter established opinion more directly. There is no reason to hold that the youth is a nobleman, and the text furnishes grounds for controverting the familiar assumption that he is. I will bring into question his heterosexuality and seduction by the mistress, prove that the poet carnally enjoys him as well as her, and uncover a sexual basis for the rivalry with the second poet. The widely propounded theory that the Sonnets exemplify a cult of "Renaissance friendship" will not withstand inspection. In Sonnets 1–126, where the unremitting object of attention is the young man, the mistress plays a very minor role; only three sonnets, 40–42, allude to her, and only in them, prior to Sonnet 127, do the repeated eruptions of jealousy and suspicion have relevance to her.

My account of the standard commentary leaves out the readings given to individual sonnets in whole or in part. Interpreters are conditioned and sometimes inhibited by confinement within the usual perimeters, described above. My readings, because undertaken without the same set of preconceptions and imperatives, will often differ from theirs, sometimes radically.

To expose accumulated misconstructions is, while requisite to this study, subordinate to its chief aim. That aim is to execute a searching and persuasive exposition of Shakespeare's Sonnets, one elucidative of their aesthetic coherence, their moral values, and their psychological depths.

One of several striking features peculiar to this Renaissance love-sonnet sequence is its bipartite structure. The first, longer, and paramount division, which comprises Sonnets 1–126 and is devoted to the friend, is here to be designated Part I; the remainder, Sonnets 127–54, about the affair with the mistress, will be denominated Part II. The two parts, besides varying in length and topicality, will be shown to present contrasts of a thematic, durational, and organizational character. Part I has three divisions, corresponding to the three distinct phases of the growth of love (Sonnets 1–19), its maturity (Sonnets 20–99), and its decline (Sonnets 100–126), or to a beginning (discussed in chapter 2), a middle (discussed in chapters 3–6), and an end (discussed in chapter 9). Part II—the twenty-eight sonnets of which are coordinated on quite different principles—will be discussed in chapters 7 and 8, that is, before, rather than after, the closing phase of Part I. This plan reflects a thesis (argued in chapter 7) that the action dramatized in Part II is concurrent with the episode of Sonnets 40–42 and hence takes place early in the middle period of Part I.

Common to both parts and preeminent throughout is the sonneteering "I," whose voice alone is heard from start to finish, whose mechanism of response engages the diverse situations, whose point of view rules, and whose "fine intelligence, either as agent or as the object of action or as both,"[6] is the lifeblood of the whole. Nowhere else does Shakespeare create such a first-person figure as the fixed center of consciousness—not in the plays, obviously, or in the narrative poems, where the narrator has an ancillary and more peripheral function. If he ever wrote autobiographically, he did so here. Can we then equate the fictive composer of the sonnets, significantly named Will in Sonnets 135, 136, and at 57.13, with that (William) Shake-speare named on the title page of the Quarto, who in truth composed the Sonnets? There are reasons to think that we might, and later they will be adduced in full; but since outside documentary corroboration is lacking, no certainty on the matter is attainable. It is this uncertainty that prompts me normally to use such terms as *speaker, persona,* or *poet* rather than *Shakespeare.*

The friend too is called Will—at 135.1–2 and 143.14. He may well be the Mr. W. H. of Thorpe's opaque dedication in Q. If so—and "that eternity / promised / by / our ever-living poet" is never promised otherwise than in verse to him—we would learn something more than the initial of his surname: that he was an actual person

and was not a peer.[7] But the appellation is too unwieldly and contro-
versial to be regularly employed. And I consider the familiar name
Will, for the persona and the youth alike, to be usable only in special
contexts. For their part, the mistress and the rival poet do not admit
of proper names at all, textually or extratextually.

The period of composition is not a major concern here, but I shall
broach it occasionally and incidentally and shall find many reasons
to place composition in the last few years of the sixteenth century
and the first years of the seventeenth.

The Sonnets will be cited from the edition that W. C. Ingram and
Theodore Redpath first brought out in 1964.[8] It is in my opinion the
most perspicaciously annotated and, all in all, the most praisewor-
thy one since Hyder Rollins's monumental variorum edition, published in two volumes in 1944, a prodigious feat of scholarship and a
mine of erudition. The notes in Rollins, as befits a variorum, are
largely a compilation of those of earlier commentators, and he re-
prints Q exactly.[9] Ingram and Redpath modernized the spelling and
punctuation, a course that I decided, after some hesitation, is also
advisable for this study. They, like most of the recent editors, are
more respectful of the 1609 text than their predecessors generally
were—more restrained in emending and more willing to abide by
the rule that grants a privileged status to a first edition, particularly
to one, such as this, that is the sole source of the work. Even so, I
will often modify the citations, usually silently, to the end of bringing them still closer to the originals. Again like the other recent
editors, they are also less reticent about glossing the sexual allusions in Part II. But those in Part I, relative to the sexual passion
between males, everywhere go unremarked, even by the glossarists
of Shakespeare's bawdy language, such as E. A. M. Coleman and Eric
Partridge.[10] Still, to the latter I am, as to the three editors mentioned
above, under a heavy obligation.

2

The Beginning
(Sonnets 1–19)

All nineteen sonnets of the opening movement give expression to one compelling case, that of saving from time and wrack the rare and ravishing beauty of the youth addressed. The first mode of preservation entertained is procreation, which is urged without letup in the first fourteen poems and twice again, almost immediately; this gives way in Sonnet 15 and thereafter to the second mode, which is perpetuation through verse. That Shakespeare's love-sonnet sequence begins in this way—and continues in this way for so long a stretch—poses a problem.

My investigation of this problem will entail looking into the arguments adopted (and those omitted) for propagation; into how, why, and with what result the alternative of poetic immortalization is later substituted; and into a number of complementary developments. Sonnets 1–19 exhibit a complex of abiding and changing attitudes toward the youth, such as the abiding awe of his looks and regard for his sexuality, and then the attitudes of respect and affection that come with the commencement and burgeoning of reciprocal male love. This love, gradually disclosed in these initial sonnets, becomes the dominant subject of Part I. These sonnets also shed light, as they progress, on various overriding interests, including the friend's social status and the poet's ethical and religious outlook, and they quietly and deftly serve to draw attention to the holistic nature of the sequence.

Shakespeare's Sonnets hardly look promising as a holistic work when Sonnet 1 is perused. It lacks the introductory features regularly found at the outset of other Renaissance love-sonnet cycles—*Astrophel and Stella*, for instance, or *Amoretti*. It makes no reference to love, or a lady, or verse, or the muse, or the poet himself, and, instead of stating some overall intent, it presents an argument that is curious, autonomous, and disorienting:

> From fairest creatures we desire increase,
> That thereby beauty's *Rose* might never die,
> But as the riper should by time decease,

His tender heir might bear his memory:
But thou, contracted to thine own bright eyes,
Feed'st thy lights' flame with self-substantial fuel,
Making a famine where abundance lies,
Thy self thy foe, to thy sweet self too cruel:
Thou that art now the world's fresh ornament,
And only herald to the gaudy spring,
Within thine own bud buriest thy content,
And, tender churl, mak'st waste in niggarding:
    Pity the world, or else this glutton be—
    To eat the world's due, by the grave and thee.[1]

Ushered into a *terra incognita*, we overhear someone, with a pressing sense of mortality that marks him as older, attempt to persuade another, who is young and fair, to propagate. And the other turns out to be a male. Line 11 gives the merest hint of this, for the "content" (as 'contents') kept buried within the "bud" of himself is something generative when brought forth and so seems to allude to his seed; but the hint is soon confirmed, if not in the next sonnet then, undeniably, in the third.

The discourse is not without some slight resemblance to that of Petrarchan poets, first in its lavish praise of personal beauty, though masculine, even to adducing the usual "bright eyes," and then in intermixing the praise with blame for, in effect, refusing sexual relations. The differences, to be sure, are far more conspicuous. Intercourse, which is now implied but is soon noted overtly, is to be engaged in not with the speaker but with some unspecified female. If some other sonneteer did strive for sexual gratification (as Astrophel does, though atypically), reproduction was definitely not the objective. Moreover, the lady in Renaissance sonnets, because she is lovely, arouses carnal desire, but, because she is chaste, virtuously disallows its indulgence. The male beauty of Shakespeare's Sonnet 1, however, is not virtuous in declining copulation but at fault, since youth and comeliness make it incumbent upon him to procreate. Hence he can be accused, in the paradox of 1.12, of squandering by hoarding ("waste in niggarding") and, in the implicit allusion to Narcissus in 1.5–6, of self-absorption.

The speaker's complimentary and censorious attitudes are outgrowths of his fondness for the young man, a feeling defined by the phrase "thy sweet self" in 1.8. Is he then being avuncular, a wise friend, a busybody? And yet do any of these roles jibe with the undivided attention he gives to the other's astonishing semblance? In any case, this fondness is far removed from the impassioned responses of the poet-lover who in other cycles woos his mistress with sonnets—far removed for the time being, at any rate. The gap, as Shakespeare's sequence continues, gradually closes and, with Sonnet 20, disappears.

Sonnet 1 does—as, reading on, one comes retrospectively and ever more fully to realize—serve an introductory function after all, at least for Part I, and, if it does so unconventionally, it might on that very account be seen as a befitting way to begin the least conventional of Renaissance love-sonnet sequences. What it does is to inaugurate: (1) a profusion of metaphorical motifs that will recur in upcoming sonnets, particularly in the next fourteen or so; (2) the concepts of beauty and time and their interrelationship, as also the emblem of the rose, all of which carry weight in Part I; and (3) the theme of reproduction, to be taken up in all except one of the sixteen ensuing poems.

The metaphors come on thick and fast in Sonnet 1 and employ a diversity of vehicles: flowers/vegetation, inheritance, betrothal, famine/food/eating, fuel and flames, the season of spring, and the hoarding of wealth. This is a store of figures that later sonnets will draw upon. For example, tropes taken from hoarding, along with spending, show up again in Sonnets 4 and 6 and at 2.5–12, 9.9–12, and 13.13, and they sometimes merge with the additional tropes from inheritance found at 2.12, 4.14, and 6.13. Other conceits based on flowers, now those distilled for perfume, occur in 5.13–14 and 6.1–4, while vegetal-seasonal conceits recur, for example, at 3.9–10, 5.5–8, 6.1–2, 12.2–12, and 15.5–8. Such schemes of repeated imagery operate as a linking device among sonnets, especially among the earlier ones. The pattern is obvious, has been sufficiently noticed in commentaries, and need detain us here only long enough to point out that Sonnet 1, by virtue of its unusual vehicular diversity, in conjunction with its position, presents more metaphorical motifs that are subsequently picked up and developed than any other sonnet does.

Two key concepts for Part I, though negligible for Part II, are signified by the abstract nouns *beauty* and *time* in the initial quatrain of the Sonnets (1.1–4). Time, which later is frequently personified (in Sonnet 19, for example) and is sometimes also granted, in passing, a beneficent side (for example, at 60.5–8 or 65.9–10), is viewed here, and most often in Part I, as a destructive element. Beauty is vulnerable to time but not helpless—not initially, in any case— since it has recourse to reproductive "increase" for survival; and, rather than being personified (except in rare instances, such as 65.3 or 106.3), it is normally imagined as incarnate in the person of the youth. To save his resplendent self in some way from the relentlessness of time is long the persona's project, but one that he gives up in the end. When one comes to see the opening four verses of Part I in relation to its closing twelve verses—those of Sonnet 126, where "my lovely boy" is finally surrendered, defenseless, to Time's devastation—one finds the overall structure of the Sonnets adumbrated.[2]

The very first image of the sonnet cycle is "beauty's *Rose*" at 1.2, and it is thus capitalized and italicized in the Quarto. That the rose stands for beauty is made explicit by the possessive form of that word, and that it stands for the other's beauty is underscored when he is represented as a flower in 1.9–11. He is "the world's *fresh* ornament," the "only [floral] herald of the gaudy spring," and a "bud" (from the prior context almost surely a *rose*bud). The rose, which is also variously associated with him in Sonnets 67, 95, 98, and 99 and is his analogue in Sonnet 54, is climactically identified with him in the fervent utterance at the close of Sonnet 109:

> For nothing this wide universe I call,
> Save thou my Rose: in it thou art my all.

That an idea in Sonnet 1 should undergo this kind of elaboration may by now come as no surprise; what may surprise is that the rose, a well-established female symbol, is made emblematic of a male.

Sonnet 1 initiates the theme of procreation treated in sixteen of the first seventeen sonnets, and it does so in a way that is in line with its lead-off position. The premise enunciated in the first quatrain underlies all the arguments to reproduce, but here, and only here, it is stated in universal terms, as applicable to all "fairest creatures," or to all things, human and other, that are subject to the organic processes of growth and decay. Of course it is "we"—that is, mankind—who "desire increase," who wish consciously for beauty's survival, and in other species as well as our own. With "But thou," however, at 1.5, this all-inclusive principle is restricted not only to man but to the one man addressed, and from this point on, through Sonnet 17, that restricted application prevails.

"Persuasions to breed" is my preferred term for these sonnets: *persuasion* to indicate their direction and intent, and "breed" because the word occurs twice in the text, as a noun at 12.14, signifying 'offspring,' and as a verb at 6.7, signifying 'reproduce.'

The reason why the young man must be persuaded to breed is plainly and simply his physical splendor. The point implied in the opening verse—that it is only "From *fairest* creatures," not from others, that we seek progeny—is further elucidated at 11.9–12:

> Let those whom nature hath not made for store—
> Harsh, featureless, and rude—barrenly perish;

> Look, whom she best endow'd she gave the more;
> Which bounteous gift thou shouldst in bounty cherish.

"Store" = 'breeding,' which nature intends only for beautiful people, not for the homely, whose exclusion from it warrants the
execration "Let those . . . barrenly perish." The idea might be
termed aesthetic eugenics. Professor Edward Hubler took Shakespeare's thesis to be conformable to the Catholic stand on birth control,[3] but that would be so only if the Church's object were to
promote beauty of the flesh.

Most of the arguments designed to induce the apparently disinclined young man to breed are of two broad types, those based on
prudence and those based on moral obligation.

The prudential persuasions appeal to enlightened self-interest and
often lay emphasis on old age. For example, the youth should take
care to avoid the social stigma that attaches to being old and childless
(2.5–12). Or, children can be a source of consolation to the elderly
parent (Sonnets 2 and 3). But this consolation has nothing to do
with receiving filial affection and succor in old age; it comes from
beholding one's own former vitality and good looks renewed in one's
offspring. Or, again, the other is entreated over and over, from the
couplet of Sonnet 1 to Sonnet 13, to act in time, before age debilitates
and death undoes him. Or, analogies are drawn, most fully in Sonnets
4 and 6, between the uses of capital and of corporal perfection to point
out that the possessor of either successfully deploys his resources,
financial or sexual, only when they breed a profitable return.

The second type of persuasion, the moralistic, invokes the order
of nature. Nature, personified as the divinity who created human
beings and is therefore venerable, imposes the duty to breed. Her
"bequest" of beauty, at 4.3–4, "gives nothing but doth lend, / And
being frank she lends to those are free" (both "frank" and "free"
mean 'liberal, generous'); consequently the "bounteous largess" bestowed on the youth is "given thee to give"—reproductively.
Nature, at 11.9–14, has made some—not everyone—to be breeders
("for store"), and them she has "best endow'd," both to equip them
for a progenitive vocation and to impress them with bounty. The
couplet, depicting her as a sculptress, stipulates her end:

> She carv'd thee for her seal, and meant thereby
> Thou shouldst print more, not let the copy die—

where "copy," along with "seal," denotes the stamp or other device
that "prints" facsimiles.

Along with the debt to Nature go the obligations due other people. These may be general: to "the world," which means 'everybody,

all humanity' when the point is made at 1.13–14, 3.4, and 9.3–6. Elsewhere the responsibility is more narrowly conceived. In shirking propagation, the youth, at 9.13, holds "no love toward others," those with whom he has personal ties; and at 10.13 the persona's plea is on his own behalf: "Make thee another self for love of me."

No less fascinating and illuminating than the arguments the persuasions to breed enlist are those they exclude. It is always taken for granted that the young man is of noble birth, but nowhere do these sonnets suggest any such thing. They might easily have done so; they might have urged his responsibilities to his family, to hand on a great name, to enable the passage of a title or property along bloodlines, to provide for the maintenance of an ancestral house. True, he is pressed not to "let so fair a house fall to decay" (13.9), but this is a *fleshly*, not a *familial* house; it is his "bone-house," and his scion will inherit a wealth of personal beauty. No other form of inheritance is ever mentioned. Though negative, the evidence is telling. And where in the Sonnets is his nobility asserted?

Christian doctrine is notably absent. Yahweh's injunction in Genesis 1:28, to "be fruitful and multiply," delivered to our first parents and their descendants one and all, cries out for inclusion, but it is not here. It is not God's will but Nature's that should be done, and hers is to reserve the job of engendering to the best-looking specimens. This is a reflection of the persona's concern, which, quasi-Darwinian, is with the survival of the fairest and, more specifically, with the genetic survival of the fairest one of all, the exquisite youth.

Wedlock is rarely referred to, and the Book of Genesis (2:18, 24) is ignored on this subject too. These sonnets say nothing about matrimony as divinely instituted or sacramental, nor do they advance such reasons as wedded love, lifelong companionship, or sexual need for entering into it. The word "husbandry" comes into wordplay twice, at 3.6 and 13.10, both times with 'husband' as the *secondary* sense and both times in the context of importuning procreating. Sonnet 8, at least through its first twelve lines, appears to be exceptional in commending marriage per se; here musical and marital harmonies are likened, the "mutual ordering" of lute strings is seen as "Resembling sire, and child, and happy mother," and the hearer—himself "Music to hear"—"confounds / In singleness [= bachelorhood] the parts that thou shouldst bear"—the parts of "husband" as well as "sire." But the couplet brings this sonnet into line with the rest, for it concludes with "Thou single will prove none," which is to say, 'unwed, hence unreproductive, you will become no one / nothing, extinct,' and the celibate state is to be eschewed for that and no other reason.

For women, however, the situation is something else. They have sexual yearnings for the youth. None would "disdain" his "tillage" of her "womb" (3.5–6). These girls have a strong maternal instinct and can find emotional fulfillment in marriage, can become the "happy mother" in the family circle at 8.11, where "happy" qualifies her alone, not "child" or "sire."[4] Virtually any young virgin can fill the bill, so completely does her reproductive function overshadow her personal attributes, even her looks. Her fairness in any case matters little, for the arguments assume it to be genetically untransmissible and that the children will resemble their father, even though he himself favors his mother (3.9–10). The one desired by many a maiden evinces desire for none. But no matter—a wife is principally a requirement for keeping his own beauty alive. The attitude taken toward women here is objectionable, and, more often than not, it is so elsewhere in Shakespeare's Sonnets.

No more than conjugal love is paternal love urged as an incentive to breed. At the opposite pole from the Shakespearean view of progeny is Spenser's, put forward in the prayer that closes *Epithalamion*.[5] There the poet beseeches the heavenly "powers" that he and his bride "may raise a large posterity," which, though a blessing, is not regarded as primarily of benefit to the parents, and the father-to-be has in mind not his own survival in children but their independent well-being; for them he wants a long, happy, and meritorious life in this world, followed by an eternal reward in the next. Moreover, he gives no thought to the semblance of his offspring; for him the ultimate goal of propagation is to augment the celestial society of sainted souls.[6] Shakespeare's persona shows no such interest in the welfare and salvation of offspring; he posits no other end for generation than to conserve on earth and among men as much as possible of the mutable bodily beauty of the begetter.

The persuasions to breed are frequently styled "marriage sonnets," which gives the misimpression that their prime purpose is to endorse and recommend matrimony. The misnomer is one among many attempts by expositors—well-intentioned, no doubt—to improve the moral tone of Shakespeare's sequence in order to make it more palatable to themselves and other right-minded people.

The beauty of the young body is never disassociated from its sexuality, and the persona, all along, is intrigued by both. When he says at 11.11–12,

> Look, whom she best endow'd she gave the more;
> Which bounteous gift thou shouldst in bounty cherish,

he refers, according to Ingram and Redpath, to "creatures given by Nature *the most generative vitality*" and to the "gift" of *procreation*.

Well, perhaps—unless Shakespeare had something more specific in mind, and "the more" and the "bounteous gift," synonymous, refer to the male member, the part most apposite to generation; then to "cherish" it "in bounty" is to make liberal use of it. This reading is reinforced by Sonnet 20. There Nature "wrought" the youth, as she "carv'd" him at 11.13, and "fell a-doting" on him, whereupon she endowed him not with 'generative vitality' or the 'gift of procreation' but, more concretely, with a phallic "thing."

Shakespeare manages to evoke that same "thing" in Sonnet 16, as he did in 11, indirectly, without naming it. "To fortify yourself in your decay" is the problem, and the solution comes in the sestet, where a witty, complex conceit is fashioned from these elements: a portraitist's delineation of the youth with a "pencil" (= a thin brush), the poet's depiction of him in lines of verse from his "pupil pen,"[7] and his own sexual self-reproduction in offspring. Then, needed to "repair" (= renovate) his sometime decaying "life" are the "lines of life," which signify genealogical lineage, lines of descent, yes; but the phrase carries a more general sense that I think is primary, with "lines" defined (OED V, 26) as preservative 'courses,' generative 'directions,' sexual 'routes' taken by ongoing "life."[8] These biological "lines" latently connote the graphic and metrical lines that the artist and poet produce by pencil and pen. What then is the corresponding progenitive implement that traces or writes the living lines? It is the genital organ. The pencil is associated with the pen, and—as in wordplay elsewhere in Shakespeare, glossed by Partridge, Coleman, and others—the pen with the penis. The couplet continues in this vein: "To give yourself away [seminally] keeps yourself still [= always], / And you must live drawn by your own sweet skill." In other words, you must make a self-portrait, one that will be more skillfully done than any painted or verbal likeness—a kind of *tableau vivant* ("*live* drawn"); and the drawing instrument is, once more, implicitly the penis.

The subject matter, breeding, affords ready opportunity for imagining the young man's engaging in sexual relations. At 3.5–6 we read of the "unear'd womb" awaiting "the tillage of thy husbandry." Partridge, glossing "husbandry" as a pun on 'husband,' notes "the seeding-cultivation-harvesting metaphor in Shakespeare when he wishes to speak of semen-sowing and sexual tillage." He wishes to do so again in the second quatrain of Sonnet 16, where "many maiden gardens, yet unset," gladly "would bear your living flowers."[9] In Sonnet 6 he is the flower that in "thy summer [prime of life]" should—as blossoms are distilled for perfume—"be distill'd" of his seminal fluid. With it he can "make sweet some vial" and "treasure . . . some place / With beauty's treasure." The "place" and the glass (cf. 5.10) "vial" are the womb.[10] In the phrase "make sweet," the adjective denotes more than 'fragrant,' for it can suggest also 'the sweet pleasure of sexual intimacy' (Partridge). "Treasure" as a noun = 'semen' (Partridge) and so as a verb means here not only 'enrich' but also 'inseminate.'

"Beauty's treasure" brings up another metaphor for coitus, the one in 6.5–10 (as also in 2.5–8 and 9.9–12) in which financial and sexual transactions are made analogous. The key word in this connection is "use" in the double sense of 'pecuniary investment' and 'sexual employment or enjoyment' (Partridge, Coleman). The former sense normally operates at the figurative, the latter at the literal, level. The affiliated word "usury" can, besides referring to moneylending, refer to 'sexual indulgence or intercourse' (Partridge). And, corresponding to the capital sum to be laid out in the economic sphere, the fecund beauty is to be coitally disbursed in the biogenetic sphere.

The procreative intercourse that he seems reluctant to undertake is not the only form of sexual activity imagined for the youth. There is another form, one that he is suspected of practicing at present and by himself, and it is most fully detailed in Sonnet 4, which could be aptly dubbed "A Disquisition Forbidding Masturbation."

Sonnet 4 is figuratively organized throughout by conceits that correlate economic and carnal operations, and it abounds in inconsistencies. "Unthrifty loveliness," as the handsome spendthrift is called in 4.1, becomes "beauteous niggard" in the vocative of 4.5; he spends lavishly on himself and gives nothing away (4.1–6), on the one hand, and is the "Profitless usurer" who invests large "sums" yet cannot "live," i.e., 'make a living,' on the other; the "sum of sums" he does "use" in 4.7–8 stands for the very "beauty" that in 4.13 is "unus'd." These contradictory details will be resolved when the topic of the discourse is grasped, as it will be once Partridge's glosses on "spend," as 'discharge seminally,' and on "traffic," as 'sexual commerce,' are brought to bear. Thereupon the clauses of 4.1–2, to "*spend* . . . thy beauty's legacy" of generative sperm "Upon thy self," where "upon" = 'over' as well as 'with respect to,' and of 4.9, "having *traffic* with thyself alone," where "alone" = 'in solitude' as well as 'solely,' make the most open reference to autoeroticism. Being infecund, it involves both the expenditure of seed for self-gratification and withholding it from reproduction. Thus the youth can at one and the same time be a prodigal and a miser, can be extravagant with himself yet unable to "live" in posterity, and can utilize while refraining from utilizing the sexuality of his fetching self. Since this sonnet, like the others, enjoins the copulative transmission of beauty, the masturbation is disapproved.

Elsewhere, too, the persuasions to breed touch on the theme of self-abuse, though never in so sustained a manner. The term 'self-abuse,' incidentally, dates from the eighteenth century according to the OED; yet the verb "abuse" in 4.5–6—"why dost thou abuse [as a masturbator] / The bounteous largess given thee to give [as a procreator]?"—bears a cognate sense in 1609. This question is put at 3.7–8: "Or who is he so fond [= foolish] will be the tomb / Of his self-love [the dead-end of his autoeroticism] to stop posterity?" "Be not self-will'd" is the main clause in the couplet of Sonnet 6, and Ingram and Redpath annotate "self-will'd" as "just possibly playing on (1) 'obstinate,' (2) 'bequeathed to yourself alone,'" to which I would add, (3) 'sensually self-desired.' At 9.11–12 the "user" of beauty "destroys it" in keeping it "unus'd," and one gets the paradox upon realizing that this use/nonuse is the way of the onanist. The first of the allusions to the theme occurs in Sonnet 1, which keeps yielding up its initiatory richness: "But thou . . . Feed'st thy lights' flame with self-substantial fuel" (1.5–6). The "lights' flame," synonymous with the "bright eyes" of the previous verse ("lights" = 'eyes'—OED 4), is kindled by the other's "substance" when he gazes narcissistically upon his own attractive person and evidently enjoys it concupiscently as well, thereby "Making a famine where abundance lies" (1.7).

The reproofs for masturbation bear so close a kinship with another set of reproofs, those for celibacy, that one cannot always tell which fault the speaker has in mind. An example is the counsel he proffers at 6.3–4, "treasure [= fecundate] . . . some place [womb] / With beauty's treasure [= sperm] ere it be self-kill'd," either by nonemission or by noncopulatory emissions. In Renaissance medical opinion orgasms were thought to be debilitating, to shorten life, and this belief would be pertinent to 9.2, "That thou consum'st thyself in single life," if "single" connotes 'solitary' as well as 'unmarried.' In that case, the idea of the bachelor's self-consumption in unfruitfulness would combine with the idea—which finds support in 9.11–12—of self-consumption by onanistic "waste"; and the one who, at the close of Sonnet 9, "on himself such murderous shame commits," does so by abstinence or autoerotic indulgence. At lines 11–12 of the pregnant Sonnet 1, "Within thine own bud buriest thy content [= seminal contents and self-contentment], / And, tender churl [= miser], mak'st waste in niggarding [= hoarding]," the other is reproached for his continence. So, this opening poem, with its nice ambiguity, anticipates both kinds of the subsequent reproof.

At times Shakespeare appears to be thinking simply of celibacy, as when he writes, at 10.7–8, of "Seeking that beauteous roof [your body] to ruinate [by shunning sex] / Which to repair [by reproduction] should be thy chief desire," or asks, at 13.9–10, "Who lets so fair a house [the body] fall to decay [through chastity], / Which [coital] husbandry in [marital] honor might uphold . . . ?" But these passages are not unequivocal, especially when the latter question is answered at 13.13, "O none but unthrifts [= spendthrifts]."

That the Sonnets deal at all with such unsavory subject matter is a very well-kept secret.[11] The first to notice that they do was Eric Partridge in *Shakespeare's Bawdy.* His glossary adduces two instances, the first under "traffic," where 4.9–10 is cited. But Partridge thinks that the masturbational import there is "secondary" instead of primary, that it is restricted to those two lines instead of being the pervasive theme of all fourteen, and that Sonnet 4 is addressed to a woman! The second instance is glossed under "usury," where "forbidden usury" in Sonnet 6 "may euphemize 'masturbation.'" But the phrase decidedly does not. The "not forbidden usury" at 6.5 is explained two lines later: "That's for thee to breed another thee, / Or ten times happier be it ten for one." Hence usury, no matter how exorbitant the rate of return on the loan—even if 900 percent—is legitimate in terms of the youth's anticipated reproduction, and great profiteering, "ten for one," in offspring; and so this justified "usury" stands for prolific breeding, which is just the opposite of self-abuse. Stephen Booth's glosses follow suit in both instances, and he catches glimpses of two others, those at 6.13 and possibly 9.14. And that is about as far as the commentary has managed to go on this score.

Neither those two glossarists nor, of course, anyone else has attended to the implications of the autoerotic issue in Sonnets 1–9. In the light of it, A. L. Rowse's insistence on the "overwhelming obviousness" that the poems in Part I, "in their whole argument and character . . . are duty-sonnets written by the poet to his patron,"[12] will strike one as implausible. What are the odds that an Elizabethan writer and social inferior would bid his noble patron to quit masturbating? If only this issue had been perceived, how much rumination on the youth as an earl, not to mention the speculation about which earl, would we and the Sonnets have been spared.

But at least we have been spared the observation that Shakespeare supports the Catholic position on self-pollution. Never does he advert to sin or any religious proscription—including the one in the account of Onan in Genesis 38:9–10[13]—to make his point. In the Sonnets, masturbation and virginity need hardly be differentiated;

for, where the youth is concerned, they are, as deviations from the reproductive course that someone so splendid-looking is duty-bound to pursue, equally blameworthy, and for exactly the same reason. The persuasions to breed are remarkably consistent and consistently secular in their arguments.

Doubts about the arrangement of the Sonnets in the Quarto of 1609 do not normally extend to these persuasions, for the reason that they dwell on the single theme of procreation and hence should go together. The reason has little merit. The treatments of poetic immortalization also share a theme but do not on that account belong together and do not occur together, being artfully distributed over much of Part I. Moreover, the accepted rationale ignores two questions essential to the problem of sequentiality: Why are these persuasions put at the beginning? and Are they, in relation to one another, placed at random or according to a plan?

The argumentative ingenuities, figurative inventiveness, ubiquitous wit, and astonishing command of language and versification might be enough to carry off the sixteen lyrics of repetitive thesis even if nothing more happened in them to hold our attention. But in fact a great deal more *does* happen, for they unfold a dramatic change of heart in the speaker, and, if less distinctly, a change also in the youth in response to the escalation of esteem and devotion in the verse composed on his behalf.

Sonnets 1–9 do not establish a definitive relationship between the persona and the young man who is the constant and exclusive object of his interest. His interest, excited by the other's comeliness, is intense enough to elicit the successive persuasions to breed; and while some measure of fondness is consciously entertained for that "sweet self" (1.8, 4.10), love plays no part—certainly none is made explicit before the end of Sonnet 9 and the whole of Sonnet 10. From there on the persona progresses toward the position, occupied in Sonnet 20, of being impassioned of a "Master Mistress." In the opening movement he passes through a stage of initial fascination (Sonnets 1–9), a second stage, the emergence of love (Sonnets 10–14), and then a third, in which the loving poet undertakes to immortalize his friend (Sonnets 15–19).

The stage of initial fascination (Sonnets 1–9). Here the situation, in comparison with what will follow, is fairly static, and the interaction between the speaker and the spoken-to has an ambiguous, unsettled quality. Still, this segment contains some developments of note and lays the groundwork for others. All of the admonitions on self-abuse, for example, are delivered in these sonnets, the last possi-

ble one occurring at 9.14. The speaker is self-effacing to the extent
that he never once employs the first-person-singular pronoun. The
youth is thought of more in relationships with women, though in
passive and potential relationships, than he is in the rest of Part I. In
Sonnet 3 he is envisioned in a maternal context that includes both
the mother anticipated for his future children and his own mother.
He resembles her, and she finds solace in that fact. The only reference to his father, in the couplet of Sonnet 13, is in his role of pro-
genitor ("You *had* a father"), and no current affiliation with him is
postulated. Nowhere else are the parents mentioned (and nothing
said of them intimates blue blood). In Sonnets 3 and 8 and, for the
third and last time, in 9 (unless 16.6–8 should be counted) the young
man is envisaged as wived. In Sonnet 3, and again in 16, he holds
allure for many marriageable girls, though never the reverse, they
for him. In metaphors before Sonnet 7 he is associated with mun-
dane things, but there he is raised to celestial heights, being figured
as the sun and transfigured thereby when such phrases as "gracious
light," "sacred majesty," and "adore his beauty" are predicated of
the vehicle; this octaval solar conceit suggests what a dazzling figure he has become in the sight of his admirer.

The admirer, though, ascribes no virtue to the youth; on the contrary, he finds faults in his character, such as selfishness and folly in
his refusal to breed. The excellence he adulates is exterior rather
than inward. Still, the adulation cannot but be gratifying to the recipient, while the badgering—particularly if he is loath to marry,
copulate, and procreate—and the vivid reminders of the aging (first
in Sonnet 2) and dying (first in Sonnet 3) that await him, would have
to be less welcome. Is he being manipulated, on the one hand by
flattery, on the other by challenges to his feelings of aversion and
fear? We may wonder, too, whether the admixture of compliment
and rebuke serves purely the cause of reproduction or whether that
cause is perhaps undertaken, even if unawares, as a way of forging an
emotional link with the youth. In praising his beauty while continually adverting to its procreational use, masturbational misuse,
and celibate nonuse, the praiser manifests a mental habit of yoking
that youthful masculinity with sex. This repeated reaction, in poem
after poem, to another male is problematical. It is not to be accounted for as Renaissance friendship, and commentators who hold
that it is never produce the requisite precedents.

When Shakespeare himself treats of arguments for sexual reproduction in other words, such as *Twelfth Night* and *Venus and
Adonis*, he does so in scenes where the characters are caught up in
erogenous circumstances. In *Twelfth Night*, Viola/"Caesario" asso-

ciates beauty with propagation when, as Duke Orsino's emissary, she/"he" first beholds the face of Olivia and declares,

> Lady, you are the cruell'st she alive
> If you will lead those graces to the grave
> And leave the world no copy.
>
> (1.5.244–46; cf. Sonnet 11.13–14)

Although the point is that she should take Orsino as a husband, this speech, along with others of the "male" go-between, so enthralls Olivia that she falls madly in love with "him." In *Venus and Adonis*, some five stanzas (lines 163–74, 751–68) are given over to procreational arguments by Venus, many of which closely resemble those in the Sonnets. Here, as in them and in *Twelfth Night*, a comely but sexually resistant young person is addressed; but Venus is enamored of Adonis, and, when she addresses him, she does so with seductive intent ("breed with me"), and she does not restrict her persuasions to this one issue but also speaks about the sensual delights of heterosexual love, a subject on which the persuasions in the Sonnets remain curiously silent.

The theme of procreation in both the play and the poetic narrative is broached under conditions of courtship, and Sonnets 1–9 seem very different in this respect. And yet their thematic kinship with these other Shakespearean works invites certain questions and speculations. Is the young man of the Sonnets, like Adonis, unaffected by the persuasions to breed, or might he, like Olivia, become attracted to the speaker? Does the persuader have the emotionally detached attitude of Viola, even though his praises of the other's beauty are far more copious and fulsome, or is his interest in some way, even if subconsciously, erotic? Moreover, he may well be supposed to be a man really captivated for the first time by another man, for he reacts as he might have when attracted to someone of the opposite sex: by associating youthful beauty with reproductive sexuality, just as Viola and Venus do; but his reaction would have to be adjusted to the novel situation in which the reproduction requires a third party, some female participant.

The stage of emergent love (Sonnets 10–14). This stage is prepared for in the couplet of Sonnet 9—

> No love toward others in that bosom sits
> That on himself such murderous shame commits—

which finally produces the most significant word for the work as a whole: "love" (hence the title of my book, which comes from 88.3).

The youth's shameful self-murder, whether committed by chastity or onanism, is not only a crime against himself but a failing in good will toward others. The lack of love is his, and the unloved "others" fall into four classes, decipherable in this and the next poem: first, all men (= "the world" in 9.5–6, where "The world will be thy widow and still weep / That thou no form of thee hast left behind"); second, some wife, the potential "widow" of 9.1–2; third, the "many" who hold him in affection at 10.3 and, among these, fourth, the speaker himself (10.13). The "love" conceived of here is not erotic; rather, it consists of a charity that might be universal in scope and that should, especially, be directed toward those with whom one has interpersonal bonds.

Sonnet 10 takes up and develops the thought of Sonnet 9's couplet, and here incipient intimacy takes a big step forward. The word "love" occurs in this text four times—as a noun twice, as a verb once, and once as "belov'd." The octave expresses a version of loving one's neighbor as oneself, in the sense that self-hatred is incompatible with charity: "So possess'd with murderous hate" turned "'gainst thyself," thou "none lov'st" and "bear'st [not] love to any." The volta, 10.9, pleads, "O change thy thought, that *I* may change my mind." The result clause should arrest the reader's attention, for here occurs the very first use of the pronoun "I." Only here does the relationship take on an explicit "I-thou"—or "thou-I"—character. The sestet is replete with innovations. The advice "Be as thy presence is, gracious and kind," ascribes qualities other than physical to the youth, and this has not been done before. These qualities inhere in a "presence" and so apparently relate rather to manners than to morals; the speaker now admires more than mere looks. The very next line, "Or to thyself at least kind-hearted prove," seeks a moral-emotional reaction, and not an exclusively self-directed one, since "at least" signals hope of some wider generosity. But the biggest surprise of all emerges at 10.13: "Make thee another self for love of me"—yes, *"for love of me."* The persona, we discover, not only presumes the youth's affection but even appeals to it as an inducement for his keeping "beauty" alive "in thine or thee." In just fifteen lines this rapid development comes about: from the charge of having "no love toward others" at 9.13 to the confident recognition of "love of me" at 10.13. Love for the youth has yet to be declared outright, but "thou art belov'd of many" implies, at 10.3, that among "the many" is the speaker himself. In Sonnet 10 the theme of beauty and its reproduction becomes confluent with that of love, and henceforth the youth may be appropriately designated the "beloved" or the "friend."

After such a crescendo of revelations, recognitions, personal breakthroughs, what will happen next? What happens is that the persona, as though he had gone too far, beats a strategic retreat. In Sonnet 11 he returns to familiar grounds, becoming once again the interpreter of Nature's will, that beauties must propagate, and making no reference to love or to himself. Sonnet 12 does resume the first-person reference of Sonnet 10, but its most interesting function, as will be seen, is to prepare the way for Sonnet 15. Sonnet 13 is the first expressly to discover the speaker's return of affection, and it does so in the form of two vocatives, "love" at 13.1 and the yet more tender "dear my love" at 13.13. Such terms of endearment will be common hereafter, but this is their first appearance.

Sonnet 14 offers an idealization of the other that both continues and surpasses the previous praises. That most commonplace of Petrarchan figures, eyes as stars, dominates, and so the exaltation by celestial comparison, which began in Sonnet 7, recurs, and the "bright eyes" of 1.5 might be recalled. The conceit is given two unusual twists. The shining eyes, ordinarily those of a mistress (cf. 130.1), here belong to a male, and, as "constant stars," they are susceptible to a reading by astrological "art." The "knowledge" so derived concerns the friend's "truth and beauty," which "shall together thrive" if only he would "convert" himself to "store" (for breeding), "Or else of thee this I prognosticate, / Thy end is truth's and beauty's doom and date." The "truth" that now complements "beauty" takes the broad sense of 'honesty, uprightness, virtue' (see OED 4), and so, beyond the friend's qualities of personality in Sonnet 10 and his personable attributes everywhere stressed, he is credited for the first time with moral excellence.

Cognizance of the connate connection between beauty and love surely antedated Diotima's instruction to the young Socrates, in which she defines love as desire for "the everlasting possession of the good" or of the "beautiful," with which "good" is an interchangeable term.[14] In Renaissance psychology—upon which the *Symposium* exercised considerable influence, as book 4 of *The Courtier* shows, where love for Castiglione is "nothing else but a certain coveting to enjoy beauty"—what initially arouses love is visual perception of a fair form.[15] This psychology is operative in Olivia's soliloquy on the departure of "Caesario":

> Even so quickly can one catch the plague?
> Methinks I feel the youth's perfections
> With an invisible and subtle stealth
> To creep in at mine eyes.
>
> (*Twelfth Night*, 1.5.299–302)

The "plague" that enters through Olivia's eye is romantic love, even though the "youth" happens to be a girl and the "perfections," while disguised in male attire, are feminine. Shakespeare has the young lady, hitherto impervious to passion, falling in love with one of her own sex, and the sexual confusion by no means impedes, but rather facilitates, her erotic awakening. We have yet to learn that the male perfections, so constantly eyed by the Sonnets' persona, likewise educe erotic love. He does not, it is true, so "quickly . . . catch the plague." In *As You Like It*, Phebe, quoting the "saw" of the "dead shepherd" Marlowe (from *Hero and Leander*, 1.176), asks, " 'Who ever lov'd that lov'd not at first sight?' " (3.5.81–82). Well, Astrophel for one, who details in his second sonnet the "degrees"— the first of which is sight once more, that of Stella—by which Love "had full conquest got" (lines 4–10):

> I saw and liked, I liked but loved not,
>   I loved, but straight did not what *Love* decreed:
>   At length to *Love's* decrees, I forc'd, agreed,
> Yet with repining at so partiall lot.
>   Now even that footstep of lost libertie
> Is gone.[16]

In Shakespeare's Sonnets the speaker's love also develops "by degrees." Only after it emerges into consciousness does he afford the friend such qualities as moral goodness (= "truth") in the couplet of Sonnet 14 and a "presence . . . gracious and kind" at 10.11, along with a "temperate" temperament at 18.2 and "inward worth" at 16.11. Once cause and effect are distinguished, the beauty of the friend, reinforced by his affectionate response, will be seen as the *cause* of the love, and the *effect* of love is the idealization of him as estimable of personality and virtuous of character.

Stage three, the immortalization of the beloved in verse (Sonnets 15–19). This third stage has been preceded by the stepped-up frequency of the first-person pronoun, from two occurrences in Sonnet 10 to four in 12 and seven in 14. The effect is to draw increasing attention to the self of the speaker in preparation for Sonnet 15 and later, when he takes it upon himself to safeguard the friend from the inroads of time.

Unless the striking parallels in syntax, organization, and thought between the quatrains of Sonnet 15 and those of 12 are noticed, a dramatic effect of this stage of the cycle will be lost. The two texts exhibit virtually identical sentence structures: each has (1) dependent "When"-clauses in the octave, one at the start of each quatrain (though Sonnet 12 has another at line 3), (2) a principal "Then"-

clause, making up the third quatrain, and (3) a clausally independent couplet attached by "And." Moreover, in the octave of each, the "I" ponders the universality of temporal decay, especially the kind that is ruinous to plant and human life; in the sestet he switches from universal to particular, and also to second-person address, to focus these melancholy reflections specifically upon the friend:

> Then of thy beauty do I question make
> That thou among the wastes of time must go,
> Since sweets and beauties do themselves forsake,
> And die as fast as they see others grow.
>
> (12.9–12)

> Then the conceit of this inconstant stay
> Sets you most rich in youth before my sight,
> Where wasteful time debateth with decay
> To change your day of youth to sullied night.
>
> (15.9–12)

Each couplet sets forth, finally, the solution to the problem of the friend's decay. In Sonnet 12:

> And nothing 'gainst Time's scythe can make defense
> Save breed to brave him when he takes thee hence.

Oh, yes, of course: "breed," by now the predictable panacea, as again in Sonnet 13, and again in Sonnet 14. With fixed expectations we approach the conclusion to Sonnet 15:

> And all in war with Time for love of you,
> What he takes from you I engraft you new.

Suddenly one does a double take: is a new resolution proposed, one different from the biological engenderment that till now has been invariable? This astonishing moment is a dividend paid to one who has been closely following the sequence of the Sonnets. The couplet, however, despite the surprise, is somewhat puzzling. "Engraft," a botanical term, refers to a method of renewing old trees by inserting a scion of one tree as a graft into another (OED 1). "Breed" at 12.14 and "engraft" here both allude to a kind of organic renewal, that of mammals and that of plants, respectively; the renewal in the one case is natural, in the other by artifice, and the former word is used literally, the latter figuratively. We learn who will "engraft" ("I") and why ("for love"), but what exactly this second mode of combating decay consists of cannot be made out, not until the metaphor gets its tenor at 16.4. It turns out to be "rhyme," and then we realize that a term from horticultural art stands for poetic art.

It is the poet—for so the persona might be called, now that he finally presents himself openly in this role, one that most sonneteers assume at the outset—who takes to himself the function of perpetuator, a function that before would have had to be undertaken by the youth with a girl. "Time," personified in each couplet, is inimical to the friend. In Sonnet 12 he commands the means of "defence," but in Sonnet 15 another will do battle on his behalf, the champion who declares himself "all in war with Time for love of you." The locution is interesting. "In love with" sounds more natural than "in war with"; the latter phrase must be modeled on the former; and to translate 15.13 into "and all in love with you I war on Time" does not improve it—quite the contrary—but does bring out its meaning. After Sonnet 9 it becomes clearer and clearer that the protagonist, as he may now be styled, is falling in love with the young beauty.

"But," Sonnet 16 begins, immediately attaching itself syntactically to 15, "wherefore do not you a mightier way / Make war upon that bloody tyrant Time"—"mightier," that is, than the "way" just proposed in the couplet. Now the war-making capacity is shifted from the poet back to the friend, from the "way" of verbal creativity to that of procreativity. A personality trait of the speaker's, already glimpsed in Sonnet 11, reasserts itself: emotional breakthrough and advance, followed by recoil and retreat; and the retreat, which proved momentary before, will prove so again.

Meanwhile, we witness a contest between breeding and rhyme, the former winning the first round, the latter ascendant in the second (Sonnet 17) and, in the third (Sonnet 18), so triumphant that breeding is permanently retired. But that is to look ahead. In Sonnet 16, breeding, so long unchallenged, comes on strong. It is the "mightier way" and the "means more blessed," the poet concedes. He suddenly loses nerve, and it does no good that he allies himself with a fellow artist, the painter—a curious alignment, really, since painting is dragged in here only for special local effects, being otherwise immaterial. The tools of both, "pen" and "pencil" (brush), are deemed inferior to the fecundating penis for delineating the friend's "outward fair" and "inward worth" (equivalent to "truth" at 14.11, 14); and the "maiden gardens, yet unset" contrast with "my barren verse," the rival and inferior means of perpetuation. The young virgins have more to offer the youth, and the poet, in seeming discouragement and surrender, directs him back to them.

In Sonnet 17 propagation and rhyme reach a sort of *modus vivendi*. They will cooperate to ensure the perpetuation of the friend's beauty. The humble stance of the poet is not altogether given up, for he does confront two problems—one of credibility, the other of artistic inadequacy. The inadequacy, however, is not personal, for his "numbers" are "fresh"; it has to do, rather, with the inherent incapacity of the poetic medium to deliver the full message of the other's splendor—to "write the beauty of your eyes" or to "number all your graces." Even though the verse is "as a tomb / Which hides your life and shows not half your parts," it will not be believed in "the age to come," but "scorn'd" as the hyperbole of some old "poet's rage" (= *furor poeticus*). Yet these difficulties are remedied in the couplet:

> But were some child of yours alive that time,
> You should live twice—in it and in my rhyme.

Now rhyme and reproduction cooperate to confer afterlives on the friend; in this respect they are equally effective, though the very equality would represent a gain for rhyme, which, at 16.12, could not, as reproduction could, "make you live yourself in eyes of men." Verse is given primacy, in fact, in Sonnet 17, and less because all fourteen lines are devoted to it, whereas only the two final lines include a reference to breeding, than because of what "But" intimates in 17.13 (vis-à-vis 17.1): that the "child" is relegated to the subordinate function of making "my rhyme" in later years believable.

The question that begins Sonnet 18—"Shall I compare thee to a summer's day?"—has a conversational ring, as if to ask the listener whether he mightn't enjoy such a comparison. But when we reach the couplet, we discover that "this" is spoken, not written, discourse, and then, in hindsight, it dawns on us that the question initiates the process of composition and that the poet is musing on the aptness of his simile. He chooses to go with it, and he works it out on a threefold basis: of visible loveliness; of temperateness as a quality of mildness and evenness that may belong to a day or to someone's disposition; and of durability. The friend excels on each basis. How he does so on the third—how his "summer" of youth can be "eternal," how he can escape the general rule that "every fair" thing must "decline" from fairness, either accidentally or in the regular course of nature—is explained in the couplet:

> So long as men can breathe or eyes can see,
> So long lives this, and this gives life to thee.

The pronoun "this" refers to the entire poem, qua poem, which can provide an existence for the friend coterminous with the human race ("eternal" in 18.9 and 12 = the 'indefinite' rather than the 'infinite future duration' of OED 3) and "gives life to thee." The "eyes" of men enable them to read; and "breathe," which may denote only vital respiration, probably also means 'to give forth audible breath, to speak' (OED 7). What, then, will "give life" is not simply the verse on the page but the verse as a score to be played whenever mentally or vocally sounded by future readers. Thus can rhyme come alive and have, beyond a memorializing, an animating power (cf. 81.9–14, 55.5–14)—a power asserted at the very moment that poetic immortalization triumphs over and displaces the cause of breeding.

Sonnet 19 is an apostrophe to "Devouring Time." It is the first poem that does not directly address the youth (neither does Sonnet 5, but it is hardly an exception, since it forms a double sonnet with Sonnet 6, which does); he is referred to here as "my love." The poet is acting on his commitment at 15.13, to be "all in war with Time for love of you" (that phrase might almost serve as a title for Sonnet 19), when he challenges, in an effort to keep his friend intact, the universal devourer. He begins, bravely enough, with a series of imperatives, one to a line through 19.6; but they are concessive, since they simply direct Time to "do whate'er thou wilt . . . To the wide world and all her fading sweets." A reversal occurs at 19.8 with the command, "But I forbid thee one most heinous crime," the savaging of "my love." Yet the bold and forceful command gives way in the third quatrain to the milder, rather imploring, tones of "O carve not," "Nor draw no lines there [= wrinkles on the forehead] with thine antique pen," and "Him . . . untainted do allow." That the protector becomes aware that his effort is fruitless is made evident in a second reversal at 19.13: "Yet do thy worst, old Time: despite thy wrong," where both "thy worst" and "wrong" are equivalent to the "most heinous crime" above. The speaker returns to the concessive imperative, now resigned to the fact that the youth, though he might serve as "beauty's pattern to suceeding men," will not be spared. "Time," after being characterized first as monstrously "Devouring," then neutrally as "swift-footed," becomes simply "old" in 19.13, the adjective implying an almost affable attitude toward him just when we might expect the greatest disparagement. The attitude is accounted for by the last line, where a third reversal occurs: "despite thy wrong / My love shall in my verse ever live young." There is, after all, a recourse available to the poet for keeping "old Time" at bay and his beloved alive. Distinctions of a semiparadoxical nature are latent in the couplet: the protagonist's words as apostrophized utterance fail to deter time, but words organized into poetry will do the job; the youth cannot escape decay in his human actuality but can do so in his existence as an aesthetic object; verse cannot prevent the deleterious effects of time (and his "antique pen") on the freshness of "my love," but his fresh beauty will be beyond the reach of time once it has been recreated in verse.

For the space now of five sonnets, 15–19, poetry, in its capacity to confer perennial life on its subject, is the continuous text. The persona comes out as a poet, abruptly, at the end of Sonnet 15, to take upon himself the formidable task of doing "war with Time" as champion of the vulnerable other, and he does so out of "love for thee"—the motivation that underlies the subsequent immortalizing sonnets. It does not matter that the idea of reproduction briefly returns in Sonnet 16 to cast doubt on his enterprise, since, after Sonnet 17, that idea can be discarded once and for all.

The steps taken by Shakespeare's persona in the opening movement of the Sonnets may now, in summary, be retraced. From the start, as throughout Part I, he is preoccupied with the imposing beauty of the youth. His first reaction is that this beauty requires reproduction and that the youth should find some woman and breed, even though he, the giver of this counsel, has little to urge in favor of women, marriage, family life, or heterosexual gratification. Next, this bodily beauty, together with affection on the part of its possessor, elicits love in the speaker. He thereupon idealizes the friend, first by ascribing to him a "presence . . . gentle and kind" in Sonnet 10 and then virtue—the "truth" in Sonnet 14 and "inward worth" in 16; and this new esteem for the friend's disposition and character is the result rather than the cause of love. Moreover, faults are no longer imputed to him—never after Sonnet 11, and even this sonnet is a temporary throwback to the earlier stage, a retreat that follows upon and briefly suspends the sudden emergence of love. Finally, love prompts the poet to essay an alternative means of salvaging the beloved, a means solely at his command and independent of the biological means that would require the youth to beget children on one of those eager maidens. The adoption of eternalizing rhyme as the vehicle, enabling exclusive interaction between the maker and the receiving subject, suggests an intensification of the protagonist's love and, as it is born of and nourished by beauty, its amorous character.[17]

And what do the nineteen sonnets say about the stages through which their recipient passes? He is certainly not persuaded to breed. Instead of following the instructions to do so, he takes increasing interest in the instructor. The narcissistic impulses perceptible at 1.5–6 and elsewhere in the initial stage seem to undergo modification; he appears to change over from being self-involved to being involved with his praiser. This inference is supported by the fact that the last allusion to his autoeroticism occurs just before, and none occurs after, the emergence of love in Sonnet 10, line 13 of which makes the first mention of his "love of me."

Keeping in mind Plato's conception of love, in the *Symposium*, as desire for the everlasting possession of the beautiful, we may perceive the following psychological states as those the protagonist undergoes in the course of falling in love: (1) his desire for the hereditary continuation of the youth's beauty; (2) his desire for the genetic survival of his beautiful friend; and (3) his desire to render his beloved everlasting in poetry. A fourth stage is inaugurated in Sonnet 20, and it consists of a passionate desire for the person of the youthful beauty, with the erotic love to keep on yielding up, periodically, eternalizations in rhyme.[18]

3

Passion and Its
Master Mistress
(Sonnet 20)

Because so much depends on Sonnet 20—it is pivotal in the sequence—and because it has become a locus classicus of essays that seek to define the emotional relations between the poet and his young friend, I am according it a full chapter of discussion.

Interpreters can be divided into two groups, very unequal in size. In the smaller one are the few who, sometimes to their discomfort, find sexual attraction revealed toward the friend; in the larger one are the many who reassure themselves and us that such an attraction, far from being affirmed, is in fact denied. Two eighteenth-century annotators, among the very earliest, can illustrate these conflicting views. George Steevens remarked on 20.2: "It is impossible to read this fulsome panegyrick, addressed to a male object, without an equal mixture of disgust and indignation." Some years later Edmund Malone came to Shakespeare's rescue, writing:

> Some part of this indignation might perhaps have been abated, if it had been considered that such addresses to men, however indelicate, were customary in our author's time, and neither imported criminality nor were esteemed indecorous.[1]

No supporting instances of these customary addresses are cited by Malone, but no matter; his position has been the dominant one among editors, scholars, and critics ever since.[2] While less condescending toward the "indelicate" language of a less polite age, they defend the Sonnets against imputations of indecency and abnormality in much the same vein. They have frequent recourse to a cult of male friendship that enjoyed a certain vogue in the Renaissance, when the amicable ideal was more assiduously practiced and consciously esteemed than in later times; but the thing about this friendship that above all appeals to expositors is their conviction that it was free of all traces of eroticism. The friends in Shakespeare's sequence are assumed to adhere to and to exemplify this cult. Whether or not they do so will be investigated in subsequent chapters more generally, but here with respect to Sonnet 20 in particular.

The sonnet begins,

> A woman's face with nature's own hand painted
> Hast thou, the Master Mistress of my passion.

The word "passion" carries in this context its most glaringly obvious sense, that given by Schmidt (who cites this instance) in his *Shakespeare-Lexicon* as 'amorous desire,'[3] and that given by Partridge (who ignores this instance) in his glossary to *Shakespeare's Bawdy* as 'sexual love, physical desire.' Both Shakespearean lexicographers establish this usage with multiple citations from the plays and narrative poems. The "passion" is directed toward a "Mistress"—a 'man's illicit woman, the woman one loves,' again from Partridge, again based on usage in the plays; and he might have cited Sonnets 127.9 and 130.1. That gloss must be modified to fit this case, and Schmidt handles the problem with a separate entry for "Master-mistress," which he defines as 'a male mistress, one loved like a woman, but of the male sex.' The word "Master" is not hyphenated to "Mistress" in the Quarto as it is in Schmidt and most editions. The hyphen makes the two nouns coordinate, in apposition to "thou," the man who serves as the androgynous object of the ardor; but this obliterates other possibilities, such as taking "Master" as an adjective qualifying this "Mistress" as 'preeminent,' or taking "Master" in the titular sense, abbreviated "Mr.," as in "Mr. W. H." in Thorpe's dedication, and hence the "Mr. Mistress." In no way does "Master" desexualize the associated nouns "Mistress" and "passion"; rather, it indicates that the erotic role played by the lady of other sonneteers, even in Shakespeare's own Sonnets 127–54, is here taken by a man.

Although it is difficult to imagine that the speaker could have anything else in mind than the plainest possible disclosure of his sexual attraction to the friend, we have yet to reckon with the evasive ploys of the exegetes. T. G. Tucker, who is more perspicacious than most, comments, "It is of importance for the relation between the men to remember that the word ["passion"] simply = Lat. *passio* '(strong) feeling.'" That the "importance" is moralistic and that the etymology is obedient to that imperative Tucker confirms by adding, "the end of the sonnet is a negation of the worst."[4] The end may turn out not to eliminate the "worst," which, like Malone's "criminality," dares not speak its name. The language of Sonnet 20, as of the rest of Part I of the cycle, Sonnets 1 through 126, is, as C. S. Lewis justly observes, "too lover-like for that of ordinary male friendship," and he further says, "I have found no real parallel to such language between friends in sixteenth-century literature." This might serve as a corrective to those, such as Malone, who postulate those parallels without adducing any, and to those, such as Tucker, who are all too eager to absolve the diction of its "lover-like" burdens. But Lewis himself declines to draw the obvious inference from his observation.[5]

Some editors, seeking to mute "passion" at 20.2, have turned for help to old Thomas Watson, who uses the word interchangeably with "sonnet" to denote the individual eighteen-line lyrics, a hundred of which compose his *Hekatompathia or Passionate Century of Love* (1582). These poetic "passions" treat of romantic responses to a "mistress"; so if Shakespeare followed this lead—a big if, for the philological evidence is tenuous—he would simply be designating Sonnet 20 as amatory verse. There is, however, no precedent, in his work or anywhere else, for labeling a poem of friendship a "passion." Moreover, the literary sense of the term does not, as Dover Wilson and Stephen Booth among others suppose, supplant the libidinal sense but in fact reinforces it.[6] The gloss, first introduced in Edward Dowden's 1881 edition, according to Rollins (1:57), is less efficacious than commentators like to imagine for rehabilitating the verse; for even if "my passion" should denote 'my love-lyric,' "Master Mistress" is not thereby explained—or exorcised. Furthermore, Watson could employ the term *sonnet* synonymously because it too had the meaning, now obsolete, of 'love-lyric' (OED 2) in addition to the surviving one of 'fourteen-line stanza' (OED 1), the OED including, after the first definition, this note: "In many instances between 1580 and 1650 it is not clear which sense [1 or 2] is intended, as the looser use of the word would appear to have been very common." Thus Watson called his own poems "sonnets," not because they approximated this formal norm, for they exceeded it by a quatrain, but because of the topic, and Donne styled his collection *Songs and Sonnets*, although it contains no quatorzain. The title *Shakespeares Sonnets* would have conveyed to Elizabethans the loverly subject matter at least to the same extent as the specific verse form, and they would not have expected to find this form disjoined, as happened increasingly in the seventeenth century, from that subject. Sonnets were generally, in Spenser's word for his own, "amoretti."

Perhaps only retrospectively can one recognize the first two lines of Sonnet 20 as introductory to its bipartite organization. The octave compares the youth with women, to their disadvantage; the sestet offers a fable of his creation. The two sections have parallel movements; each begins by remarking the youth's feminine aspects and closes by distinguishing male from female reactions to his person. The octave proceeds:

A woman's gentle heart but not acquainted
With shifting change as is false woman's fashion;
An eye more bright than theirs, less false in rolling,
Gilding the object whereupon it gazeth;
A man in hue all hues in his controlling,
Which steals men's eyes and women's souls amazeth.

The superior (or "Master") feminine (as "Mistress") qualities are ascribed not only to the bodily externals of "face" (20.1) and "eye" but also to the psychical and inward "heart." Although elsewhere "My Mistress' eyes are nothing like the sun" (130.1), here the hyperbolical Petrarchan compliment is not withheld, and the eyes of the "Master Mistress" are very much like the sun, having both brightness and powerful rays to send forth for "Gilding . . . objects." "More bright" than women's, his eye surpasses theirs in brilliancy, and, "less false in rolling," it evinces the capacity, lacking in them, of being true. This comparison of 20.5 has both a physical and moral basis; in 20.3–4, where the womanly virtue of gentleness abides in his heart without women's vice of inconstancy, the comparison has a moral basis; and in 20.1 the implicit comparison between his naturally colored face and their artifically colored ones has, primarily, a physical basis, though the hint of rouging would connote imperfection. On either basis, he comes off best.

Out of context, the catalogue of female characteristics in 20.1–6 could almost cast doubt on the sex of the "thou"; but clues to his maleness beyond the multivalent "Master" are present, the first in the fact of his being measured against womankind, the second in the unlikelihood that praise for a lady would fasten on the *womanliness* of her countenance and disposition. But then one might think about what sort of man would find praise such as this pleasing. At any rate, at 20.7 his masculinity is directly confronted with the phrase "a man in hue." "Hue" can hardly denote 'color,' for the color predicated at 20.1 is feminine; so "hue" should denote, instead, 'form' or 'shape' (OED 1). The female head rests upon, and the female heart is inside, a male bodily form, whose essential feature, its genitals, remains implicit for now but will soon be explicitly remarked. The noun "hue" serves as the antecedent for the two pronouns, "his" (= its) in the same line and "Which" in the next. The plural "hues" that are "in his [the hue's] controlling" can signify 'species' (also at OED 1) as the two subdivisions of the human genus, for the "Master Mistress" subsumes both sexes within his own person, and he also, in 20.8, has a pronounced effect on the members of both. The plural "hues" can also signify 'colors,' his person ruling and harmonizing all the tinctures that invest it. In the latter reading, 20.7 does not jar with 20.1 but complements it with the observation that, in him, feminine facial coloring does not strike a discordant note. His most fair shape "steals men's eyes and women's souls amazeth." The distinction implied may be that of Tucker's annotation, "In women's case the effect goes deeper than the eyes."[7] And yet the men's response can by no means be dismissed as superficial. Not only is their gaze compelled by this rare handsomeness, but, according to the psychological theory of the period, erotic love is born of the visual apprehension of beauty, and the poet's own love has precisely that origin: he has been engaged unremittingly, since Sonnet 1, in contemplating the youth's comeliness. It has stolen his eyes *and* amazed his soul, so that he combines the men's and women's reactions, and he transcends them as well; for he has been more than amazed—he has been aroused to "passion."

Nature, personified, is introduced in 20.1, where hers was the hand that painted the "woman's face." She does not reappear until the third quatrain, where she is depicted not merely as painting but as fabricating her handiwork:

> And for a woman wert thou first created,
> Till nature as she wrought thee fell a-doting,
> And by addition me of thee defeated,
> By adding one thing to my purpose nothing.
>> But since she prick'd thee out for women's pleasure,
>> Mine be thy love and thy love's use their treasure.

In this flattering fable of the youth's creation, Nature is the efficient cause, and her original intention, to fashion a woman—the formal cause—was partially executed, at least to the extent of the face, eyes, and heart, the parts itemized in 20.1–6. Then she "fell a-doting"—rather like Pygmalion, except that, here, maker and made are of one gender—and somewhat revised her plan. The revision entailed no more than the "addition," which the creatress, smitten, had not the heart to withhold, of the "thing" required, and alone required in this conception, to turn the female into a male.

The "thing" that he was "prick'd out" with becomes the focal point of four verses, which not only constitute about 30 percent of the total number but are placed in the culminating position. Such attention in itself might well argue something other than lack of interest in this organ. Yet 20.11–14 are the very lines adduced by most explicators as conclusive evidence that the sonneteer's attachment to his friend is not sexual. Their position, if tenable, at least should be seen as lending the poetic argument a certain paradoxical drollery.

The effect of Nature's gift on the poet is disclosed in 20.11–12. He finds himself "of thee defeated," and the verb, bearing the sense 'disappointed' or 'defrauded' (OED 7), registers regret on his part and protest at the unfair action of a rival. But the regret and the protest are mild. Nature, far from a villain, is represented as a kindred spirit, one with whom the poet identifies or on whom he projects salient aspects of himself. She is a fellow artist; and while she "creates" in fine art as distinct from his literary art, she and he choose the same subject, on whom alike they dote. Her "addition," too, gains approval in being regarded as a good tenderly conferred. Does the poet, however "defeated" by it, wish it away? His "passion" has certainly not been deflected by it; to the contrary, it was initially excited by the "*Master* Mistress." When he goes on to say that the defeat is accomplished "By adding one thing to my purpose nothing," the question that arises is what he might mean by "my purpose." An answer must take the couplet into account.

The couplet offers a practical program for dealing with the situation at hand. This program, based on final causality, respects rather than opposes Nature's intention when she "prick'd . . . out" (= selected and genitally endowed) the youth "for women's pleasure" (20.13). This aim differs from that ascribed to her earlier in the sequence. At 4.3, "Nature's bequest gives nothing but doth lend" for reproductive purposes, and at 11.9 she makes beauteous persons, if not others, "for store." Now the phrase "for women's pleasure" posits something else: a voluptuous rather than a procreative objective. The notion, incidentally, goes counter to the Victorian one, since here sexual enjoyment accrues only to the female, not to the male, partner. Then 20.14 proposes a distribution of the friend's favors. "Mine be thy love" is the first proposal, and it has telling implications. The end of the discourse is to solicit for the poet the undivided and exclusive love of the youth, and love is disassociated from sexual activity, which the second proposal concedes to women in the plural, to no one of them in particular: "and thy love's use their treasure." Here "use" = both 'sexual employment' and, in combination with "treasure," = (figuratively) 'monetary investment.' The diction and the financial metaphor echo the rhetoric formerly devoted to "breed." At 6.3–4 "beauty's treasure" alludes to the young man's semen fecundating a womb, and at 2.6–10 the "treasure of thy lusty days" ought to be put to propagative "use." We would be back in familiar territory if Sonnet 20 did conclude by urging a generative utilization of women, whose compensation would consist of "pleasure" and valued progeny but no love. However, "their treasure" in this instance does not allude to their fecundation but to the precious gratification they would derive from "thy love's use." Sonnet 20 deviates from the persuasions to breed in important respects: the biological perpetuation of beauty is neither advocated by the poet nor demanded by Nature, and the entire stress falls on the bestowal of pleasure as the natural function of the virile member.

In 20.12 the speaker cannot be reverting to the "purpose" he had in mind in Sonnets 1–17, which was to urge reproduction, since the genitals, far from being "nothing" to that purpose, are vital to it. Could he then be adverting to the male reproductive "purpose," defined in those earlier sonnets, as applicable to himself? That is very unlikely, for, having made no previous mention of his own obligation to breed, why would he bring it up at this moment? A far-fetched reason for doing so might be based on the supposition that the youth has initiated amorous advances that are being delicately declined. But such advances are nowhere intimated, and the idea of declining is in any event clearly at odds with the conceptual and tonal drift of the poem.

I take "my purpose" to be that of the persona, seized by "passion," and I take 20.12 to be construable in two distinct but compatible ways. The "one thing" donated by Nature is "to my purpose nothing" in the sense 'immaterial to what I have in view,' and, as the slight transposition "nothing to my purpose" makes plainer, in the sense 'immaterial to the purport of my written discourse' (cf. OED 1, 6).

Still, whether held in mind or set down in writing, the poet's "purpose" has not as yet been discerned, and it is never specified positively. There can be no doubt of his intentions to reveal passion and to request love, and the "purpose" must pertain to them; but its expressed stipulation is negative, a negation of designs on the penis.

Then the reason for this abnegation seems to be that given in the couplet, to abide by the will and purpose of Nature, who "prick'd thee out for women's pleasure." This reason in no way precludes carnal yearnings on the part of the confessedly impassioned lover. The reason may be taken at face value, or taken as adduced to reassure the youth that he should not be anxious about sexual overtures, perhaps unwelcomed, or to rationalize the persona's disinclination to act on impulses in himself that are as yet strange and confusing. The argument of the sestet seems to call for "And since" as a more apt opening of the couplet than "But since." The differing nuances are subtle and hard to describe; yet "But since" does lightly hint at some other possibility in the mind of the poet than the one he chooses to state at the close.

To conform to the Renaissance ideal of friendship, Sonnet 20 would have to rule out, on the one hand, seductive intent, which it does, and, on the other, sexual attraction, which it nowhere does and in line 2 avers. Even though Nature's creative "addition" may be represented as an obstacle to fleshly intimacy between the friends, its presence does not divert the poet's "passion" but may, indeed, serve as a principal cause of its arousal.

The figure depicted in Sonnet 20 is, in its simplest outlines, that of a woman with a penis.

That figure was far from unfamiliar to Shakespeare in another sphere, that of his theater, where boys impersonated women. A young male in "hue" (= form) would show a "woman's face," "eye," and, in his speeches, "heart," and everyone recognized that his dress concealed a sex opposite to that of the character he enacted. The playwright, in conceiving every feminine role of his imagination, had to think of it as performed onstage by a boy. He was accustomed to thinking in terms of this dramatic convention, but in Sonnet 20 he portrays a personage who does not, like the boy actors, *play* a woman's part but instead conjoins, within a single self, female characteristics and the primary male differentia.

Strikingly delineated in this poem is the classic figure of homoerotic fantasy. No less an authority than Freud himself writes on the subject as follows:

> It is clear that in Greece, where the most masculine men were numbered among the inverts, what excited a man's love was not the *masculine* character of a boy, but his physical resemblance to a woman as well as his feminine mental qualities—his shyness, his modesty and his need for instruction and assistance. . . . In this instance . . . as in many others, the sexual object is not someone of the same sex but someone who combines the characters of both sexes; there is, as it were, a compromise between an impulse that seeks for a man and one that seeks for a woman, while it remains a paramount condition that the object's body (i.e. genitals) shall be masculine. Thus the sexual object is a kind of reflection of the subject's own bisexual nature.[8]

This passage is as obviously as it is astonishingly apposite to Sonnet 20. Gentleness, the "female mental quality" alluded to by "a woman's gentle heart," is akin to Freud's "shyness" and "modesty," and the youth's "need for instruction and assistance" was undertaken in the earlier instructions to "breed." In this psychological explanation—and its applicability, the context makes clear, is not restricted to the ancient Greeks—the genital "thing" is affirmed to be the "paramount condition" of the attraction, and the poet in no way disallows that possibility when he views this organ as an impediment to overt sexual relations. He rather provides impressive corroboration of Freud's theory in proclaiming a "passion" aroused in himself by one whom he perceives as both a lovely "Mistress" and, genitally, as a "Master," i.e., by a "sexual object" who is "a kind of reflection of the subject's own bisexual nature."

The poet discloses in manifold ways, explicit and implicit, his erotic attachment to the young man. Two of them have already been discussed, the first, and most explicit, being the language of 20.2, and the second, tacit, consisting of the phallic awareness suffusing 20.11–14. Two other components of that attachment are admiration for the feminine aspects of the friend and the poet's bias, in respect to him, against womankind.

The object of the passion was "Created for [= to be] a woman" and is rendered womanly of face, eye, and heart. This detail is descriptive and laudatory. It describes someone hardly of a virile complexion and one who, though young, is past boyhood, for he is likened to a woman, not a girl. He is imagined by the poet, and must be thought of by the reader, as taking satisfaction not only in the praise heaped on him but also in the title "Mistress," though modified, of course, by "Master." The recipient of the praise, having a marked female element in his makeup, inflames the male praiser, and the dynamics of the stimulus and response are those described by Freud.

The proposal that the friend go off to pleasure women, when it is made to one who has feminine attributes and who seems to have been unaffected by so many arguments to breed, might impress us as a bit disingenuous. This late access of concern for the opposite sex represents something of a turnabout from the animus earlier entertained against it. Comparison of the friend with women in 20.1–6 was intended to establish at once his resemblance and his superiority to them. That his face is painted "by nature's own hand" carries the implication—confirmed in the very next sonnet, which alludes (21.1–2) to the "painted beauty" of many another "Muse" (= poet)—that their faces need, or undergo, cosmetic coloring by human hands. Further, they are "false"; their hearts, unlike his, are "acquainted / With shifting change"; and their eyes, less bright than his, are "false in rolling." This is an odd preliminary to, if not an actual undermining of, the counsel of 20.14, that he go off to give them orgasmic delight, but it is an apt preparation for the rest of the counsel, that he hold back his love from these creatures.

The poet's attitude toward the other sex is ambivalent, and the favorable side is revealed in a rather oblique manner. The traits that make the friend adorable are in large measure woman-like. But that need not imply effeminacy, which is hardly a basis for compliments and is usually considered unbecoming. A certain feminineness in a young man can exert a powerful appeal on some sensibilities—and the poet has one—that are also responsive to female charms. And Nature is personified, playfully and respectfully, as a slightly comic but also reverenced "she." Aside from the slight chagrin, vented in the verb "defeats," at her phallicizing his inamorato, the persona represents himself, in various respects, as her disciple or else represents her as his alter ego; for each is a maker, and the self-same youth serves both of them at once as subject of art and object of infatuation. The fact that she initially made the youth female does not prevent Nature from falling in love, and, once in love, she cannot doom her unfinished creature to the "deprived" state of womanhood but must add the perfecting touch that will transform "her" into a "him." Thereupon she decrees, in a show of concern for her own gender after all, that the masculine "addition" is to be employed in intercourse with women. All that, of course, is the invention of the poet, as is the corresponding role he assigns to himself. He follows her example by falling in love with one of the same sex as himself and by introducing the penis at the end of his own creative process; he also shows a readiness to abide by her decree in his willingness to keep his distance from that "mastering" organ. However, this threefold conformity to Nature—psychological, artistic, and moral—generates a conflict, a tension within him.

The dramatic tension inherent in the text of Sonnet 20 is between, on the one hand, the attitude embodied in the second line's salutation, "thou, the Master Mistress of my passion," and, on the other, the last line's resolve—but not resolution—"Mine be thy love, and thy love's use *their* treasure." Can the enamored poet be content with "thy love" while giving up "thy love's use"? And how could he develop an erotic passion, and for how long could he sustain it, in the absence of any means whatsoever of giving it sensual expression? It would be a hopeless and tormenting desire that had for its object a "Master Mistress" who responded with affection but bestowed his sexual favors elsewhere.

In sum, in the sonnet that Shakespeare placed in the twentieth position of his sequence the speaker confesses himself impassioned of a "Master Mistress"; a man of salient feminine traits is entreated to grant all his love to another man; the beseecher betrays considerable ambivalence toward the opposite sex; Nature herself sets an example for homoerotic "doting"; and the penis of the beloved is dwelled upon at length. This poem seems a curiously inappropriate one for annotators and critics to single out as the principal prop of their contention that the friendship treated in the Sonnets is innocent of erotic content. But on second thought it is not so surprising that Sonnet 20 figures so prominently in their efforts at whitewashing, for it confronts so openly the question of eroticism in the relations between the friends that until, or unless, it can somehow be rendered innocuous, their efforts are doomed to failure.

The skepticism entertained by most expositors with regard to the authenticity of the 1609 order of the sonnets has to do in large measure with their moralistic resistance to any amorous transaction between the friends. The arrangement, if perused attentively and without preconceptions, discloses such a transaction, and the eroticism, in turn, contributes a key to the intelligible arrangement of the Quarto. I will constantly be bringing forth evidence in favor of these propositions, some of it now, in observing connections between Sonnet 20 and the sonnets that lead up to it.

If the women's "treasure" in 20.14 did allude to fructifying insemination, the final allusion to reproduction would occur here rather than in Sonnet 17; but the word "treasure" here is simply equivalent to its rhyme word "pleasure," so that a *contrast* occurs between Sonnet 20 and its predecessors. Another such contrast occurs when Nature's aim is shifted from procreation with women to delectation of them. Contrasts of this sort do not evidence discontinuities in the Quarto arrangement but, quite the reverse, subtly dramatize the ongoing and intensifying eroticism of the protagonist's relations with his beloved. In the process, reproduction is gradually phased out, women are relegated to less crucial roles, and Nature is made a less formidable force and her generative aim undergoes revision. The disclosure of his feminine attributes casts the youth in a new light and helps account for the poet's attraction to him and for his hitherto unexplained withstanding of the pleas to "breed." Having argued forcefully against celibacy and onanism as barren, the lover might well be reluctant, upon acknowledging his own passionate propensities, abruptly to reverse himself by pressing for sexual union, which could not but be barren also, and thereupon he assumes the intermediate position of 20.14: 'love me, but make love in the way endorsed before—with *them*.'

The evolution of the persona's love that I traced out in chapter 2 culminates when the full intensity and erotic character of his response is discovered in Sonnet 20. From the very beginning he had been so preoccupied with the youth's outward beauty that he could think, according to the record we have, of nothing else. What was to be done under these circumstances? What he did was to write sonnets to the young man that insisted on his keeping his loveliness extant by the genital means at his command. Beauty and sex have been yoked all along in the sonneteer's mind, and that is a clue to what would come later—and, doubtless, was going on in him unconsciously from the outset. Looking for a motive for the persuasions to reproduce, some commentators have speculated that the youth's noble parents may have requested, or paid, Shakespeare to urge the family's scion to marry. Nothing could be more fanciful. We receive additional clues to what the initial project was all about as we perceive the speaker gradually falling consciously in love with the youth and then abandoning the admonitions to breed in favor of perpetuating the beauty by a means at his own command—his verse. Then, when "passion" for the "Master Mistress" is divulged, the seed of the physical beauty that had caught the eye of the beholder by Sonnet 1, and that had begun palpably to grow as love from Sonnet 9 onward, blossoms or, rather, buds, since physical relations are as yet debarred. The full flowering comes later, for the erotic evolution does not stop here, and its continuance will be demonstrated in the following chapters.

The speaker of Sonnet 20 presents himself in an unstable plight. He has that prerequisite of Renaissance sonneteers, a lovely mistress of whom he is enamored and to whom he addresses his fervent verse. But this particular mistress is "prick'd out" for women, and that fact creates a dilemma for the lover. His passion has been evoked but wants an acceptable mode of expression. The compromise proffered at the end, "Mine be thy [nonsensual] love," cannot but be, under these conditions, provisional and temporary. Something will give; either the passion will subside, or the friends will engage in physical enjoyment of each other. Sonneteers are, I am aware, notoriously capable of sustaining themselves in a worshipful state of ungratified desire. But this sonneteer, with a *"Master Mistress"* plus a dark mistress, who is neither idolized nor disdainful of sexual advances, is hardly a conformist to Petrarchan conventions.

4

The Expressions of
Homoeroticism

Does Sonnet 20 bring up passion at the outset only to bury it at the end, as commentators are wont to maintain, or does Shakespeare rather set the stage for amorous interaction between the male friends? Though erotically aroused by the Master Mistress, the poet finally makes a principled or prudent decision to forgo physical intimacies, leaving the "pleasure" of "love's use" to "women." Now this decision either holds up or breaks down, and which alternative comes to prevail will be made known later in the sequence. Should erotic pressures turn out to vanquish that resolve, the outcome should occasion little surprise after the perusal of Sonnet 20 in chapter 3.

Until now I have been taking up the sonnets more or less as they successively occur in the Quarto, in furtherance of my long-range purpose of upholding Q's order of presentation, but I cannot, of course, continue in this vein through all 154 poems of the cycle. From now on my demonstrations of the rightness of the original order will have to be selective, and at this point I will make a leap to Sonnet 52. It, along with other sonnets, can be shown to disclose sexual relations between the friends, with the result that the arrangements stipulated in the couplet of Sonnet 20 will prove to have been provisional, and in this my exegesis veers sharply away from the settled views of the commentators. Their views and ways of reasoning will be surveyed in the second section of this chapter.

I

The couplet of Sonnet 52—

> Blessed are you whose worthiness gives scope,
> Being had to triumph, being lack'd to hope—

may be paraphrased: 'Fortunate' you are to be in possession of the 'excellence' that gives one 'room' or 'free play' ("scope"—OED 7) either "to triumph" when you are "had" or to "hope" for you when you are "lack'd." In the three paraphrases of the couplet quoted by

Rollins, "had" is taken as 'present,' a sense I cannot find in the OED, and "lack'd" as 'absent.' Schmidt more feasibly defines "have" as 'to possess, to own' (2a), but that sense is not consonant with the periodic lacking. The most feasible meaning of the verb here is one recorded in the Supplement to the OED (14e), with two citations from the plays, as 'possess sexually.' Then "Being had to triumph" refers to the feeling of exaltation attendant on carnal possession of that erotic prize, "you," and "being lack'd to hope" refers to the lover's anticipation, during intervals of deprival, of possessing "you" once more. This reading of the couplet is solidly supported by 52.1–12:

> So am I as the rich whose blessed key
> Can bring him to his sweet up-locked treasure,
> The which he will not every hour survey,
> For blunting the fine point of seldom pleasure.
> Therefore are feasts so solemn and so rare,
> Since seldom coming in the long year, set
> Like stones of worth they thinly placed are,
> Or captain jewels in the carcanet.
> So is the time that keeps you as my chest,
> Or as the wardrobe which the robe doth hide,
> To make some special instant special blest,
> By new unfolding his imprison'd pride.

In the simile of 52.1–4 the speaker likens himself to a man of wealth who rarely inspects his hoard for the cautious if improbable reason that he will thus protect his delight from satiety. What the hypothetical "he" has in a literal sense—the "key" and the "treasure"—and the way "he" puts them to use serve to represent what "I," in a corresponding and figurative sense, have and "my" manner of employing them. "His . . . treasure" consists of precious stones or metals; "mine" in some way consists of "you," the beloved who is being addressed. The "key" is, curiously, "blessed" (= happy, fortunate) that "Can bring him to" the contents of a treasure chest; and what "key" has the speaker, in what way is it "blessed," and to what place, "sweet" and "up-locked," can it "bring" him? If these questions seem suggestive, they are intended to, for the quatrain is replete with terms of sexual import, as the following listing, with glosses by Partridge, indicates: "sweet" can = 'filled with sexual pleasure'; "treasure" can = 'a woman's . . . "secret parts",' here applicable if adaptable to an erogenous part of a man, and can also = 'semen'; "lock" can = 'pudend' (with 'pick a lock' a phrase that = 'force a woman's chastity'); "point" can = 'head (or glans) of the penis, with vague allusion to the entire phallus'; "pleasure" can =

'sexual pleasure.' Could Shakespeare have collocated all these bawdy terms in the space of four verses without design? If he did so unconsciously, which I regard as next to unthinkable, the very unconsciousness would be significant.

Still, it must be shown how the raw definitions are intelligibly integrated in the text. The poet's "key," and one more naturally called "blessed" (meaning 'fortunate') than the metal instrument, would be his phallus, for it is his means of entry, nonforceful and very likely posterior ("can bring him"), to the sensually "sweet" and enclosed "treasure" of the friend's body. These lines may be construed in another way if "treasure" is taken, figuratively, to designate, as the word does at 6.3–4, 'semen'; then the fortunate phallus of the lover, aroused and evoking a responsive passion, would be the "key" to unlocking the "sweet" fluid confined genitally in the beloved. In either case, whether the "treasure" is fleshly or seminal, the concern is that if it is too frequently "surveyed," or erotically experienced, the "pleasure" may lessen (unless this is a rationalization for not enough sexual contact). The fourth line, while completing the simile, adds a metaphorical dimension; for "pleasure" ('covetous' for the rich man, 'libidinal' for the lover) is conceived of as a sharp instrument, such as a sword or lance, whose "fine point" will be blunted by overuse. Partridge remarks that Shakespeare's "most potent idea in penis-terms is that of acuity."[1] The fact that the metaphor takes a phallic object for its vehicle would seem to lay more stress on the "pleasure"—the tenor—that is genitalic than on the miser's "pleasure" in his wealth.

The second quatrain reinforces the principle implied in the first, that enjoyments, to keep their edge, must be seldom savored. Feast days remain "solemn" (= grand, imposing—OED 4a) and "rare" (= uncommonly fine—OED 6) because, being "thinly placed" in the necklace of the "year," they are "Like stones of worth" or like "captain jewels" in a neck ornament, the "carcanet." The word "worth," signifying the material preciousness of gems in 52.7, should guide us to the sense it bears when recurring in the form of "worthiness" in 52.13, where it signifies the youth's physical rather than moral excellence.

The intricacies of language in the third quatrain are breath-taking. The single sentence has a brief main clause, which occupies only the first two feet of 52.9: "So is the time." "So" refers back to what has been established, that scarcity breeds appreciation, and "the time" refers ahead to the infrequent occasion that in one way or another discloses "you": one way according to one reading, which I shall label A; the other way according to reading B.

Reading A. It is the "time that keeps [= withholds] you" during a period of separation, which is likened both to "my chest" and to "the wardrobe" that "doth hide" the "robe," corresponding to "you," hiding it until the particular, happy ("blest") moment when the wardrobe of time opens and its ("his") contained "pride," the 'gorgeousness' of the robe, figuring your own splendid self, is exhibited with renewed glory to my sight. Here 52.9–10 would be scanned "Só is the tíme that kéeps you aś my chést, / Or aś the waŕdrobe. . . ." The *as*-phrases may be adverbial, modifying "keeps," or adjectival, modifying "time."

Reading B. Here the same lines would be scanned, "Só is the tíme that kéeps yóu as my chést, / Oŕ as the waŕdrobe. . . ." The *as*-phrases now are adjectival and modify the stressed pronoun "you," and "the time that keeps [= maintains] *you*," as "chest" or "wardrobe," does so in order to reveal, at a future moment, the wondrous contents inside, specifically the "robe," which must stand for your body. Thus "you" are closed when clothed and disclosed when sometimes undressed. Freud sheds light on this paradoxical equating of a "robe" with the state of being disrobed when he finds clothes in dreams, and so in the unconscious, symbolic of nakedness.[2] The manner in which "time" displays the youth at "some special instant" depends on alternative meanings of "pride," whether as 'magnificence, splendor' (OED 6, 7, 9) or, in Coleman's gloss, as 'phallic turgidity' (cf. 151.10). Consequently, 52.12 permits these complementary constructions: (1) "By new unfolding" (= revealing) of the formerly "imprisoned" (= clad) "pride," where "pride" is the 'splendor' of the young body now bared; (2) "By new unfolding" (= lengthening-out) of the "pride" formerly "imprisoned" (by garments), where "pride" is the youth's 'aroused phallus.'

Readings A and B need not be mutually exclusive; A may well be devised by the author as a discreet screen for B. But B better adapts to the couplet, the first word of which, "Blessed," characterizes "you" as 'fortunate,' specifically in the area of erotic love, and this sense can apply to the two previous uses of the adjective: at 52.11, where "special *blest*" is the "instant," interpretable as the instant of erotic interaction, and at 52.1, where the "key" that is "blessed" will bear, in line with Freudian dream symbolism, phallic overtones.[3] Not only does "worthiness," as already remarked, derive from "worth" at 52.7 a corporal reference, but "to triumph," the infinitive dependent on "had" at 52.14, expresses sexual transport no less than in Sonnet 151, where to "*Triumph* in love" means that the poet's penile "flesh . . . rising . . . doth point out" the mistress as its "*triumphant* prize" (151.8–10). Whatever camouflage might have been furnished by the reading labeled A virtually vanishes with the verb "had," the most transparently sexual allusion in this text. In Sonnet 52 we learn—and numerous other poems will be seen to make the same discovery—that the "passion" felt for the Master Mistress in Sonnet 20 is subsequently enacted rather than suppressed.

The verb "had," used transitively and with an auxiliary, as at 52.14, and with the same denotation, turns up again in the couplet of Sonnet 87:

> Thus have I had thee as a dream doth flatter—
> In sleep a king, but waking no such matter.

To look on past joys as a dream and to feel like a king when contented are common enough notions, and these verses include them but say more. Shakespeare recognizes, with Freud, that dreams "flatter" in being wish-fulfillments; to be "In sleep a king" is to command what the sleeper's heart desires; and the dream material, or "matter," is conceived of as libidinal in character, for what is dreamt of is having "had thee" in the erotic sense of the verb. The dream psychology here has a figurative status, being incorporated into a simile made to convey the poet's impression that, once "waking" to the current reality of the youth's unavailability, the memories of sexual fruition with him take on a dreamlike aura.

The bawdy wordplay in Sonnet 87, no more restricted to the couplet than that of 52, is introduced at the very outset: "Farewell, thou art too dear for my [carnal] possessing." This gerund carries the same idea as "had" in 87.13. In between, at 87.9, appears the clause "Thy self thou gav'st," and Partridge and Coleman agree that 'giving oneself' in Shakespeare can = 'sexual yielding.' In this setting, 87.5, "For how do I hold thee but by thy granting," admits of the reading, 'I take you in my arms only with your consent.'

Sonnet 87 has a formal affinity with Sonnet 20, whose rhymes also are all feminine, and with Sonnet 52 it has affinities of diction, which include the word "worth," used twice in both, in Sonnet 87 at lines 3 and 9 to signify 'value' or 'excellence' based on personal beauty. Allusions to beauty occur also in "that riches," "this fair gift," and "thy great gift" (87.6, 7, and 11), where the gift is that of the comely body that was amorously granted out of an underestimation of yourself ("thy own worth then not knowing") or your overestimation of myself ("where is my deserving?").

Why the self-abasement? Shakespeare could hardly be unaware of his superlative genius, and, to leave the question of autobiography aside, the fictive persona shows himself elsewhere to be fully confident of his capacity to compose undying verse. Class differences cannot be the answer, unless one is prepared to argue that the friend remained unaware of his noble rank until *after* he had yielded himself in love. The poet's self-depreciation, rather, issues from the same source as his awe: from the passionate response to the youth's exceptional good looks on the part of the older man, who feels himself deficient precisely in the physical qualities that elicit his desire. Once the beloved realizes how rare his attractiveness is, can he remain satisfied with such a lover? The lover who fears rejection anticipates and even justifies it, though surely he does so in the hope of forestalling it.

Sonnet 75 is particularly dense with sexual innuendo. Here, to begin with, is the third quatrain:

> Sometime all full with feasting on your sight,
> And by and by clean starved for a look,
> Possessing or pursuing no delight
> Save what is had, or must from you be took.

Shakespeare here makes "delight" allude to 'sexual pleasure,' as Partridge records he does elsewhere, atypically including among the citations 36.8, where the "sweet hours" of "love's *delight*" consist of amorous play between the lovers. With this annotation alone the erotic drift of the quatrain is established. The verbs *possess* ("possessing"), *have* ("had"), and *take* ("took") also admit, and synonymously, of sexual meaning. But whereas it is "you" (or "thee") that is *had* or *possessed* at 52.14 and 87.13, in Sonnet 75 the locutions change; "delight" is now the object of "possessing," and it is now "had" or "took" "from you." In this altered phraseology the verbs and verbal might be thought to lose their bawdy sense, but I think, rather, that it survives and reinforces the carnal import of the passage; for 'to have/take/possess sexual pleasure from you' hardly differs semantically from 'to have/take/possess you.'

The first two lines of Sonnet 75's third quatrain are obviously charged with libidinal intensity. Two appetites are implicitly compared, the nutritive and the sexual, the latter being described metaphorically in terms that belong to the former, both appetites being assumed to undergo the same rhythms. The sexual rhythms take the form of lust of the eyes, those of the lover now "feasting" on the "sight" of the youth and, again, "clean starved for a look" at him, where both the context and the phrasing suggest that the ocular hunger is too avid to be satisfied with less than a "look" at the other's beauty fully bared.

The motif of nourishment found here, and again in the couplet, is introduced in the opening lines:

> So are you to my thoughts as food to life,
> Or as sweet season'd showers are to the ground. . . .

Not only are "my thoughts" refreshed and fructified as they dwell on you, but they do so of necessity. Then a second motif intervenes in 75.3–8, where the lover compares himself to a miser:

> And for the peace of you I hold such strife
> As 'twixt a miser and his wealth is found—
> Now proud as an enjoyer, and anon
> Doubting the filching age will steal his treasure,
> Now counting best to be with you alone,
> Then better'd that the world may see my pleasure.

In the phrase "the peace of you," the noun = 'contented tranquillity,' obtainable from you, and it may entail wordplay on 'piece' as 'a person of supreme excellence' (Schmidt) or 'masterpiece.'[4] The poet's paradoxical "strife" for this "peace" resembles the miser's conflict between rejoicing in his wealth and fearing ("doubting") its theft in these dishonest times. "Now proud as an enjoyer" takes one meaning with respect to the figurative miser; with respect to the literal "I," it takes the analogous and bawdy meaning that incorporates these glosses: *enjoy* 'sexually' (Coleman); "proud" = 'sensually excited' (Ingram and Redpath, p. 361). Like the miser, the lover is apprehensive lest his "treasure," the beloved, be stolen by another; and yet, though "counting best to be with you alone," he then counts it still better to take the youth out in public. Along with cognizance of the danger of showing him off goes the explicit desire to do so. What "the world" will "see" is "my pleasure," and this can = 'you,' 'my obvious delight in you,' and the 'erotic bliss derived from you' that will be evident to everybody.[5]

The couplet of Sonnet 75 again employs metaphors from feeding—

> Thus do I pine and surfeit day by day,
> Or gluttoning on all, or all away—

to convey the experience of passion. This experience includes the visual sensations treated in 75.9–10, but these are only one aspect ("thoughts," feelings, acts are others) of the sensual complex that is the poem's subject. The language of the conclusion is figurative *and* the principal words are puns, as these glosses from Partridge indicate: "pine" = 'to waste away for love'; "surfeit" = 'to indulge excessively in physical love'; and, as an adjective, "glutton" = 'amorous-greedy.' The extremes of desire and satisfaction are of frequent occurrence, "day by day"; and the "gluttoning," a kind of passionate devouring, is "on all." "All" refers to the totality of the other's physical self, which is removable and on some days is removed: "or all away."

By now it should be plain, even though but a modicum of the evidence is in, that sexual relations do occur between the friends, that the program proposed at the end of Sonnet 20 is subsequently discarded, and that the conclusion the commentators customarily base on that sonnet—that it proves once and for all the absence of such relations—is unwarranted.

Sonnets 52, 87, and 75 can be perceived as chaste only at the cost of their considerable attenuation. A phrase like "clean starved for a look," when discharged of its erotic energy, becomes little more than 'I am eager to see you again,' while "gluttoning on all" is reduced to 'it's most enjoyable to be in your company,' and "Thus have I had thee as a dream doth flatter" to 'knowing you was truly delightful.' Filtering out the passion makes the texts comparatively dull, stale, and flat and creates an odd discrepancy between the ardent language and the amicable sentiments it is taken to convey. Nonetheless, readers for generations have been content to receive these poems as expressive of nonsensual male friendship. The explanation is not far to seek. First, they are conditioned to do so by an inbred bias against amorous relations between men. Second, they have been assured over and over by the most distinguished scholars, who themselves usually share the same bias, that nothing sexually amiss is to be found in the lyrics that Shakespeare composed for the youth. Persuasion is very easy under these circumstances, and almost anything passes muster so long as it serves the cause of denying eroticism between the male friends.

The increasing interest shown of late in the bawdy vein in Shakespeare, thanks above all to Eric Partridge, is a happy development, enhancing our appreciation and understanding. Yet scholars and critics who so often seem liberated from the old fault of prudery are but partially so. The greater attentiveness to sexual innuendo has not affected readings of Part I of the Sonnets. If Part II has profited from the broader attitudes, that is because it treats of an affair that may be illicit but is mercifully heterosexual. Hence the limitations of the new open-mindedness become apparent; it extends only to a vocabulary of "normal" sexuality and does not countenance references to the erotically "abnormal."

The glossaries of Shakespearean bawdy at once illustrate and legislate this restriction, doing so (1) by failing to cite, when defining terms, their usage in Sonnets 1–126, and (2) by failing to take account of the possible homosexual relevance of terms in formulating their definitions. Editors and other expositors then offend in yet a third way, which relies on annotating, the trick being to withhold from a given word or phrase its bawdy sense when supplying it would compromise the male friends. These procedures amount, in effect, to glossarial censorship, however undeliberate it may be in most cases.

Shakespeare's transitive use of the verb *have* as a past participle in the couplets of Sonnets 52 and 87 ("you . . . Being *had*," "Thus have I *had* thee"), is a case in point. The word may appear in love lyrics, and at climactic points, but no matter; for since the love in question is not heterosexual, the carnal import goes unremarked. Had these sonnets been written to a mistress, the verb would surely be noted, in lexicon and edition, as an instance of the bawdy use of *have*; but they are written to the friend, and so this denotation must be suppressed. Paul Ramsey concedes that the clause "Thy self thou gav'st" at 87.9, "if said of a woman would certainly suggest consummation." Why should the identical clause take one meaning in amatory verse to a woman and automatically take another if the recipient is a man? It is a curious idea, that words gain and lose significations according to the sexes of speaker and hearer; if this were so, new labels might be called for in dictionary entries, such as *ref. restr. to opp. sex.* Ramsey also spots "had" in the two instances above, observing that it "suggests to a modern ear physical possession."[6] But modern and Elizabethan ears are attuned in this instance, as Partridge, Coleman, and the OED all bear witness.

Have is glossed by Partridge as 'possess carnally,' by Coleman simply with the qualifier 'coitally' (though he gives *take* the broader qualifier 'sexually'), and by the OED Supplement with the infinitive phrases (synonymous?) 'to have sexual intercourse with, to possess sexually.' 'Coitally' and 'sexual intercourse' delimit the sense, but otherwise the definitions seem broad enough to cover other sexual practices. However, all of the definers probably had copulation in mind. The supporting citations, which are all taken from Shakespeare's plays by Partridge and Coleman, refer exclusively to heterosexual relations. Partridge admits to but two "definite" and "exceedingly few indefinite references to male homosexuality" in the plays and none in the Sonnets, while Coleman, though receptive to more erotic possibilities in the Sonnets, breaks no semantic ground. There is no reason to restrict the sense of *have* to either intercourse or heterosexuality, and the restriction reflects less the usage of the age than the habits of mind of the glossarists, who refuse to confront linguistic evidence that does not fit their predilections. It is generally made to look as if Shakespearean English, though so fertile in heterosexual bawdy, was incapable of producing homoerotic statements.

In actual fact, most sexual acts that a man can perform with a woman can also be performed with another man, and one and the same word serves to denote both kinds. He may have *intercourse* with a member of either sex and, *per anum*, with both. That our most notorious four-letter word admits of such dual usage is demonstrated by Rochester in "The Disabled Debauchee" (1675):

> Nor shall our love-fits, Chloris, be forgot,
>   When each the well-looked linkboy strove t'enjoy,
> And the best kiss was the deciding lot
>   Whether the boy fucked you, or I the boy.[7]

If that, of all verbs, could do such double duty, and in the seventeenth century too (though later than Shakespeare), the verbs *have, take,* and *possess,* which are milder and probably have less specific sexual denotations, need not be conceived of as more specialized. As the boy might have been said to *have* Chloris, just so might the male speaker *have* the boy.

Although Rochester clearly uses the verb to signify intercourse of one man with another, that meaning is omitted from glossaries of bawdy diction, and omissions of this kind are customary. Moreover, in alluding to a sexual act between men, he perforce has recourse to the terminology of heterosexual experiences, and by doing so he makes manifest that the term that names the act can be neutral as far as gender is concerned.

A passage from Marlowe provides further illustration. In *Dido, Queen of Carthage,* Venus bursts in on Jupiter as he dallies with Ganymede and exclaims: "You can sit toying there / And playing with that female wanton boy . . ." (1.50–51). Partridge glosses the verb "toy" as follows: 'To play, or disport oneself; especially, amorously; not merely to copulate but also, and predominantly, to kiss and caress playful-passionately.' He glosses the verb "play" as 'To disport oneself sexually' and the adjective "wanton" as 'lewd; sexually light; amorously playful." In each case he elucidates Shakespearean usage that refers to heterosexual behavior; but Marlowe uses these same terms—there just were no others—to refer to the homosexual behavior of bisexual Jupiter. Or again, Partridge's definitions of "whore" as 'a prostitute,' and 'hence, occasionally, a very loose woman,' and of "mistress" as 'a man's illicit woman' and 'the woman one loves' hardly allow for the "masculine whore," a very loose man, that Patrocles is in the opinion of Thersites (*Troilus and Cressida*, 5.1.16) and even less for the "Master Mistress" of Sonnet 20. Where bawdy language appertains to erotic interplay between male lovers, the annotators prove to be off-color blind.

Continuities, thus far neglected in this chapter, will now be taken up again as I return to Sonnet 52 in order to view it in its immediate contexts. Beginning with the pair of poems that precede it, I shall survey many of the poems in the 50s, which are particularly fertile in erotic allusions.

Companion pieces, Sonnets 50 and 51 might better be regarded as a double sonnet of twenty-eight lines, with the "turn" at 51.5. The literal circumstances remain the same throughout, the persona depicting himself as making an outward journey on horseback. In the first eighteen lines he is "heavy" with sadness, weighed down with "woe," because of departing from "my joy behind";[8] then, in the last ten lines (51.5–14), his mood changes as he has a powerful fantasy of the return trip to the beloved, when even the speed of wind or wings will seem too slow, and "no horse" can "with my desire keep pace."

That "desire" is figuratively equine, as 51.9, just quoted from, intimates, and in 51.11 it "Shall neigh":

> Therefore desire, of perfect'st love being made,
> Shall neigh, no dull flesh, in his fiery race; . . . .

The Q printing, "Shall naigh noe dull flesh in his fiery race," is in Rollins' mind when he surveys at some length "the efforts made by editors to clear up this puzzling line." "To clean up," he might better have said, and the efforts include, besides repunctuation, annotation and sometimes verbal revision. I need not go over the same ground except to remark that in virtually all cases "desire" is construed as fleshless, as having "no . . . flesh." I, to the contrary, take "no" to modify "dull" rather than "flesh." The metrical stress lends some support: "no dúll flesh." The two verses above may thus be paraphrased: 'Composed of the most perfect love, desire, fleshly and embodied in flesh that is not dull, shall neigh (like a horse in heat) during its passionately inflamed run (toward you).' "Race" has the sense of OED 1: 'The act of running; a run. Freq. in phr. *in, on, with a race.*" Ingram and Redpath, though offering an interpretation basically at odds with mine, do define "desire" as 'pure *eros*.' They also produce two texts that strongly reinforce this annotation, citing *Venus and Adonis*, 262–65 and 307, for Shakespeare's recognition that "a horse . . . often neighs from the impatience of sexual desire," and, "for application of the word ['neigh'] to human desire," citing Jeremiah 5:8: "They were as fed horses in the morning; every one neighed after his neighbor's wife." Partridge glosses "dullness" as 'sexual torpidity.' In Sonnet 151 the "flesh . . . rising at thy name," that is, the mistress's, and able "To stand" is phallic and the poet's, and the "flesh" that is not "dull" at 51.11 is likewise the poet's and phallic, the stimulating object, there female, being here male. Modernized punctuation should set off the phrase "no dull flesh" with commas or dashes as a way of indicating its apposition to "desire"—desire conceived of as carnal and genitally stimulative.

Sonnet 52 avers that the rareness of the friends' coming together betters rather than impairs their love, and the poem gains poignancy from its position immediately after the "journey" of Sonnets 50–51. In fact, Sonnet 52 might be considered epistolary, sent from the traveling poet, as the preceding two sonnets were, or else an address delivered on his return; but, either way, it is related to the separation treated just before. And, of course, the eroticism expressed in Sonnet 51 suffuses Sonnet 52, and it then carries over into Sonnet 53:

> What is your substance, whereof are you made,
> That millions of strange shadows on you tend?—
> Since every one hath, every one, one shade,
> And you, but one, can every shadow lend:
> Describe Adonis and the counterfeit
> Is poorly imitated after you.
> On Helen's cheek all art of beauty set,
> And you in Grecian tires are painted new.
> Speak of the spring and foison of the year—
> The one doth shadow of your beauty show,
> The other as your bounty doth appear,
> And you in every blessed shape we know.
>   In all external grace you have some part,
>   But you like none, none you, for constant heart.

This discourse upon shadows has to do rather with "love's philosophy" than Plato's. The central conceit rests on the everyday observation that "every one," person or thing, casts one and its own shadow. However, the friend is unique, seemingly composed of some unheard-of "substance," since not one but "millions . . . of shadows"—"strange" ones, other than his own—attend him. To the poet's mind all beautiful phenomena, human and other, in art and nature, are shadows of the beautiful beloved. The conception is not Platonic because the "substance" shadowed is a particular physical body and cannot mean "yourself as archetypal Idea," since, in that case, shadows would be not "strange" but regular and expected reflections.

Out of the "millions," four shadows are specified, two from art and mythology in the second quatrain (Adonis, Helen) and two from the seasonal cycles of nature in the third (spring, autumn). Adonis and Helen present these contrasts: one is male, one female; the "counterfeit" of the first is a verbal depiction unrestricted as to bodily parts, and the second is "painted," but only her head, as is indicated by the details of "cheek" and "Grecian tires" (= head-dress); each is a paragon of "external graces" (53.13), he that of the handsome youth, she that of feminine beauty; the one is famous for shunning seduction (by Venus), the other for yielding to it (by Paris). The youth is told that artistic delineations of Adonis and Helen are but "shadows," that is, images "poorly imitated after you." This superlative compliment to the more resplendent Adonis-Helen recalls Sonnet 20, where a "woman's face," like Helen's in a painting, is ascribed to him, together with the masculine form ("hue") of an Adonis. Once again, this time with allusions to classical myths, the Master Mistress is portrayed as embodying features of both sexes.

Yet other implications may attach to Shakespeare's choice of these particular figures to serve as comparisons. "Describe Adonis," he writes, and he has done so, in the descriptive details scattered through *Venus and Adonis*. That poem, if elucidative of the allusion here, makes it tempting to infer that the friend, sharing more than beauty with Adonis, is likewise unsusceptible to eros. But he is then immediately likened to Helen, who to the contrary showed herself only too susceptible to erotic enticement. The indifference in the one case is to a female, the attraction in the other is to a male; the youth would harbor tendencies akin to those of both mythic figures if he turned out sexually to be indifferent to women and attracted to men. That interesting possibility will be explored further, but the failure of the earlier persuasions to breed might here be pertinently recalled.

In the third quatrain of Sonnet 53, where each "shadow" is seasonal, that of the spring shows "your beauty," the lovely season being assigned the same function as the Adonis and Helen. The autumnal "foison" has a different function, for in it a new quality, "your bounty," appears. The word "bounty" means 'generosity with something abundantly possessed.' That 'something' is certainly not a fortune, as those who suppose the poems to be concerned with patronage would have it. In annotating 53.1 Ingram and Redpath give, among other definitions of "substance," that of 'wealth,' adding, parenthetically, 'he has many servant shadows to attend him.' *Millions* of them? And just how could 'wealth' be imagined to cast "shadows"? A. L. Rowse comments, "I think we may infer that the poet [Shakespeare] had been the recipient of his patron's [Southampton's] bounty."[9] Such readings stem from the presumption that the friend is a nobleman. To the contrary, his "bounty" consists not in dispensing funds but rather in yielding the richness of his physical beauty to his lover, of giving himself personally and sexually, and this sense accords with the commendation of him at the end of Sonnet 52, where his "worthiness"—not financial worth but corporal excellence—admits of "triumph" when he is carnally "had."

Lines 12 and 13 of Sonnet 53 express, in different words, the very same idea, that "you" appear "in every blessed shape" and participate "in all external grace," both phrases making reference to the visually beautiful. The last line, by contrast, extols the friend for a virtue that is interior and unshared: "But you like none, none you, for constant heart."[10] Here "none" has a strictly human reference, denoting 'nobody else.' Such a heart distinguishes the friend both from inconstant Helen and from Adonis, who might be termed "nonconstant" for declining the commitment to love that fidelity presupposes.

The "constant heart" that terminates Sonnet 53 anticipates 54, which begins:

> Oh how much more doth beauty beauteous seem
> By that sweet ornament which truth doth give.

The meaning of "truth" required by the prior context and the present one is 'constancy' or 'troth' (OED 1). After the introductory observation, that truth in this sense enhances human pulchritude, the poem veers into a comparison between roses and "canker blooms," or 'dog-roses,' that runs through the next ten lines, 54.3–12. The critical problem, then, is to determine how this central passage ties in with the two opening verses and the closing couplet.

> The rose looks fair, but fairer we it deem
> For that sweet odor which doth in it live.
> The canker blooms have full as deep a dye
> As the perfumèd tincture of the roses,
> Hang on such thorns and play as wantonly
> When summer's breath their maskèd buds discloses:
> But for their virtue only is their show,
> They live unwoo'd, and unrespected fade—

> Die to themselves. Sweet roses do not so;
> Of their sweet deaths are sweetest odors made.

Although no more splendidly colored than the canker, the rose is superior in two respects: it is "sweet," in the sense of 'fragrant,' and so perfumes ("odors," 54.12) can be distilled from it. But this discourse is not about botany; it is rather about, as the initial lines indicate, the relation between constancy in love and personal comeliness. The floral details are meant metaphorically. The two kinds of beautiful blossoms, one kind sensuously preferable to the other, represent two types of beautiful people, one type morally superior to the other; and the aromatic quality of the rose stands for the virtue of fidelity that distinguishes the superior human type, to which, in 54.13, the "beauteous and lovely youth" belongs.

The diction in 54.7–12 that is literally descriptive of the flowers abounds in sensual connotations applicable to the flowers' human referents. When they bud in the warmth of "summer's breath," the "canker blooms" will *play* as *wantonly* as the rose, but they will "live *unwoo'd*" and "*Die* to themselves"; by contrast, of the "*sweet deaths*" of "*sweet* roses" are "*sweetest odors* made." To "play" can = 'to disport oneself sexually' (Partridge), and "wantonly" reinforces that meaning. The verb "die" can = 'experience an orgasm' (P), and since "deaths," in the very next line, denotes the roses' dyings, the plural noun can be allowed the same import. "Sweet" can = 'filled with sexual pleasure' (P). "Odors" denotes the 'scent' distilled from the rose, and at 6.1–2 the youth is implicitly a summer flower that must be "distill'd" of the essence of his generative fluid. The conceit of 54.3–12 incorporates these verbal senses, and it cannot be fully decoded until they are taken into account. Once they are, the following reading emerges.

The canker-types are good-looking young rakes, all "show," sexually active and dissolute, incapable of fidelity, who doom themselves to "live unwoo'd, and unrespected [= disregarded] fade [= grow old]," and, ultimately, to "die to themselves" in masturbatory isolation. The rose-types, also fair, also sexually active, but faithful in love, "do not so," that is, do not live unwooed and unrespected and do not die to themselves; instead, they *die to another*, a lover, with "sweet" orgasmic "deaths," and the "sweetest odors" made thereby consist of the ejaculatory distillations. The phrase "And so of you," at 54.13, indicates that the "beauteous and lovely youth" addressed is one of these—a rose, sainted by amorous commitment, who dies in the odor of sexuality.

The final line—

> When that shall vade, by verse distils your truth—

consists of an independent and self-contained sentence that modernized punctuation would do well to set off by placing a period at the end of the preceding line. The antecedent of "that" is "youth" in 54.13, where the word denotes 'young man'; but to serve as the antecedent, the word retrospectively suffers a semantic change to 'youthfulness.' The word "truth" has the same sense as in 54.2, 'constancy'; but it seems also to purport, in 54.14, your 'actual nature' (OED 11c, d), where fidelity and loveliness meet. The verb "distils," which signifies the technical process adverted to in 54.12, of obtaining perfume from roses, is intransitive, so that "your truth," the verb's subject, either 'undergoes distillation' (OED 6) or perhaps 'becomes a distillation' (Tucker), i.e., figuratively becomes a perfume derived from you by the distilling agency of "verse." Hence the line might be paraphrased: 'When your youth shall in the future fade, your commended faithfulness / your lovely, lovable, and true self in essence does ever subsist (in an eternal present) by means of immortal poetry.'[11]

The tenses of 54.14—future in the dependent clause, present in the main clause—carry further significance. If in later times "your truth" distills by verse, what about at present, when youth and beauty are yet in full bloom? Even now, as always hereafter, the "sweetest odors" are distilled from "your truth" by means of the preservative powers of poetry, including this poem, and now by other means as well, by acts of love; for "your truth" entails, above all, your unalterable commitment to perform those acts with one and the same lover, the poet himself.

When the idea of orgastic distillation of the friend was enunciated earlier, at 6.1–2—where "let not . . . thy summer" be defaced "ere thou be distill'd" meant 'do not permit your youth to perish before your generative fluid is discharged'—he was being counseled to "breed." In a dramatic reversal of that stand, Sonnet 54 celebrates his practice of sexual fidelity, and to the very one who had then counseled propagation.

It is possible that with the allusion to "verse" at 54.14 Shakespeare had in mind not so much this sonnet as another, or others, more fully and centrally devoted to the theme of immortalization of the friend in "powerful rhyme," and it is no accident that the sonnet that comes up next, 55, "Not marble, nor the gilded monuments," turns out to be one, and one of the most renowned, on this subject. Once again the wonderfully artful arrangement of Q cries out for notice—too often to deaf ears. For the second time in a row Shakespeare makes the final line of one a link and prelude to the succeeding poem. As Sonnet 53 concludes with the phrase "constant heart," which heralds the theme of "truth" in 54, so does 54 conclude with the idea of perpetuating "verse" in preparation for 55, which amplifies the idea.

Sonnet 55 claims to do more than extract an essence from the youth; its "powerful rhyme" can keep his life ("you live in this") and the way he looks and moves ("you shall shine . . . bright" and "pace forth") in endless aesthetic existence. The poet-lover also specifies the fit audience when he writes, in 55.14, "you" here and forever "dwell in lovers' eyes." The anticipated readership, both contemporaneous and in time to come, will consist of lovers, because it is they who will be attuned to and engrossed by the erotic feelings that motivate and suffuse this tribute. Unfortunately, the most vocal readership has been that of scholars, most of them dead set on negating the loverly feelings.

The "Sweet love" apostrophized in the octave of Sonnet 56 is neither the friend nor Cupid but the erotically "sweet" feeling of being in love. Apparently and alarmingly ebbing, it is beseeched: "renew thy force [= vigor, or potency]; be it not said / Thy edge should blunter be than appetite." "Edge" in Partridge = 'sexual desire in a man, with special reference to erection—the semantics being "edge of sexual appetite."' Love is compared (56.3–8) with the "appetite" for food,

> Which but today by feeding is allay'd,
> Tomorrow sharpen'd in his former might;
> So love be thou; although today thou fill
> Thy hungry eyes even till they wink with fulness,
> Tomorrow see again, and do not kill
> The spirit of love, with a perpetual dulness.

Struck with the awkward notion that *friendship* is likened to hunger, commentators miss the obvious: the parallel drawn between two bodily appetites, the need for nutriment and sexual needs. The common rhythmic pattern in which each is alternately "sharpened" with craving its object and then "blunted" with gratification furnishes the basis of comparison. Because his carnal desire now fails to follow this pattern by failing to go on to the phase of arousal, the troubled poet presses it on in the second quatrain with metaphors taken from eating. "So love be thou"—be continually, tomorrow just as today, on the model of the daily yearning for bread, reenkindled with libidinal energy.[12] "Thy eyes" at 56.6, "hungry" (which = 'avidly amorous' [Partridge]), are not the poet's but love's, who "fills" them, by analogy with feasting to drowsiness, "even till they wink [= close] with fulness [= satiety]." Then "Tomorrow see again" is urged upon "love"; that is, be concupiscent once more upon beholding the beloved, "and do not kill / The spirit of love, with a perpetual dulness."[13] Shakespeare makes a distinction between (A) "love," spoken to and endowed with visual power and the power to "kill" the "spirit of love," and (B) "the spirit of love," which is spoken about and is, as the naming suggests, an integral part of "love," the two conceived of as differentiated aspects of a single entity. "Dulness" at 56.8 completes the metaphorical design of the octave, and in the sense of 'sleepiness from overeating' the word refers back to "wink with fulness" in 56.6, and, in the sense of 'lack of sharpness' (Rollins), it refers, further back, to the implied 'blade' ("edge . . . blunter . . . sharpen'd") of 56.2 and 4, while, on the literal level, "dulness" denotes 'sexual torpidity' (Partridge).

The "spirit" of "love" may be taken to allude to its 'soul' or 'spiritual element,' to feelings toward the other such as tenderness and wonder, for these inform eros and also depend on it, since they will not, it is feared, survive the permanent subsiding of desire. However, "spirit" again can = 'semen,' along with the closely allied physiological 'spirit generative' that the word also conveys,[14] and it may possibly = 'the male member.'[15] Annotated thus, "the spirit of love" would have reference not to affectionate sentiments but to sexual sensations, and it would be deadened when no phallic reactions arose as a result of gazing on the beloved. The subject, the lover's feeling of apathy, is intimately connected with, if not one with, the idea of genital dormancy, an idea that has lurked just below the surface all along—what with love's "force" in need of renewal at 56.1, the blunted "edge" of desire in 56.2, and the "dulness" at 56.8.

If "spirit" may signify both 'idealizing sentiments' and 'sperm' (with or without its organ), two corresponding readings, diverse but not incompatible, emerge. In reading A, "love" alludes to the sensuous/sensual responses of the lover, and the "spirit of love" refers to his appreciation or admiration of the youth's "spiritual" qualities. In reading B, "love" designates the sensuous, and especially the visual, apprehension of the youth by the lover, and the "spirit of love" designates the latter's attendant sensual responses.[16] Here are two different facets of love, and Freud has made pertinent observations on each. With respect to the notions in reading B, he speaks of the eye as an "erotogenic zone" (equivalent to love's "hungry eyes" at 56.6) which

> in the situation of wooing . . . is liable to be the most frequently stimulated by the particular quality of excitation whose cause . . . we describe as beauty. This stimulation is on the one hand already accompanied by pleasure, while on the other hand it

leads to an increase of sexual excitement or produces it if it is not yet present.[17]

In Sonnet 56 the erogenous eyes fail to stimulate, so that desire remains inert. Elsewhere Freud says that "visual impressions remain the most frequent pathway along which libidinal excitement is aroused."[18] But in the poem that pathway is blocked.

With respect to the notions in reading A, Freud says that he has

> always been struck by the phenomenon of sexual overvaluation—the fact that the loved object enjoys a certain amount of freedom from criticism, and that all its characteristics are valued more highly than those of people who are not loved, or than its own were at a time when it itself was not loved.

He also calls this same "tendency," signified by one sense of "spirit of love" in 56.8, "that of idealization." He considers, moreover, its cause and function:

> If the sensual impulsions are more or less effectively repressed or set aside, the illusion is produced that the object has come to be sensually loved on account of its spiritual merits, whereas on the contrary these merits may really only have been lent to it by its sensual charm.

Shakespeare is under no such illusion, recognizing in the second quatrain this dependence of idealization on sensual responsiveness. The "overvaluation" serves the function of "directing a lasting cathexis upon the sexual object" in order that it may be loved during the "passionless intervals" between the satisfaction and revival of sexual need.[19] This, of course, bears strikingly on Sonnet 56. The lover is undergoing just such an interval, and the "spirit of love," not tiding him over it, not serving as a means of continuity, seems itself to be falling victim to the inertia of desire.

The two readings should not be regarded as alternatives, for both are supported by text and contexts; they enrich each other, and the elimination of either would impoverish the poem.

In the sestet the poet drops the second-person address to love, though he continues, as before, to muse to himself, now dwelling on the chance that his unhappy plight may prove fruitful:

> Let this sad interim like the ocean be
> Which parts the shore, where two contracted new
> Come daily to the banks, that when they see
> Return of love, more blest may be the view;
>   As call it winter, which being full of care,
>   Makes summer's welcome thrice more wish'd, more rare.

Hope is expressed with the conceit that likens the temporal "inter-im," which is "sad" on account of the torpor that interrupts the passion for the friend, to the spatial "ocean" that keeps apart two hypothetical lovers—evidently heterosexual ones, since they are "contracted new" (= lately engaged). Every day, while the separa-tion lasts, each visits the seashore, presumably to look over the water toward the distant, unseen other, so that "when they see / Return of love" at their later reunion, "the view" of the reciprocated affection will be "more blest" than if they had not suffered the ab-sence or had not faithfully observed the seashore ritual of yearning. The poet entertains the possibility that his current lack of passion will prove to be temporary, an interval that may be, as the ocean is for the fictive couple, conducive to renewed and heightened love.[20] The couplet adds a second and congruent simile: "Or call it [i.e., the "sad interim"] winter," the very burdens of which serve to render summer's return triply delightful.

Although his passion has flagged, the lover clearly wishes it re-stored, whether from feeling himself deprived by its loss or out of care for the other, or both; and this wish, embodied in the imper-atives of 56.1, 5, and 7 and in the optative of 56.9–12, presages the revival of love's "force."

Shakespeare places Sonnet 56 brilliantly, between 55, which, in a mood of confidence, ringingly confers immortality on the beloved, and the paired 57 and 58, which, in a bitter mood, upbraid him for high-handed mistreatment. The center of indifference on the poet's part modulates between his prior euphoria, unlikely to be sustained, and his subsequent anguish when the conduct of the friend seems to betoken indifference. Between the happiness and the hurt, he suffers the hiatus of Sonnet 56. Unlike its neighbors, this sonnet does not address the youth, nor does it seem meant for his perusal; for to what end would he be apprised of the unfortunate "interim" of inap-petence that the lover is suffering? The soliloquy occupies a se-cretive breach in communion with the other, between that in Sonnet 55 and that resumed, though in a very different key, in 57.

From Sonnet 57 we learn that the "interim" was just that and not the dreaded "perpetual dulness," for the emotional lethargy has come to an end, though not in the way anticipated—with the "re-turn of love"—but rather with stirrings of jealous suspicion. The interrogative opening of the poem is weighted with sarcasm:

> Being your slave, what should I do but tend
> Upon the hours and times of your desire?

The persona is irate and remonstrative as he ironically dons the mask of a "slave." The projected relationship, with the friend tacitly his master, does not in the least suggest an actual difference of social position, as that of commoner and nobleman. To evoke class distinction here would considerably attenuate the force of the irony, though not entirely eradicate it; for even then the polar opposites of "your slave" and "my sovereign" (57.6) would be, though less so, hyperbolical. The projected relationship, rather, caustically contrasts the role of each in practice with the role that properly belongs to each of two who are joined in erotic intimacy.

Carnal leanings and deeds are ascribed to the youth throughout this sonnet and the next: "your desire" is fleshly at 57.2; "in your will" = 'sexual urge' as well as 'willfulness, choice,' at 57.13; "your . . . pleasure" is lascivious, or suspected to be so, at 58.2, and "your pleasure" is definitely so if "ill," at 58.14; "your liberty" = 'your freedom of movement / libertine behavior' (Tucker, who cites 41.1) at 58.6; the "self-doing crime" at 58.12 consists of sexual misdemeanors. Moreover, the "services" of the poet at 57.4 would include 'sexual attentions' (Partridge), and "your servant" at 57.8 gets this annotation from Ingram and Redpath: "As frequently in Elizabethan English both (1) slave and (2) lover."

Not only does the friend go where, and do what, he pleases, but, with respect to sexual offenses, he assumes the prerogatives of the highest offices. He must be judge as well as offender to "pardon" his own "crime" (58.9–12); and since he is not to be held accountable (58.3) and is beyond indictment (58.8, 14), his state is kingly. If he does try to lord it over his lover, he is taking advantage of the privilege, not of aristocratic rank, but of personal charm. The poet protests what he regards as an unjust exercise of erotic power. At 57.5–10 he vents his grievances in ironic terms. Feeling himself degraded, as though to the status of a menial, he "dare" not complain about interminable periods when he is kept waiting—whether for a meeting or at a meeting place—or about the "bitterness of absence" after dismissal; nor dare he even speculate on the master's whereabouts or activities elsewhere, except for the obsessive thought of "where you are, how happy you make those."

Sonnet 58 continues the subject and the ironic mode of discourse of 57 but subtly intensifies the protestations. The poem begins:

> That god forbid, that made me first your slave
> I should in thought control your times of pleasure.

These verses resemble those that open Sonnet 57: "your slave" occurs in line 1 of each poem and "times of" in each line 2, with the kindred objects "desire" and "pleasure," respectively. The "god" who imposed the enslavement, first mentioned here and with an ambivalent attitude, is Love, which has just been promoted from "fool" (57.13). At 57.1–2 the "hours and times of your desire," however intermittent, will be shared by the lovers; but "your times of pleasure" at 58.2 will be enjoyed otherwise than with the poet. In 57, waiting creates the impulse to "chide the world-without-end hour," and "absence" is distasteful—a "bitterness" truly "sour" (57.5 and 7). In 58, "absence" is a prison, as every place is apart from the beloved; and the inclination is toward "accusing you of injury," and "waiting" now is an excruciating "hell." The "jealous thought" in the sestet of 57 dwells merely on the happiness afforded others by the presence of the friend, but in 58 it dwells, with intimations of immorality, on "your pleasure" taken in another place and in other company, and suspect. Suspicions of profligacy, hinted at in the sestet of 57, become increasingly pronounced in 58. More emphasis than before is put on the love-slave's powerlessness in 58. He must not exercise "control" even "in thought"; he can only resort, in stoic fashion, to disciplining his own reactions—to becoming "tame" with "patience" and cultivating resignation.

The couplet of Sonnet 58, in keeping with the rest, is more acrimonious than that of the companion poem:

> I am to wait, though waiting so be hell,
> Nor blame your pleasure, be it ill or well.

The speaker feigns acquiescence in the other's conduct, whether licit or licentious. But the true message, ironically delivered, is the outraged lover's strong objection to painful mistreatment at the hands of the beloved.

Sonnet 57 concludes:

> So true a fool is love, that in your Will,
> Though you do anything, he thinks no ill.

The poet at 58.14, in contrast, most certainly does "think ill"; the suppressed thought of 57 is given expression in 58, and, once again, the final words of one poem serve as a thematic pointer to the next. The "he" who refuses to judge adversely is personified "love" and, as well, "Will." Even though this refusal to judge is qualified as foolish, the couplet is indulgent and playful, even affectionate. These qualities, missing from the couplet of 58, become even more evident when a third meaning, besides (1) 'choice' and (2) 'libido,' is assigned "Will," capitalized in the Quarto: (3) 'Will(iam)' your lover. Here for the first time in the Sonnets does Shakespeare introduce wordplay on his given name. With meanings (1) and (2) the couplet may be paraphrased: 'Love is so genuine/faithful a fool that no matter what you do by volition/in lust, he forms no bad opinion of you.' With (3) an additional sense emerges: 'the foolish emotion of love resides in your William, so that he loves, if not wisely, too well to bring himself, however you may act, to think harshly of you.'

Sonnet 58 moves the argument of 57 to a further stage of jealousy. But the question arises, and will be taken up later, whether or not the lover has grounds for his suspicions. At any rate, he is prone to jealousy, and it is an outbreak of that passion that brings to an end the emotional lassitude recorded in Sonnet 56.

Sonnets 50–58 prove to be linked in a series unquestionably arranged by the author. This is but a sampling, as Sonnets 1–20 were another, of the fine and complex organization of the sequence on various internal principles. Moreover, the sonnets analyzed so far in this chapter—75 and 89 as well as 50–58—are replete with words and phrases that disclose sexual intimacy between the male lovers. But allusions to their erotic actions and reactions, by no means restricted to these eleven poems, are recurrent in Part I from Sonnet 20 on.

2

To postulate "Renaissance friendship" as the burden of Sonnets 1–126, a maneuver foreshadowed by Malone late in the eighteenth century,[21] is now, and long has been, routine among expositors. Douglas Bush, for example, advances this staple position in his introduction to the Pelican edition of the Sonnets:

> Since modern readers are unused to such ardor in masculine friendship and are likely to leap at the notion of homosexuality . . . we may remember that such an ideal—often exalted above the love of women—could exist in real life, from Montaigne to Sir Thomas Browne, and was conspicuous in Renaissance literature (*Euphues*, Sidney's *Arcadia*, the fourth book of *The Faerie Queene*, some of Shakespeare's plays), whether on the merely human level or linked with cosmic concord. The poet's young friend, though alive, familiarly known, and sometimes charged with vices, becomes a kind of equivalent to Donne's Elizabeth Drury, a symbol of living perfection.[22]

With misconceptions so copious, one hardly knows where to begin. Nowhere in the Sonnets is friendship "linked with cosmic concord." What is Elizabeth Drury doing there? She was personally unknown to Donne, who composed the *Anniversaries*, after the girl's death at fourteen, without ever having laid eyes on her. And can one "charged with vices" be "equivalent" to her as "a symbol of perfection"? Though Bush leaves the plays unnamed, Paul Ramsey makes a germane distinction: "The friendship of Hamlet and Horatio is beautiful, tender, and noble," but they are "not in love," whereas "Shakespeare is in love with the young man."[23] The idea that Musidorus and Pyrocles in *The Arcadia* (to choose only one of Bush's examples)—young men who are princes, cousins, of the same age and brought up together, each in love with a different princess, chivalric adventurers in a pastoral romance—exhibit the same sort of relationship as the poet and his "young friend" cannot be countenanced. It is true that Pyrocles, disguised as the Amazon Zelmane, attracts both male and female desires, so that he is a kind of mistress-master, but this basis for comparison would never occur to someone like Bush.

A shared commitment to virtue, exemplified by Sidney's young friends, is stipulated as the paramount condition of the highest friendship not only in Renaissance discussions of the subject but also in the classical theories, such as those of Aristotle and Cicero,[24] to which the Renaissance theories were often affiliated. Montaigne objected to Greek homosexuality on the basis of Christian morality and also because of the disparity in age and status between the lovers; he also thought that the passion in the older man "was simply grounded upon an externall beauty," the situation being "a false image of corporall generation."[25] Yet Bush—who, though he neglects to mention it, cannot have failed to notice Shakespeare's accent on the external beauty of the youth, and who finds him "superior in social status" and "charged with vices" (whether guilty or not is left up in the air)—disregards all niceties of distinction when he associates the "ideal" of "masculine friendship" in the Sonnets with that in Montaigne and that in *The Arcadia*. He does stumble on one valid observation: in Shakespeare's sequence the love for the other man *is* "exalted above" the love for the woman.

"Modern readers," supposedly ignorant of the history of ideas, are given to understand that erotic interplay between friends never enters into the literature of the Renaissance. However, Professor Bush passes over Richard Barnfield's *Certain Sonnets* (1595), a cycle of twenty poems in which the older lover, Daphnis, woos his Ganymede in indubitably amorous terms. One might have thought that the other Elizabethan sequence that also treats of love for a youthful master-mistress would have received attention—even particular attention—in the vast output of the Shakespearean commentators. Instead, Barnfield is a dirty little skeleton to be kept in the closet, while insistent and exaggerated claims are advanced for the concept of "Renaissance friendship." Other skeletons lurk in the closet too. One is an earlier poem by Barnfield, *The Tears of an Affectionate*

Shepherd Sick of Love, or *The Complaint of Daphnis for the Love of Ganymede.*[26] Another is *Edward II,* in which Marlowe dramatized the king's liaison with Gaveston for the public theater. Then, "in real life," another king, James I, whose reign began in 1603, was known to be erotically attached to a succession of male favorites. In the age of Shakespeare friendship was imagined and experienced with far greater diversity than learned disquisitions would lead us to believe, and "modern readers" should not be intimidated when Elizabeth Drury, Sir Thomas Browne, or the royal heroes of *The Arcadia* are trotted out to "prove" that the Sonnets are locked into a historical context that precludes homoeroticism.

That term "modern readers" undoubtedly comprehends young students, who can be supposed to leap to naive conclusions but who may in fact have clearer vision than indoctrinated savants. Even though handicapped by annotations that shy away from sexual meanings when the subject is "masculine friendship," the "uneducated" readers still have plenty of evidence for concluding that the poet and the friend are amorously conjoined. Sonnets 27 and 43, to choose from a wealth of examples, contribute such evidence. In these poems the absent lover's thoughts during the night revolve obsessively, in sleeplessness or dreams, around the beloved.

"Weary with toil" from traveling all day, in Sonnet 27, "I haste me to bed," only to embark on another "journey," a mental one, when "my thoughts" undertake "a zealous pilgrimage to thee." Rollins records a comment by Kittredge that cites this line: "That lovers are pilgrims and their lady-loves are saints was a common metaphor."[27] True enough, and, to illustrate, the metaphor is elaborated in the sonnetized love duet performed by Romeo and Juliet when they first come together at the Capulet ball (1.5.91 ff.). The implied saint of Sonnet 27, the object of the "pilgrimage" and of love, is, however, a man rather than a lady. Unable to sleep, the poet likens himself to a blind man in "looking upon darkness," with the difference that "my soul's imaginary sight" makes present the youth's image, and it is that "shadow" (produced by "my thoughts") "Which like a jewel hung in ghastly night / Makes black night beauteous, and her old face new." Bright and precious, the "jewel" metamorphoses night. The diction once again is close to that of Romeo, who at first sight of Juliet exclaims, "It seems she hangs upon the cheek of night / Like a rich jewel upon an Ethiop's ear" (1.5.44–45). This "jewel" stands for Juliet as beheld by Romeo, whose speech implies that he is stricken with passion; the poet's "jewel," also "hung" in "night," which is transmuted by it, stands for the image of the youth—and can anyone seriously maintain that the language in the play conveys erotic passion but that the cognate language in the Sonnet does not?

In Sonnet 43, apparently once more a missive sent from the poet on a later journey, his nocturnal response to the friend takes another turn. He is now able to sleep, for his "eyes," that "all the day view . . . things unrespected," can "in dreams look on thee." Sonnet 27 (along with its continuation in 28) records the restlessness of an earlier stage of love, when the persona is more emotionally wrought up by the lately begun intimacy, while Sonnet 43 records a more advanced stage, when the beloved has become so deeply fixed in his unconscious that the lover can relax into a slumber of wish-fulfilling dreams:

> All days are nights to see till I see thee,
> And nights bright days when dreams do show thee [to] me.

Those who read into the sequence the peculiarly Renaissance version of friendship would have us believe that the nocturnal agitations, the need to fantasize the beloved, the fixation of mind on him, and the coveted dreams of him were a quite ordinary part of masculine amity and betoken nothing erotic. Substantiation for this view is never provided, and where in the literature of the age can symptoms like these be found to mark the reaction of one male friend to another? Not in Sidney's *Arcadia,* and in which of Shakespeare's plays? The friendship of the two Gentlemen of Verona admits of no such behavior, nor does that of Romeo for Mercutio. When Romeo uses language similar to that in Sonnet 27, it is when he is captivated by Juliet; and he is kept awake at night, but that is when, earlier, he is infatuated with Rosaline. Close parallels between the language of the sonnets and that of the plays or narrative poems are often adduced by exegetes, but the nonlyric passage usually deals with romantic love, rarely with friendship. Sidney renders nocturnal experiences similar to those in Shakespeare's Sonnets 27, 28, and 43 in his *Astrophel and Stella.* Astrophel, too, suffers insomnia from his preoccupation with Stella, in Sonnets 39, 40, and 31 of that cycle, and he likewise relishes dreams of his beloved, in Sonnets 38 and 32. In the writing of the period such wakefulness and such dreams are common symptoms of erotic love, while they have no more place in nonerotic "masculine friendship" in the Renaissance than at any other time.

The root cause of passion in the Renaissance lover is the visual beauty of the mistress, and just so does that of the Master Mistress generate passion in the sonneteer. Rollins records an observation made in 1861 by Franz Grillparzer, that when "interpreters adduce

from the dramas many passages in which the word 'lover' is used by
man to man for 'friend,' 'favorite,' 'devotee,'" they fail to notice
that "*beauty* is never the cause of the affection."[28] This telling objection retains its force. Hubler certainly provides no adequate re-
joinder in remarking that "the young man's beauty is far from being
the sole source of the poet's admiration and affection."[29] His beauty, if not the "sole," is clearly the primary source, and it is stressed
ubiquitously. Among the Elizabethan sonneteers, who admires his
lady *solely* for her beauty or accords it greater prominence than
Shakespeare does that of the young man? Moreover, who else, Barnfield and Marlowe excepted, envisions a "masculine friendship" in
which physical beauty is both causative and fundamental?

In striving to stave off distressing recognitions, some scholars
have recourse to even odder positions. For Rowse, the entire sequence consists of "duty-sonnets written by the poet to his patron,"
and he says of Sonnet 43, "That this is duty is obvious." What must
be "obvious" is the duty of a poet to dream about his patron.[30]
J. Dover Wilson dissents. He hears another "voice" throughout, not
that "of a client seeking patronage" but that "of an ardently affectionate uncle or guardian."[31] A polar-opposite position is taken up
by C. S. Lewis. He affirms that in the Sonnets Shakespeare deals
with no specific love relationship but with one that is all-inclusive
and that he

> ends by expressing simply love, the quintessence of all loves,
> whether erotic, parental, filial, amicable, or feudal [*sic*]. Thus
> from extreme particularity there is a road to the highest univer-
> sality. The love is, in the end, so simply and entirely love that
> our *cadres* are thrown away and we cease to ask what kind.[32]

This fusing of every type of human love with every other type is
obfuscatory. The "erotic," though noted, is but another and equal
ingredient in the brew that contains the "paternal," "filial," etc.
Unless the "extreme particularity" is apprehended first, the "road
to the highest universality" will inevitably be missed. Nonetheless,
Lewis has pointed, though in a way he never intended, to a salient
aspect of the poet's responses to the youth, for these are often conveyed in metaphors that do derive from a variety of other affectionate relationships and that do intimate that this love *in some manner*
comprehends other kinds. The kinds presented in the Sonnets are
enumerated below, starting with those itemized by Lewis. Neither
an uncle nor an applicant for patronage shows up in the list, an absence that might make the stipulation of these as the roles domi-
nantly or exclusively assumed by the persona look even more far-
fetched.

1. *Parental.* At 37.1–3, the poet imagines himself "as a decrepit father" who "takes delight / To see his active child do deeds of youth." A comparable figure occurs at 22.11–12, when the speaker, "Bearing thy heart," pledges to "keep [it] so chary / As tender nurse her babe from faring ill." The "child" represents the friend, the "babe" his "heart"; but the figurative language that characterizes the lover's attitude as paternal delight and nurse-like tenderness does not imply a return of *filial* affection. The poet elsewhere ascribes such affection to himself—as in Sonnets 97 (see below) and 143 (here toward the "mother" that in the conceit stands for the mistress).

2. *Amicable.* This type might best be illustrated by Sonnet 31, where the current love for the friend is conceived of as resurrecting and synthesizing all previous friendships enjoyed by the persona:

> Thou art the grave where buried love doth live,
> Hung with the trophies of my lovers [= friends] gone,
> Who all their parts of me to thee did give,
> That due of many now is thine alone.
> Their images I lov'd I view in thee,
> And thou (all they) hast all the all of me.

3. *"Feudal."* If the term at first sight seems strange, that is because it is really a misnomer for *Courtly Love.* A pertinent sonnet is 26, the first two quatrains of which go:

> Lord of my love, to whom in vassalage
> Thy merit hath my duty strongly knit,
> To thee I send this written ambassage
> To witness duty, not to show my wit—
> Duty so great, which wit so poor as mine
> May make seem bare, in wanting words to show it.
> But that I hope some good conceit of thine
> In thy soul's thought all naked will bestow it.

To take this to mean that the poet and friend are engaged in a feudal relationship is to confuse the vehicle of the metaphor with the tenor. The lover exhibits, in troubadour fashion, the 'humility' and 'obedience' that are conventional in courtly love, wherein

> There is a service of love closely modelled on the service which a feudal vassal owes to his lord. The lover is the lady's 'man.' He addresses her as *midons*, which etymologically represents not 'my lady' but 'my lord.' The whole attitude has been rightly described as a 'feudalization of love.'

This quotation comes from the first chapter, "Courtly Love," of *The Allegory of Love,* and few will need reminding that the author is

C. S. Lewis.[33] Thus he can be cited as a corrective to himself, and the reason is not far to seek. It is hardly a lapse of memory, despite the lapse of eighteen years between the statement just quoted (1936) and the one quoted earlier (1954). The lack of consistency stems from the different literary works Lewis had in mind on each occasion. Once his topic is the Sonnets, he prefers "feudal" to "courtly love" because he knows only too well that the latter entails poetic adulation of the lady on whom romantic passion devolves; but when the same feudal language ("Lord," "vassalage," "duty") also shows up in a poem to the young man, it cannot but bear the implication that he is now the object of impassioned courtly love.

A variation on the "service of love" appears in two sonnets I have already discussed, 57 and 58, where the poet presents himself not only as "your vassal" (58.4) but also as "your servant" (57.8) and "slave" (57.1, 11; 58.1) but does so in vexation and to object to the mean roles implicitly thrust upon him by the beloved, "my sovereign" (ironic) and a 'master,' regarded for the moment as presumptuous and neglectful. Another variation occurs in Sonnet 106, when the "blazon of sweet beauty's best," descriptive of "ladies dead and lovely knights" in chivalric romances, is finally actualized in "such a beauty as you master now."

The "attempt to preserve the mystique of courtly love and much of its traditional imagery by transferring them to a male beloved" has been remarked by Leslie Fiedler, and it constitutes for him "what is peculiar" to the sequence. He adds that "in language, too, Shakespeare emulated his great [Provençal] predecessors, referring to his beloved as a rose, a muse, an angel, a Helen of Troy; but, unlike them, he found his rose-muse-angel-Helen in a boy rather than a woman."[34]

4. *Marital.* That this type is ordinarily passed over in the commentaries should by now come as no surprise. The most famous allusion is located at the outset of Sonnet 116, as "the marriage of true minds." The sonnet belongs to Part I, and the "marriage" alluded to is the kind that permanently unites the male friends. No one is disturbed by this if they are joined spiritually rather than in flesh, but 116.9–10 undercuts this comfortable supposition:

> Love's not Time's fool, though rosy lips and cheeks
> Within his bending sickle's compass come.

Whose "rosy lips and cheeks," and what is their function? They are the youth's, and they initially ignited the poet's love. This marriage, like others, may survive the fading of youthful loveliness, but it began, as erotic love in the Renaissance is conceived of as beginning, in the eye of the lover, an eye entranced by physical beauty.

At 93.1–2 the poet says,

> So shall I live, supposing thou art true,
> Like a deceived husband,

and such a depiction of himself implies a complementary role in his mind for the friend—that of unfaithful wife: "Thy looks with me, thy heart in other place." The couplet reinforces this implication:

> How like Eve's apple doth thy beauty grow
> If thy sweet vertue answer not thy show.

"Eve's apple," like the youth's "beauty" unattended by "virtue," proves ruinous, and initially to Adam, her "deceived husband."

When the poet, again, would express his loneliness and desolation in his absence from the beloved, he writes, at 97.5–12:

> And yet this time remov'd was summer's time,
> The teeming autumn big with rich increase
> Bearing the wanton burthen of the prime,
> Like widow'd wombs after their lord's decease:
> Yet this abundant issue seem'd to me
> But hope of orphans, and unfathered fruit,
> For summer and his pleasures wait on thee,
> And thou away the very birds are mute.

He adumbrates his sadness in a subjective description of the scenes of nature he beholds; he projects his feelings onto the landscape, and they are both *filial*, those of the fatherless child, and *conjugal*, those of the pregnant widow.

5. *Love for a mistress in the manner of the sonneteers.* This type, transmuted in Part I in more than one respect but, most obviously, with respect to its male object, the Master Mistress, is so complex and pervasive that it can be only partially sketched in this survey. I will begin with the colors emblematic of eroticism, red and white, as these figure in the third quatrain of Sonnet 98:

> Nor did I wonder at the lily's white,
> Nor praise the deep vermilion in the rose;
> They were but sweet, but figures of delight
> Drawn after you, you pattern of all those.

The "blazon," commonplace in Petrarchan praise of female beauties, is spoofed in Sonnet 130 and disallowed the dark mistress, yet it is adduced in praise of the Master Mistress not only explicitly in Sonnet 106 but implicitly in 99:

> The forward violet thus did I chide:
> Sweet thief, whence didst thou steal thy sweet that smells
> If not from my love's breath? The purple pride

Which on thy soft cheek for complexion dwells
In my love's veins thou hast too grossly dyed.
The lily I condemned for thy hand,
And buds of marjoram had stol'n thy hair;
The roses fearfully on thorns did stand,
One blushing shame, another white despair;
A third, nor red, nor white, had stol'n of both,
And to his robbery had annex'd thy breath,
But for his theft in pride of all his growth
A vengeful canker ate him up to death.
     More flowers I noted, yet I none could see
     But sweet or color it had stol'n from thee.

Let those who will suppose that such poetic bouquets were regularly offered to nephews, patrons, or the companion in "masculine friendship" of the time; but the failure to produce corroborative data should not pass unnoticed. Echoes of the language and sentiment of Sonnet 99 are easily enough located, but in love sonnets—for example, in Spenser's *Amoretti*, the very first line of which makes mention of "those lilly hands" (of course his lady's), while in LXIIII,

Comming to kisse her lyps, (such grace I found)
Me seemed I smelt a gardin of sweet flowres.

Spenser goes on to present an olfactory "blazon," in which he likens the smell of each particular feature of the lady, from brows to breasts, to a different species of flower, and concludes:

Such fragrant flowres doe give most odorous smell,
But her sweet odour did them all excell.

The "kiss" of the first line, which occurs just after her acceptance of her suitor, introduces him into this aromatic paradise. Shakespeare's emphasis on "my love's breath," referred to in 99.3, 11, and 14 (with "sweet"), makes sense only if the intimacies of kissing and caressing engaged in by the Spenserian lovers are also engaged in by the friends.[35] Accounts of nocturnal eroticism in the form of sleeplessness and dreams, such as occur in Sonnets 27, 28, 43, and 61, are likewise common in Petrarchan sequences. The verse immortality accorded the Master Mistress is also accorded the ladies of other sonneteers, particularly those who follow upon Ronsard.[36]

   6. *Divinity and votary.* The worshipful attitude toward the friend is really but another aspect of the lover's response to his mistress regularly found in Renaissance sonnets. She is endowed with numinous qualities, being regarded as a saint, angel, or goddess. Shakespeare himself alludes to such glorifications at 130.11–12:

> I grant I never saw a goddess go—
> My mistress when she walks treads on the ground.

She may not excel the human, but the Master Mistress does. He is "A god in love" and "my heaven" at 110.12–13 and an angel in Sonnet 144 (where she is a devil); and in Sonnet 106 he is the prophesied and prefigured messiah of beauty, analogized to Christ himself. Though usually a masculine divinity, as befits his gender, in Sonnet 38 he is "the tenth muse," in line with the feminine element also in his makeup.

Of the six types of love distinguished above, and *all culled from the Sonnets*, three are erotic in nature—the marital, the courtly, and the Petrarchan. The remaining three types—the parental, the amicable, and the religious-devotional—are not innately erotic but are brought, through metaphor, into the passionate commitment. Wilson and Rowse err in defining the friends' relationship univocally and, in disregard of the textual evidence, arbitrarily. Bush is representative of those who err by viewing the relationship less in terms of what Shakespeare wrote than in terms of the very different notions of "masculine friendship" found in works written by others at roughly the same period. The full panoply of affectionate relationships comprehended by the poet's response is broader than Lewis recognizes and richer in amorous kinds, and he errs, principally, in slighting the particularity of *this* love in order to soar to the "highest universality" of love.

The vision of the beloved in the couplet of Sonnet 31 as "thou (all they)"—

> Their images I lov'd I view in thee,
> And thou (all they) hast all the all of me—

becomes amplified in the sequence as a whole; for not only is he for the poet my friend of friends, but also my child, my wife, my lord, my mistress, my god, "my all." The feeling that this one relation encompasses all others manifests an emotional intensity that is rather a characteristic than a transcending of erotically passionate love. Complementing the sense of inclusiveness of "thou (all they)" is the sense of exclusiveness of "my all":

> For nothing this wide universe I call,
> Save thou my Rose; in it thou art my all.

The concentration on the one, "my Rose" of beauty and love, along with contempt for what's not he, the rest of the world (109.13–14), is another concomitant of great passion. To seek elsewhere for this

paradox of love as all-inclusive, all-exclusive, we need look no farther afield than John Donne:

> Sh'is all States, and all Princes I,
> Nothing else is.
>
> ("The Sun Rising," 21–22)
>
> Let us possesse one world, each hath one, and is one.
>
> ("The Good-morrow," 14)
>
> You . . .
> Who did the whole worlds soule extract, and drove
> Into the glasses of your eyes,
> So made such mirrors, and such spies,
> That they did all to you epitomize,
> Countries, Townes, Courts . . .
>
> ("The Canonization," 39–44)

Donne's lover is not discoursing on some universal or abstract quin-
tessence of love; he is enunciating his own experience of sexual love
for the one woman spoken to or of (they are in bed together in the
first two of these poems). When Shakespeare's lover utters kindred
thoughts and sentiments, and with like fervor though to a man, he
too is passionately caught up in a concrete love relation, and one
that he experiences both as if "Nothing else is" and as the epitome
of many types of love—familial and romantic, familiar and strange,
old and new, lived and known from verse. And so, once again, the
closest analogues to the "passion" for the Master Mistress turn out
to be furnished by Renaissance poems for a female beloved.

Shakespeare renders the erotic union of the male lovers with such
vividness and resonance as to evoke a shock of recognition in readers who are, have been, or would be in love; and whether it is with
someone of the opposite or of the same sex turns out not essentially
to matter. This is not to say that heterosexual and homosexual loves
are to be differentiated only by the genders of the participants—
other differences will be considered in the following chapters—but
rather to suggest that both kinds draw in large measure upon the
same range of feelings. Just as readers of homosexual orientation can
find their own amorous impulses and responses reflected in the
verse of a Donne or a Sidney, so can those of heterosexual bent find
theirs given consummate expression in Shakespeare's love lyrics to
the young man. Thus they perform the valuable service of revealing
how much alike the two modes of loving can be, the considerable
extent to which they are affectively indistinguishable. Herein the
true universality of the Sonnets may be glimpsed in yet another

way, but a way once more at variance with Lewis's postulation, the love being quintessential not because it is not homoerotic but because it is, and not because it surpasses the particulars of the poet's passionate attachment to the friend but because it is so firmly grounded in them.

Shakespeare takes up this very issue in closing Sonnet 55 with the words "lovers' eyes." These "eyes," in which "You . . . dwell," are the eyes of those who will read the sonnet, and they are "lovers' eyes" because lovers are the ones who most naturally will be drawn to amatory verse. "Lovers" is a signifier contextually certified as erotic, and the signifieds are conceivable as indifferently male or female and, again indifferently, as those who, like the persona, are attracted to someone of the same sex and those whose attraction is heterosexual.

Edward Hubler errs in asserting that "To Shakespeare *and his contemporaries* the words 'love' and 'lover' *as used between men* did mean 'friendship' and 'friend,' and were so used throughout Shakespeare's works."[37] My italics emphasize two assumptions that Hubler makes: the one questioned earlier, that verbal meanings depend on the genders of the communicators; the other, that the given meanings hold for the vocabulary of the age. "Love" in the sense of eros between men was certainly used by Shakespeare's contemporaries, as by Marlowe in *Dido, Queen of Carthage* (1.2), *Hero and Leander* (2.167, 182, 191, 221), and *Edward II* (all through the dialogues between the King and Gaveston), and by Richard Barnfield throughout *The Affectionate Shepherd* (1594) and also in *Certain Sonnets* (1595). In the latter work the word "lover," in the sense of one man in amorous relationship with another, appears twice, with reference both to Daphnis the older wooer (13) and to Ganymede the young shepherd wooed (11). Shakespeare's use of the word is more various: it could, and as a plural probably does, = 'friends' at 31.10, but the plural at 55.14 carries the erotic denotation indicated above; as singular, at 32.14 and 126.14, "lover" alludes to the poet and cannot be denied its current sense, available to Shakespeare and found in the plays, nor can it at 63.12, where "my lover" is synonymous with "my sweet love" and where both allude to the friend. Then the word "friend" itself could = 'a lover or paramour of either sex' (OED 4); both male and female characters in the play can be heterosexual "friends" in this sense and are often so called, and the youth and mistress are suspected of being such at 144.11. Marlowe, again, has Gaveston referred to by Edward as his "sweet friend." Thus "friend" could signify "lover" regardless of the sexes involved, and it surely takes that meaning at 50.4 and 110.11 and most likely does elsewhere in the Sonnets. But even more interesting is the substantive use of "love," especially as a vocative, in the sense of 'the person loved.' Schmidt defines the word when so used between men as "friend," but all his citations come from the Sonnets, with one exception. The OED (sb. 9) has this entry: "A beloved person; *esp.* a sweetheart; chiefly applied to a female person but sometimes to a male." The rare application to a male cited is the same as Schmidt's exception, from *The Merchant of Venice* (4.1.273), where Antonio wishes Portia might judge "Whether Bassanio had not once a *love.*" The word in the sense employed here, as 'a male friend to another man,' does not occur anywhere else; besides, the word here may well take another meaning, that of 'friendship' rather than 'friend.' The sonneteer not only keeps referring to the beloved as his "love" but habitually utilizes the vocative, calling him "love" (13.1, 22.9, 89.5), "my love" (40.1, 3), "dear my love" (13.13), or "sweet love" (76.9), and for this form of address between men I can find no precedent whatever. This term of endearment was never employed by friends in the Renaissance, though it was by lovers to their ladies and vice versa. The vocatives supply fresh and substantial evidence of eroticism in the conversation between the poet and his young "love."

Expositors are rarely adverse to confronting in some way, usually to deny or else to curtail, "the notion of homosexuality." The quoted phrase comes from the Pelican introduction, and there Douglas Bush appends to it this parenthetical remark, omitted from the excerpt cited earlier: "(a notion sufficiently refuted by the sonnets themselves)." He does not say how or where it is refuted, and why should he bother to do so when he can count on the reader to share his bias and welcome the pronouncement without question?

J. Dover Wilson, however, is less sanguine, since he does provide "two good reasons" for his certainty that "Shakespeare was not a conscious paederast." His reasons are the ones most commonly urged. The first is that Sonnet 20 makes it "unmistakably clear" that the "passionate admiration" expressed is dissociated from "sexual desire." The second and "even more cogent" reason is that "the Poet's infatuation for a woman" is "a major theme." Most of these commentators either have never heard of bisexuality or prefer to say nothing about it. The infatuation for the mistress, which is a distinctly minor theme in Part I, being treated only in Sonnets 40–42, is made into a "major theme" when Wilson locates another nine "liaison-sonnets" that bear upon it—33, 34, 35, 48, the "yoked pair" 57 and 58, 61, 92 (unyoked by violence from 91), and 93. All, he says, are misplaced in Q, and so he assembles and reorders them toward bringing out "the outlines of the story."[38] He assigns the Dark Woman a far bigger role in the story than Shakespeare allows her in Part I; his license for doing so is Thorpe's alleged derangement of the poems; and he argues that the sonneteer can be exonerated of pederasty because heterosexual infatuation plays such a prominent part in the sequence as reordered by him. This ploy demonstrates how rearrangement and the refutation of homoeroticism can go hand in hand.

The editors of the two most prestigious editions of the Sonnets in recent times, Ingram and Redpath and Stephen Booth, prove to be noncommital on the subject. In their preface, I/R decline "to offer or argue for a view of the relationship" between the poet and the friend, though in their notes they "have naturally tried to face particular aspects of it"; yet they caution against "supposing any consciously or overtly sexual quality in the relationship."[39] In his Appendix I, Booth includes a section subtitled "Homosexuality." He starts out by declaring, "William Shakespeare was almost certainly homosexual, bisexual, or heterosexual." But the Sonnets shed no light whatsoever on these theoretical possibilities:

> The sexual undercurrents of the sonnets are of the sonnets; they probably reflect a lot that is true about their author, but I do not know what it is; they reveal nothing and suggest nothing about Shakespeare's love-life.[40]

The endeavor here is clearly to eliminate the issue of homoeroticism. However, the approach bypasses a crucial step. While we may not be able to tell if or where Shakespeare records his own experience, each and every sonnet does reveal something about the erotic experience of the persona, so that we learn a great deal about him and the ways in which he relates to the fair friend and the dark lady. A consideration of the character and conduct of the poet, missing from Booth's discussion, is, on the one hand, a necessary precondition of speculation about authorial self-revelations and, on the other, it is fundamental to any inquiry into homosexuality in the Sonnets.[41]

Some few scholars and critics, from G. Wilson Knight in 1955 to Kenneth Muir in 1979, do discern a homoerotic response of sorts in the Shakespearean sonneteer.

Knight terms this response "homosexual idealism," by which he means that it is a "strong sexual impulse" wholly divorced from "physical vice" or carnal enactment, or a "fine physical ardour" that is "less a matter of desire than of adoration." (As to "desire," let 45.3, 51.9–10, and 57.2 set the record straight.) An impulse without an outlet, without, even, sublimation, may be the formula for frustration, but Knight can "somehow feel" that the "love is grander and more perfect" in this condition.[42] C. S. Lewis argues against "pederasty" on the curious grounds that "Shakespeare, and indeed Shakespeare's age, did nothing by halves," and if he had intended to be "the poet of pederasty, I think he would have left us in no doubt."[43] I think that he left us in none. Yet Lewis has a point, if one that again goes contrary to his intention: the poet is homoerotic not by halves but in both desire and its gratification. But Knight's Shakespeare does go halfway: he feels the sexual impulse but is inhibited from acting on it.

A major difficulty with the critical readings that concede the poet's response to the friend to be erotic is that the concession makes so little difference. Kenneth Muir can write, concerning Sonnet 20, that "the Poet recognizes frankly that his love is erotic as well as spiritual." He quickly adds, "yet there seems to be no thought in his mind of the possibility of a physical consummation of his love, *or even that he would have been tempted if the possibility had existed.*"[44] In what way, then, is the love *erotic?* This brief affirmation of its being so is the sum and substance of what Muir's book-length study has to offer on the subject. The exposition proceeds without further elaboration, and excision of the statement would change next to nothing. If Muir had chosen to deny eroticism of the love, only a sentence or two would have to be modified, and the illogicality could then be excised. Some other critics may devote a bit more space to discussing the postulated eroticism, but the results are much the same: it does not affect the poet's conduct, and it has a negligible effect, if any, on their readings of the sonnets.

Paul Ramsey devotes a four-page section of *The Fickle Glass* (1979) to "Homosexuality," and this discussion, while it reaches a conclusion at odds with my own, surpasses any other I know of. He realizes that "citing Renaissance friendship is mostly beside the way" and that "lover" and "friend" are multivocal signifiers. He considers the "general likelihoods" that passionate love such as the poet's might be expected to seek consummation in the long run and that the infidelity complained of may mean "to make physical love with someone other than the person entitled to one's physical love." He considers "hints of language," such as the words "desire" at 57.1–2 and "had" at 52.14 and 87.13. He has detected and weighed some of the pertinent evidence, even to linguistic data, and this sets him apart from other commentators. Interpretation is something else. Ramsey seriously entertains the possibility of overt homosexual relations but decides that "the evidence against overtness is the stronger evidence." There is far more evidence in favor of it than he discovers, and what he does bring forth is less susceptible of dismissal than he supposes. He comes, after all, to the lame—and to me, of course, untenable—conclusion that "the love has a familial quality" and that the poet is governed by "a great and passionately held ideal of chastity."[45] He ends up belonging, then, with Knight and Muir, along with Leslie Fiedler,[46] Martin Seymour-Smith,[47] and Philip Martin,[48] to the small band that, over some twenty-five years, has at least been willing to grant the persona erotic feelings, even though these feelings are sexually suppressed and, at most, are allowed indirect and indistinct verbal expression—if even so much as that.

Oscar Wilde may be regarded as the ancestor of this group of commentators, for he writes of Shakespeare's love for the youth, in *The Portrait of Mr. W. H.* (1889; expanded 1895), that "there was a kind of mystic transference of the expressions of the physical sphere to a sphere that was spiritual, that was removed from gross bodily appetite, and in which the soul was Lord."[49]

Finally, another poet, whose affinities with Wilde include more than a shared interest in Shakespeare's Sonnets and whose view of them may owe something to Wilde, cannot be ignored in this context. W. H. Auden, in his introduction to the Signet edition (1964), writes that "we are confronted in the sonnets by a mystery rather than an aberration": a mystery because the *"primary* experience" rendered was "mystical" (surely as eccentric as "avuncular" and "cliental") and because the sequence is about the "Vision of Eros" and Shakespeare's "agonized struggle to preserve it." The "aberration" that is repudiated is inversion. Auden chides the "homosexual reader," assumed to be "determined to secure our Top-Bard as a patron saint of the Homintern," with being "uncritically enthusiastic" about Sonnets 1–126 and with preferring to ignore "the unequivocally sexual" sonnets to the Dark Lady and the fact of Shakespeare's being "a married man and a father."[50] So was Wilde, and Auden certainly knew about the phenomenon of bisexuality. Further, Auden's characterization of the friend derives from some other experience than that of reading the text, for the good-looking, unpleasant, frivolous, cold-hearted, self-centered, manipulative young male he describes is pretty much the same as the persons of the "canker"-type, in contrast to the friend as a "rose"-type, depicted in Sonnet 54.

Auden's is an eccentric and unpersuasive critical performance, and the reason why may be supplied by Robert Craft. In a memoir of an evening spent at the Stravinskys' on January 31, 1964, Craft reports that Auden said that "it won't do just yet to admit that the top

Bard was in the homintern."[51] If this is accurate, and the repetition of the same facetious phrasing makes it look so, the statement is startling, and less for what it says than for gainsaying the stand taken in the Signet introduction, which was written at about the same time. If Auden did not believe what he wrote there and prudently falsified his opinion—and we can never be certain which of the two views he held—we have here not necessarily the only instance of a discrepancy between what an expositor wrote and what he privately thought, but it is the only instance I know of where the discrepancy can be documented as being at least feasible.

My account of the ways in which the commentary disposes of homosexuality in the sequence should be instructive to two classes of readers: those who have been induced by the most distinguished literary authorities to dismiss the idea of inversion, and those who are familiar to a greater or lesser degree with the Sonnets but not with the criticism and who find it hard to believe that the idea is so generally resisted in scholarly exegeses.

The thesis argued in this chapter, and to be continued, that the friends' love arrives at homoerotic expression in diction and deed, discloses a further stage in their ongoing intimacy. This might now be correlated with the earlier stages of the developing "lovership" hitherto traced out. The beauty of the youth is always uppermost in the mind of the poet, and his responses to it are successively these: (1) you are so beautiful that your beauty must be preserved—so engender; (2) you are so beautiful that your beauty must be preserved, and I'll be the one to preserve it, with my verse; (3) you are so beautiful that I have fallen passionately in love with you, my "Master Mistress," and I seek your love in return, though I am willing to leave your genitals to women's pleasure; (4) your beauty and responsive love overwhelm any qualms I might have had, and I have come to realize experientially that the sexual enactment of our impassioned love entails no guilt and brings supreme fruition.

The first two stages belong to the first movement of Part I, the next two to the second, which Sonnet 20 initiates. The physical relations between the lovers have certainly begun before Sonnet 52 and will later be discovered to have begun before 33; moreover, as soon after Sonnet 20 as 24.5–12 they are represented as gazing deeply into each other's eyes.

5

The Bisexual Soul

Having established its homoerotic character through textual analysis, I shall now approach the male friendship from the additional standpoint of a close psychoanalytic reading of the text. This approach, strange to say, has rarely been ventured. My primary recourse will be to the masterly writings of Sigmund Freud. I cite them so particularly because my own intellectual orientation is principally Freudian and because of a remarkable coincidence between Freud's theories of inversion and the bisexual psychology adumbrated in the Sonnets. Although post-Freudian and non-Freudian contributions have had a pronounced effect on both psychological theory and practice, to date they have not provided as cogent an account of homoerotic dynamics as Freud himself has, and so well does his account accord with the one presented in Shakespeare that the sequence could usefully be considered a proof-text for the psychoanalyst.

Freud's contributions to understanding homosexuality appear in various papers written over a number of years, and his views alter somewhat from one exposition to another. He generally deals with males whom he designates *"absolute* inverts," those attracted and gratified only by other men. The poet is not one of these, for he can be aroused by women and has the passionate affair with the mistress in Part II. But Freud recognizes another class, whom he designates *"amphigenic* inverts," and who have come to be termed "bisexual," whose "sexual objects may equally well be with one of their own or the opposite sex" and whose "inversion thus lacks the characteristic of exclusiveness." He recognizes, too, "variations which relate to questions of time," so that "a periodic oscillation between a normal and an inverted sexual object" may occur, and "the trait of inversion" may "make its first appearance late in life after a long period of normal sexual activity."[1] Such seems to be the case of the poet, who is past youth when he falls in love with the Master Mistress. His prior sexual experiences are most likely to have been heterosexual if he naively and, as things turn out, mistakenly believed what he says in Sonnet 20, that the passion confessed there could dispense with orgasmic expression.

For Freud, even "the exclusive sexual interest felt by men for women," a condition always before taken for granted as "normal" or "natural," is "a problem that needs elucidating" by psychoanalysis.[2] Its method, with both this problem and that of inversion, is to explain adult behavior in terms of past experiences, especially those of childhood. The Sonnets treat of adult love very fully, but they yield scant information, at least directly, about the childhood of the persons involved. Freud was aware that writers "can show only slight interest in the origin and development of the mental states which they portray in their completed form."[3] Yet the particular manifestations of bisexuality in the mature personality of the poet-lover afford glimpses into the early, hidden, psychical causes that would have generated that condition—a point to which I shall return.

A predominant characteristic that Freud finds in homosexual men is "the inclination toward a narcissistic object-choice," and lying "concealed" behind this factor is "the high value set upon the male organ and the inability to tolerate its absence in a love-object." And behind that factor lies the expectation, a hangover from childhood, that everyone, including women, does or should possess, as they themselves do, a penis.[4] These observations, of course, will have to be modified when the man in question is bisexual. Even so, all of them prove to have relevance to the sonneteer's love for the friend.

Freud finds that a goodly proportion of "alleged inverts" are "by no means insusceptible to the charms of women" and that "in their sexual object" they seek "feminine mental traits" ("a woman's heart") and "physical resemblance to a woman" ("a woman's face" and "eye"), together with a masculine "body (i.e., genitals)" ("a man in hue . . . pricked"), so that they look for "not someone of the same sex but someone who combines the characters of both sexes," and "the sexual object is a kind of reflection of the subject's own bisexual nature."[5] This account is especially apropos of Sonnet 20, which supplies the parenthetical quotations above. The male/female traits that bewitch the lover are noted once again in Sonnet 52, where the Master Mistress is likened to Helen as well as Adonis. And throughout Part I, through most of the sequence, this master is cast and courted in the role normally assigned to the mistress of other sonneteers.

The poet most certainly can tolerate the absence of a male organ in a love object, as he does in the case of the dark woman. There are many indications, though, that he does, despite the initial disclaimer, set a high value on the friend's organ. The disclaimer occurs in Sonnet 20, when the attraction was of a type new to him and possibly confusing; even then, however, the focus of the last four lines is on that "one thing." The earlier persuasions to breed are obsessed with the youth's physical beauty and genitalic potency. This patent sexual consciousness develops into the passion for the Master Mistress disclosed at 20.2, where "Master" denotes endowment with a penis. That member cannot but be of importance in the sexual transactions that subsequently occur, and over a long period, between the male lovers.

Children, according to Freud, who here has male children in mind, *"attribute to everyone, including females, the possession of a penis* such as the boy knows from his own body" and has learned to value as "the leading erotogenic zone" (his emphasis). One in whom the idea is "fixated" rather than countered by "influences in later life" will, because unable to do without this "essential sexual attraction," become exclusively homosexual.[6] The poet is quite obviously not such a one. And yet we may detect in Sonnet 20 a remnant of this early misconception. The sestet imagines how the lovely youth came by his phallus. Nature, personified, initially designed him as female, but then, becoming infatuated with him, she could not bear to deprive him of the virile "addition." This creation myth implies (a) that a woman is a man without a penis and (b) that women, for lack of this prized organ, are less fortunate and complete than men.

The inclination toward the female "pricked . . . out" is akin to another homoerotic inclination, that "toward a narcissistic object-choice."[7] This means that the individual seeks as a "love-object" one who, like himself, is male, and one whom, furthermore, he takes as a "model" of "what he himself is" or "once was" or of "what he himself would like to be."[8] These Freudian postulations shed light on Sonnet 62:

Sin of self-love possesseth all mine eye,
And all my soul, and all my every part;
And for this sin there is no remedy,
It is so grounded inward in my heart.
Methinks no face so gracious is as mine,
No shape so true, no truth of such account,
And for myself mine own worth do define,
As I all other in all worths surmount.
But when my glass shows me my self indeed,
Beated and chopp'd with tann'd antiquity,

83

Mine own self-love quite contrary I read—
Self so self-loving were iniquity.
'Tis thee (my self) that for myself I praise,
Painting my age with beauty of thy days.

This "sin of self-love" commands first the "eye" of the speaker, to be immediately connected with seeing, and then his "soul" and every bodily and mental "part"; and the sin is "grounded" so ineradicably in his "heart" that there can be *no remedy* for it. It consists of the illusion of personal physical perfection ("truth"), of owning a "face" and "shape" of superlative "worth." But his looking glass, a corrective text in 62.11, soon dispels the illusion, showing himself as he really is, "Beated and chopp'd with tann'd [= tawny/leathered] antiquity," and for such a one to be "so self-loving were iniquity." This "iniquity" raises a problem: is it to be equated with the "sin" of the first quatrain? And the answer is no, because the sin has no remedy, while the iniquity has a simple one: it requires only a mirror. The poet does not pronounce himself culpable in 62.12, which says that to be so vain "were [= would be] iniquity," the subjunctive denoting a condition contrary to fact; he does, on the contrary, confess the sin as something of which he is guilty and as a deep-rooted fact of his personality. The iniquity, avoided, is conceit over being good-looking; the sin, unavoidable, is narcissism in the Freudian sense.

The distinction is confirmed and resolved by the couplet. It unexpectedly introduces the "you" of direct address, so that what had seemed interior monologue must now be reassessed as intimate personal disclosure to the friend. One might paraphrase 62.13 as 'It is you, who are myself, we through love being one, that I praise when I praise myself.' That explains how the "iniquity" of 62.12 is circumvented and also how the "face," "shape," "truth," and "worth" in the second quatrain are the poet's in the sense that they belong to his beloved, who belongs to him. Now certain first-person pronouns of 62.5–8 take on new meanings, retrospectively, on the basis of "thee (my self)": "mine" = 'mine as yours who are mine,' and "I" = 'I as incorporating you.' If self-praise is simply praise for the other self, why is the "self-love" in the first quatrain deemed an irremediable sin? If the reason is to be found in the sonnet, it must be found in the final line: "Painting my age with beauty of thy days"— that is, with your comeliness and youthfulness. The only word that could possibly bear on sinfulness would be "painting." The "woman's face" of the youth, at 20.1, is "by nature's own hand painted." But the poet's "beated and chopp'd" face is painted with borrowed colors. The contrast set up in 62.9–14 is between the impossibility of viewing myself as beautiful in my mirror and the gratification of viewing myself as beautiful in my friend, that is, of adorning myself with the youth—yours—that I once had but no longer have and with the handsomeness that I may or may not once have had but can have now only by appropriating yours. The narcissistic component of homoerotic love is here distinctly realized. Self-love of this type is perceived as blameworthy because the lover uses the other exploitatively, as a means of making up deficiencies in himself. The qualities gained, or fantasized as gained, by the older man belong to the body, and the way to possess them is by sexual possession of the fair young person.

Freud writes of the homoerotic "inclination toward a narcissistic object-choice" that it "in general lies readier to hand and is easier to put into effect than a move toward the opposite sex."[9] The bisexual poet exemplifies the observation to this extent at least, that whereas narcissistic identification enters into his love for the youth, it does not carry over into his move toward the mistress. He never views her as another self or alter ego or with a sense of two-in-oneness. That may be because she means far less to him than the friend does, but it can also have something to do with her female otherness, which might make identification with her more difficult. For Donne, "difference of sex"[10] does not preclude a man's identifying with a woman. Diverse psychobiological factors underlie his phrase "We two being one,"[11] which alludes to heterosexual lovers, and Shakespeare's "thee (my self)," which alludes to homoerotic lovers. In Donne's phrase, oppositeness of gender is the basis of the attraction; in Shakespeare's, sameness of gender is. The contrast by no means escapes Donne, for in "Sappho to Philaenis" he shows that very sameness as fueling the lesbian passion of Sappho, whom he has, in wooing the girl, declare:

> My two lips, eyes, thighs, differ from thy two
> But so, as thine from one another doe;
> And, oh, no more; the likenesse being such,
> Why should they not alike in all parts touch?
>
> . . . .
>
> Likenesse begets such strange selfe flatterie,
> That touching my selfe, all seems done to thee.
>
> . . . .
>
> Me, in my glass, I call thee.[12]

Donne's Sappho may have beauty like the beauty she nonetheless desires in another, and Shakespeare's persona may lack the beauty he seeks from the other; but both make, analogously and homo-erotically, a narcissistic object-choice. The choice enables the persona, through possessing the youth, to feel himself endowed with traits both wanted and wanting and to obtain the advantage without the anxiety that may attend a move to the opposite sex.

Sonnet 62 has a mutually illuminating relationship with each of the adjacent sonnets. In Sonnet 61 the poet depicts himself as "far from home," weary, abed, but unable to sleep because "thy image" and "shadows like thee" keep impinging on his wakeful consciousness. His solacing fantasy of the second quatrain, that the beloved, jealous, sends out his "spirit . . . into my deeds to pry," evaporates when the reality principle intervenes in the third: "O no, thy love though much is not so great," it being "my love that keeps mine eye awake"; and the jealousy turns out to reside in himself, made sleepless by his suspicions of the youth, who "doth wake elsewhere, / From me far off, with others all too near." The friend's "image" that through the night obsesses the lover is the image that is introjected and subsumed into himself in Sonnet 62. In 61 the poet weighs the relative strengths of the two loves and finds his own to excel; we learn why in 62, where his needs and dependence are shown to be greater, where he profits more from the amorous transactions. And the "others all too near" cause him anguish because they might gain the benefits so essential in 62, diverting them from him.

Sonnet 63 looks to the future, when "my love shall be as I am now," that is, "With time's injurious hand crush'd and o'erworn." The octave broods on the physical deterioration in store for the beloved, when "his youthful morn" will move to "age's steepy night," or, in the shift from diurnal to seasonal metaphor, when his "beauties" will vanish that are "the treasure of his spring." The poet "for such a time" can "fortify," to the extent of memorializing "my sweet love's beauty," even if he is unable to save "my lover's life":

> His beauty shall in these black lines be seen,
> And they shall live, and he in them still green.

In Sonnet 62 the persona, though old, borrows narcissistically and with a sense of guilt the physical qualities of the fair youth; then, in Sonnet 63, he offers compensation, for these metaphorically "green" qualities, subject to the "lines and wrinkles" of age, will paradoxically be kept intact by the "black lines" on paper of the sonneteer's verse. What is taken is given back, and given back with interest, namely, perpetuation.

In addition to its neighbors, Sonnet 62 has fertile affinities with two earlier sonnets, 22 and 37. They too treat of the narcissistic advantages to be derived from amorous commerce with the friend.

As he does again in Sonnet 62, the poet in Sonnet 22 has two ways of viewing himself: as reflected in his looking "glass," which "shall not persuade me I am old," and as reflected in the loved and loving youth, who can so persuade him, and will, but only much later, when "in thee time's furrows" appear. The quasi-riddling statements of the first quatrain are elucidated in the second, the key being that the "heart" of each "doth live" in the other's "breast." The speaker's heart, consequently, is metaphorically reclothed in "the seemly raiment" of physical beauty, "all . . . that doth cover thee." (Shakespeare refrains from considering the corresponding raiment of the other, younger heart—a consideration that would prove inconvenient to his argument.) Love is conceived of as a spiritual or psychological communion that has yet to overflow into sexual expression. At this point in the cycle—only the second sonnet after 20—the poet still abides by the program set down there, that despite his own "passion" for the Master Mistress, "thy love's use" should be "women's treasure." The feeling expressed in Sonnet 22 is certainly erotic, as is evident from the narcissism implicit in the lover's wish to enclose himself in the borrowed robe of beauty and youth.

A number of salient issues are inaugurated in Sonnet 22: it is the first explicitly to confront the relative ages of the friends; it makes the first mention of the poet's death (22.4); it first divulges the youth's receptiveness to and return of love; and, in the couplet, it for the first time expresses apprehension as to the dependability of the other's loving commitment. These issues are interrelated—most interestingly, perhaps, the first and the last. Being older and physically less attractive, the poet thinks of himself as gaining greater benefit from the friendship—love received being the single benefit accruing to the youth—and he therefore fears abandonment: "Presume not on thy heart when mine is slain." He concludes on the warning note "Thou gav'st me thine not to give back again." He would have far less, if any, reason for disquietude about the discrepancy in age were the friendship devoid of libidinal content. Aging deterioration, which signals the approach of death (22.4), can be warded off by uniting with the friend, who has power over another evil as well, the death of love.

The stern caution at the close follows the appeal, more gentle and poignant, of the third quatrain:

> O therefore, love, be of thyself so wary
> As I not for myself, but for thee will,

Bearing thy heart, which I will keep so chary
As tender nurse her babe from faring ill.

The simile, which casts the poet in the role of "nurse" and casts the beloved—or his "heart," which stands for his nonphysical presence, internalized in the poet—in the role of "babe," has affinities with the simile that opens Sonnet 37—a simile that posits a paternal/filial relationship:

As a decrepit father takes delight
To see his active child do deeds of youth,
So I, made lame by Fortune's dearest spite,
Take all my comfort of thy worth and truth.

The comforting qualities, the "worth and truth," include the beauty of the beloved but are not, as in Sonnets 22 and 62, limited to it. "Truth" here signifies fidelity or, more broadly, virtue. "Worth" can comprise what 37.5–6 itemize, though partially and with disjunctives: "whether beauty, birth, or wealth, or wit, / Or any of these all, or all, or more." "Beauty" of course is comprised and "wit" also—unless the admirer means to imply that the other is witless. That leaves "birth" and "wealth" as problematic. If the youth were a nobleman, a Southampton, say, or a Pembroke, his being well-born and wealthy would be fully evident—then why the tentativeness? But if he were not a nobleman and lacked these advantages, why would they be mentioned, even tentatively? The only way out of the dilemma and to make sense of the passage that I can find is to take "birth" to mean 'natural character' (OED 6) or 'a nativity happily influenced by the aspect of the planets' (OED 9), and "wealth" to mean 'the condition of being happy and prosperous; well-being' (OED 1). Blessings of this kind are not as readily apparent as those of aristocracy and, so conceived, they better fit in with the disjunctive syntax. The solution connotes that the beloved is no noble, and nowhere do the Sonnets suggest that he is one.[13] He is profusely endowed with bodily and inward gifts but not with a title or fortune.

Then at 37.8, "I make my love [feeling of love] engrafted to this store [= plenty]," whatever it may comprehend. The speaker uses the horticultural term *engraft* to signify the attachment, by love, of his deficient self to the youth's merits, with the psychological consequences defined in the third quatrain: "So then I am not lame [figuratively, by Fortune], poor, nor despis'd, / Whilst that this shadow [my imaginations of your qualities] doth such substance [additions to my real being] give [me],"

> That I in thy abundance am suffic'd,
> And by a part of all thy glory live:
>> Look what is best, that best I wish in thee;
>> This wish I have, then ten times happy me—

"happy" tenfold, not only because my wish for you is fulfilled, but also because the wished-for goods, beauty and the rest, become mine by a process of narcissistic assimilation.

The last line noticeably formulates Freud's idea of narcissism: I "by . . . thy glory live," not by my own, and "in thy abundance am suffic'd"—an abundance properly the beloved's rather than the lover's but lent him by erotic love reciprocated and, at least since Sonnet 33, sexually expressed.

"Fixation on the mother" can, according to Freud, be conducive to a homosexual bias. A change occurs "a few years after puberty" in the young man in whom such a bent develops, when "he identifies himself with his mother, and looks about for love-objects in whom he can rediscover himself, and whom he might love as his mother loved him"—might love, that is, as his own "babe" or "child." Moreover, "the characteristic mark of this process is that for several years one of the necessary conditions of this love is usually that the male object shall be of the same age as himself when the change took place."[14] The poet loves a far younger man and can think of him as a "sweet" and "lovely *boy*" (108.5, 126.1). If, as I surmise, the protagonist has his first sexual encounter with a male in later life rather than "a few years after puberty," still, the conditions favorable to such an attraction would have had to be formed long before. It cannot be supposed that the youth created the tendencies he arouses; he would rather activate those that were latent. "In their later choice of love-objects," lovers of this type will not look for mother but will narcissistically "seek *themselves*," and will do so by projecting "their own selves" into an alter ego and then cherishing him maternally or with the care and protectiveness of a mother-substitute.[15]

The similes at 22.11–12 and 37.1–4 depict cognate situations. In the first, the poet, as a "tender nurse" or mother-substitute, will protectively keep "her babe," the "heart" of the other in his care, "from faring ill." In the later simile, the poet is a "father," but not one who is strong and authoritative; rather, he is weak, "decrepit," "lame," and indulgent.[16] He dotes on his "active child" and "takes delight" in his "deeds of youth" because the nimbleness lacking in himself can be enjoyed once again in the lad who is his.

Sonnet 143, which is in Part II, where the topic changes to an affair with a woman, affords insight into the sonneteer's childhood attachment to his mother. Like dreams, fantasies, and slips of the tongue, figurative language draws on feelings and memories lodged in the unconscious. Freud remarks as a special quality of the writer "the courage to let his own unconscious speak"—a courage that Shakespeare had superlatively.[17] In the single conceit unfolded through Sonnet 143, the persona revamps the relationships found in Sonnets 22 and 37 by representing himself as the "babe" and his mistress as its mother, while the friend, called Will, is present as an aviary figure:

> Lo, as a careful housewife runs to catch
> One of her feather'd creatures broke away,
> Sets down her babe and makes all swift dispatch
> In pursuit of the thing she would have stay:
> Whilst her neglected child holds her in chase,
> Cries to catch her whose busy care is bent
> To follow that which flies before her face,
> Not prizing her poor infant's discontent:
> So runn'st thou after that which flies from thee,
> Whilst I thy babe chase thee afar behind,
> But if thou catch thy hope, turn back to me
> And play the mother's part—kiss me, be kind.
>   So will I pray that thou mayst have thy *Will*,
>   If thou turn back and my loud crying still.

The affection for the lady expressed here differs from that for the friend, for that was narcissistic, while this "may be called the 'anaclitic' or 'attachment' type." This type, according to Freud, has its source in the child's "earliest sexual objects," those "persons who are concerned with [his] feeding, care, and protection"—that is, "in the first instance his mother or a substitute for her."[18] Just such an attachment of the child to its mother occurs in the sonnet as the metaphorical vehicle whose tenor is the attachment of the adult poet to his mistress. This vehicle can be seen as the infantile cause, of which the tenor is the maturational effect, the trope then connecting the past and current desires for a woman. At neither stage does the child/poet seek himself in her or seek to identify with her, as he did in his love for the male.

The "poor infant's discontent" and crying are due to his being set down and "neglected" when the preoccupied "housewife" runs after the fleeing fowl. He hopes, but cannot be sure, that the abandonment is temporary. She does not display—at least in the babe's eyes and at this critical moment—the excess of "tenderness" that, as Freud holds in his work on Leonardo, encourages the fixation on the mother that can lead to homosexuality.[19] Such a fixation is not precluded, however. The yearnings and attention of the child are kept trained on his mother; his misery arises solely from her forsaking him; his one wish, tinged with eroticism even at the figurative level, is that she treat him kindly by once more holding and kissing him. This childhood attachment to the mother can develop into a heterosexual adjustment or can, under certain conditions, contribute to a homosexual orientation; or it may evolve in both directions, as it seems to have done in the bisexual persona.

The dramatic situation, the literal ground of the conceit, comprises the anxious lover, the mistress, and the young man whom she desires. The "feather'd creature" that stands for him is also a phallic symbol. From psychoanalysis and kindred disciplines we know that birds and other flying objects regularly have such import in dreams, art, and myth.[20] The verbal detail of Sonnet 143 furnishes confirmation. The word "thing," which in 143.4 refers to the fowl—implicitly a cock and hotly pursued—will take the sense of 'genital organ.' Then in 143.13 "thy Will," besides the wordplay on the name of the youth, William, and on 'your wish' and 'your lust,' can also denote the 'male member.' The "babe" is the speaker, and everything is recounted from its point of view. The mother's lust does not elude his notice, and the bawdy language comes out of his mouth. The "child"—at least a toddler, since he chases his parent—is hardly an innocent if he understands what he says. Shakespeare here divines what Freud has established, that sexuality has a place in the minds of young children, and he would seem to have been in touch, while composing Sonnet 143, with traces of primitive feelings in himself.

Two congruent triangles, one superimposed on the other, can be discerned in the sonnet: the one consists of the child-mother-fowl, the other of the poet-mistress-youth. They are congruent because the emotions of the child and the poet, and their attitudes toward the other personages, correspond. Both feel "discontent" because "neglected" by the loved woman, and both are hopeful that she will "catch" the object of her desire and then "turn back . . . And play the mother's part." She will play that part in one way with the child, by caressing it, and in another way with the adult, whom she will "mother" coitally. The father is absent, and the child is emotionally detached from his feathered rival. The poet's attitude toward Will here is similarly indifferent, unless the reduction of the rival to an animal level, while the other two figures retain human forms, can be construed as indicating some resentment. Even so, the choice of image, a domestic fowl, does not constitute much of an affront.

Emotions notably missing from the triangles are jealousy, anger, and hostility. They are vented neither toward the withdrawing woman nor toward the male, aviary or human, who draws her away.

Sonnet 143 is not to be disassociated from Sonnet 144. The latter fills in emotional gaps in the former, and a reading of the two texts as complementary will furnish insight into the bisexual soul of the protagonist.

The same three characters interact in Sonnet 144—the poet (A), the mistress (B), and the friend (C). In 143, A chases B, who chases C, who flees her. In 144, A loves B, who has designs on C that may or may not succeed, and now A loves C and loves him much more; and A is a human adult, B is a feminine devil, and C is once again a winged creature, though promoted from subhuman bird to super-human angel:

> Two loves I have, of comfort and despair,
> Which like two spirits do suggest me still:
> The better angel is a man right fair,
> The worser spirit a woman colour'd ill.
> To win me soon to hell, my female evil
> Tempteth my better angel from my side,
> And would corrupt my saint to be a devil,
> Wooing his purity with her foul pride.
> And whether that my angel be turn'd fiend
> Suspect I may, yet not directly tell,
> But being both from me, both to each friend,
> I guess one angel in another's hell.
> Yet this shall I ne'er know but live in doubt,
> Till my bad angel fire my good one out.

The interval between Sonnets 143 and 144 can be conceived of in terms of two distinct orders of time. In terms of the sequence of incidents, the mistress in the meantime may have caught the friend and now may or may not be in the process of seducing him; all that we definitely learn is that the poet is racked by jealousy from suspecting that she is doing so. In terms of the poet's psychological history, we find him to have gone from the child suffering desertion by its mother to a man struggling with a crisis of bisexual love.

The child *is* father of the man, for this later crisis is an outgrowth of the earlier one. The man exhibits two emotions that before were absent: hatred of the betraying woman, whom he vilifies, and worship of the male rival, whom he idealizes. The jealousy arises not because the male is stealing away the female—rather the opposite— and the affection that had devolved on her in Sonnet 143 is transferred to him in Sonnet 144. The babe has grown into the adult who is capable of loving either sex but for whom homoerotic passion, certainly in this situation, takes precedence.

Of the "Two loves I have," that "of comfort" is "a man" physically "right fair," of moral "purity," metaphorically the "good" and "better angel" and, synonymously, "my saint," while that "of despair" is "my female evil," physically "colour'd ill," morally "of foul pride," and metaphorically "the worser spirit" and "bad angel" or devil. The "two spirits" do "suggest me still," that is, work on me constantly and to opposite effect, the one as blessed comforter and the other, diabolically, to induce "despair" and—the same thing—"to win me soon to hell." The "hell" at 144.5 is psychological and within, the torment consisting at once of deprival of love and of jealousy.

So far the figurative theology follows along traditional lines, but from 144.6 onward it becomes curiously heterodox, as if to intimate that the emotionally wrought-up lover is too preoccupied with his own plight to be bothering about precision in his angelological conceit. The peculiar means of damnation employed by this devil is to lure away the victim's good spirit, and no less peculiar is the attempt on the part of the "worser" to convert the "better" spirit into a fiend and draw him to her "hell." Carnal activity is ascribed to these spirits: the angel has male, the devil female, genitals; they are capable of copulation; and they are even subject to venereal infection. The "hell" at 144.12—"I guess one angel in another's hell"— differs from that of 144.5 in two regards: it is meant for the celestial being, and it is not psychological but anatomical, consisting of the vagina.

Whether or not it has received the friend the speaker can only "guess" but "ne'er know . . . Till my bad angel fire my good one out." To "fire out" signifies to communicate a venereal disease (Rollins et al.). The infernal burning is imagined as both genitalic and syphilitic, and the "female evil" corrupts not only morally, by seduction, but also organically. However, we cannot take at face value the idea that she is infectious; she is nowhere else said to be so, and the poet has had, and will again have, sexual relations with her without ill effect. It is his frustrated rage, when he suspects her of debauching his angel, that prompts him to think of her as a she-devil, motivated by "foul pride" (= the capital, Satanic sin) and carnal desire, and as a demon diseased. But the rage that evokes the revulsion does not fully account for the form of the fantasy and its specific focus on the female organ.

Circumstantial differences between Sonnets 143 and 144 help explain the emotional disparities they record. Since 143 addresses the mistress with the intent of regaining her, angry and abusive language would hardly serve the purpose; but 144 is a soliloquy that has no practical aim except to unpack the heart with words. In 143 the other two figures are situated within the ken of the speaker, and he can see that they are apart and at variance; in 144 they are "both from me," and that fact makes room for speculation that they are "both to each friend [= lover]"—though that remains inconclusive. Two emotions missing from Sonnet 143 and emergent in 144 are the ardor for the other male and the jealousy and rage at imagining his seduction by the female. Here the contrast between the persona as a "child" in the one sonnet and as a grownup lover in the next provides the heuristic clue.

In 1922 Freud announced his discovery of a "new mechanism" that can lead to homosexual adaptation, one that operates in this way: the mother praises other boys, usually older brothers, perhaps holding them up as models, and she thus stimulates impulses of intense jealousy in her closely attached child and also "his tendency to a narcissistic object-choice." Then, under "the influences of upbringing," the feelings of jealous hostility, yielding to "repression," undergo such "transformation" that the rivals of the earlier period become "the first homosexual love-objects."

Certain elements of this "mechanism" can be descried in the two sonnets under consideration, as follows: (1) the "child" sees that his "mother" is taken with the young man "Will"; (2) expectable jealous hostility toward the rival is absent and may well be repressed, or was later so successfully repressed by the writer as to be forgotten; and if such repression can be assumed to occur, it may occur earlier in the Shakespearean than in the Freudian child; (3) the child's rival in Sonnet 143 is transformed into the adult's first homosexual love object in Sonnet 144. And (4) the jealous hostility apparently represented in Sonnet 143 bursts forth in 144, now directed toward the woman who is a rival for the youth. Freud further writes of this "new mechanism" that, "in cases I have observed," it "led only to homosexual attitudes which did not exclude heterosexuality," as is true of the poet, and "did not involve *horror feminae*," little evident in him. Finally, Freud remarks that "this new mechanism . . . is sometimes combined with the typical conditions [of homosexual object-choice] already familiar to us."[21] Hence it is not a question of either/or, and, however applicable the mechanism may be, it would not preclude but would supplement other causative factors.

Factors cited by Freud that can be psychogenetic of homosexuality (though homosexuality is but one component in the persona's sexual makeup) include, along with the factors and manifestations I have already discussed, the following:

1. "The fixation on the mother" in childhood, "which makes it difficult to pass to another woman."[22] The difficulty may be less for someone bisexual, but the poet does represent himself in Sonnet 143 as the child infatuated with his mother and then, in Sonnet 144 as often elsewhere, as the man whose amorous preference is for the male over the female.

2. "Fear of castration."[23] This, again can be less of a problem in bisexuality, and one finds slight reference to it in the Sonnets. The nearest approach to it is the poet's fearful fantasy at 144.12–14 that his good and beloved angel, who is another self, will pay the price of venereal disease if he penetrates the female.

3. "The high value set upon the male organ."[24] Such high valuation is revealed in the sestet of Sonnet 20, where infatuated Nature introduced that organ to produce the Master Mistress with whom the poet falls passionately in love. Then, in Sonnet 144, while the sexuality of the male, along with all else about him, is angelic, the female is demonic, and her sexual organ is deemed infernal and infectious. Here, if only here, we catch sight of the *horror feminae* that Freud defines as "depreciation of women . . . even horror of them" and that he thinks is "generally derived from the early discovery that women have no penis." Not only in Sonnet 144 does Shakespeare write of aversion to the female organ, for he puts in the mouth of the mad Lear the same abhorrence, couched in quite similar terms: "Beneath [the woman's girdle] is all the fiend's; there's hell, there's darkness, / There is the sulphurous pit—burning, scalding, / Stench, corruption; fie, fie, fie! pah, pah!"[25] The vaginal hell imagined by the sonneteer is less expansively described but no less forbidding, and he gives it a further horrifying dimension as a place morbidly contaminated and contaminating.

4. "The inclination toward a narcissistic object-choice." This factor is most perspicuous in Sonnets 62, 22, and 37, as previously shown, but vestiges of it are discoverable in 143 and 144. The beloved "angel," though celestially idealized, mirrors the poet in being male, in assuming his place with his mistress, and in bearing his name, "Will" (136.14, 143.13). Freud says of "inverts" that "they proceed from a narcissistic basis, and look for a young man that resembles themselves and whom *they* may love as their mother loved *them*."[26] Certainly the poet harbors impulses of tenderness, concern, and protectiveness toward his "angel," in contradistinc-

tion to the maternal indifference in Sonnet 143, identifying with the mother to the extent of loving the young man as her "babe" wished to be loved by her.

5. "A retention of the erotic significance of the anal zone."[27] It is usually impossible to make out what specific form sexual relations between the friends take, nor should it be assumed that they take only one form. Sonnet 33 seems to allude to fellatio. But the evidence in Sonnet 52, already discussed, and in Sonnet 80, to be discussed, suggests that the lover has the Master Mistress *per anum*.

6. The absence of a "strong father," whose "presence" might insure the son's opting for heterosexuality.[28] In Sonnet 37 the poet identifies himself metaphorically with a father-figure that is not strong but "decrepit," and he does so when he feels himself to be in such a weakened condition ("lame by Fortune . . . poor . . . despised") that he must gain strength from, rather than imparting it to, the child. Sonnet 3 likens the youth to his mother. One comes across mothers in the Sonnets and the infirm father, but never a strong father.

Homoerotic desires are multiple and individually determined, as Freud himself acknowledges: "The problem of inversion is a highly complex one and includes very various types of sexual activity and development,"[29] or "What is for practical reasons called homosexuality may arise from a whole variety of psychosexual inhibitory processes," and there may be more than "one type of 'homosexuality.' "[30] It is no wonder, then, that a single profile that exactly fits the *bisexual* persona does not emerge from his pages. What Freud does is to discover etiological factors that can lead to a homoerotic object-choice, an appreciable number of which are perceptible in Shakespeare's sonnet-writing.

The persona, like most literary characters, is not given a childhood, and his unconscious is a puzzle. Though he brings up materials that seem amenable to psychoanalytic interpretation, he cannot be the subject of psychoanalysis. He lives in a lyric "present," never exploring his past as such, and, when he provides ostensible clues to it, he does so inadvertently, with figurative language and certain symptomatic modes of affective response. Yet, as the sole speaker throughout, he gives constant and exclusive utterance to his own thoughts and feelings, and in this respect he somewhat resembles—free association and other major differences aside—the analysand. The overriding question is where and how the early origins of his condition are to be located.

It is conceivable for a "past" to impinge upon the persona's present in three ways. The first is psychogenetic: sexual orientation and practice, hetero- and homosexual alike, in Freudian theory, will be determined by one's personal history, however subterranean it remains, so that libidinal effects evinced "now" necessitate causes of a "then" that would be implicit, no matter how inaccessible. The second way is authorial, in the sense that the writer may draw on his conscious and unconscious experience to endow a character he creates, even one very different from himself, with psychological dimensions that are aspects of his own personality and past. Jacques Lacan writes, with respect to "the story of *Hamlet*," that "Shakespeare's poetic skill doubtless guided him along the way, step by step, but we can also assume that he introduced into the play some observations from his own experience, however indirectly."[31] We may with more reason surmise that in the Sonnets he introduced more such observations, less indirectly. The third way of conceiving of a past for the persona, the simplest one of all, is autobiographical. This assumes that the protagonist is a version of the artist as a lover, that Shakespeare recreates in verse his private erotic experiences with an adored younger man and a tantalizing woman, and that these experiences grow directly out of his psychosexual history. Since we have, at best, only minimal and superficial information about that history, and virtually none that is psychoanalytically useful apart from what the Sonnets themselves may impart, the hypothesis cannot be ultimately substantiated. It is not improbable, though, that the remarkable pre-Freudian insights into the dynamics of homoerotic love derive from self-awareness, elicited by the amorous relationships reported. A good case can be made for the rendering of autobiographical experience in the Sonnets, but it would here be digressive, and so I defer it till later.

Psychological messages, some more salient and distinct than others, turn up throughout the sonnet sequence, and often their decoding—even their recognition—depends on the keys supplied by Freud and his followers. My psychoanalytic approach to the Sonnets, I would emphasize, proceeds on the assumption that homoerotic relations between the friends have already been established by means of the verbal data I have explicated in the earlier chapters, and I shall uncover further sexual allusions in the same vein in the chapters to come. The Freudian theory serves an ancillary function, lending some confirmation and, above all, enabling us to apprehend an order of meaning that would otherwise have remained impenetrable.

J. Dover Wilson opens his paragraph that explains away pederasty by saying, "Whatever psychologists [psychoanalysts included] may postulate about the love that inspires the sonnets . . ."—and that "whatever" is then dismissed without further ado.[32] The literary scholar, even in matters of sexuality, can get along very well without their help, thank you, as Wilson mistakenly believes he will demonstrate. What he demonstrates instead is how sorely his and other commentary is in need of the kind of psychosexual knowledge to be gained from Freud.

Freud is not only more knowledgeable about homoeroticism than members of the literary professoriat who write on the Sonnets; he is also more humane. Though he may regard it as a "perversion," which "we shall usually be justified in regarding as a pathological symptom,"[33] his notion of "perversion" implies a "norm," according to Laplanche and Pontalis in *The Language of Psycho-Analysis*, and that norm is not based on "a social consensus" or on "a deviant path in contrast to the dominant tendency of the social group"; instead, it refers to "genetic criteria" based on the psychosexual development of the individual.[34] Freud remarks further that "inversion is found in people who exhibit no other serious deviations from the normal" and in those "whose efficiency is unimpaired, and who are indeed distinguished by specially high intellectual development and ethical culture."[35] He takes his most sympathetic stand in a letter written in 1935, in reply to "a despairing mother in America" who sought his advice concerning her son. In it he says:

> Homosexuality is assuredly no advantage, but it is nothing to be ashamed of, no vice, no degradation, it cannot be classified as an illness; we consider it to be a variation of the sexual function produced by a certain arrest of sexual development. Many highly respectable individuals of ancient and modern times have been homosexuals, several of the greatest among them (Plato, Michelangelo, Leonardo da Vinci, etc.). It is a great injustice to persecute homosexuality as a crime, and a cruelty too.[36]

This statement, minus the reservations ("no advantage," "arrest of sexual development"), and the historical exemplars aside, expresses an attitude very much akin to that taken in Sonnet 121. There the sonneteer mounts a ringing challenge to contemporaries who criticize his amorous conduct, and the challenge holds, *mutatis mutandis*, for those later critics who cannot abide and so deny the sexuality of the friends' love.

> 'Tis better to be vile than vile esteem'd,
> When not to be receives reproach of being,
> And the just pleasure lost, which is so deem'd
> Not by our feeling but by others' seeing.
> For why should others' false adulterate eyes

Give salutation to my "sportive blood"?
Or on my "frailties" why are frailer spies,
Which in their wills count bad what I think good?
No, I am that I am, and they that level
At my "abuses" reckon up their own;
I may be straight though they themselves be bevel;
By their rank thoughts my deeds must not be shown,
Unless this general evil they maintain,
All men are bad and in their badness reign.

The persona enunciates two opposite estimates of his own behavior, which to his mind is defensible but is reproached by "others," and he gradually moves from a defensive stance to counterattack, until in 121.12 he reproaches his reproachers for their "rank thoughts." Rollins cites Tyler's 1890 comment: "This, as well as preceding expressions, shows that the charge brought against the poet involved sensuality in some form or other." Indeed it does, as most commentators agree; and the text is replete with words of sexual import, with "pleasure," "false," "adulterate," "sportive," "blood," and "frailty" all given pertinent bawdy glosses by Partridge. But it is the phrase "in some form or other" that goes to the heart of the problem, for everything depends on the form of sensuality that the poet is charged with, that he does not deny or deem culpable, and that his upbraiders term "vile." Any mystery about what form the sexuality takes should be dispelled once the sonnet is viewed in its proper contexts: the adjacent sonnets and Part I as a whole.

Each and every one of the hundred twenty poems before Sonnet 121, as well as the five that follow it in Part I, deals, without exception, with the protagonist's preoccupation with the youth. How starkly anomalous Sonnet 121 would be if it treated of something else, as it would if the persona were defending his own carnal relations with anyone, or ones, other than the friend, and with whom, in that case, the sonnet would be uniquely unconcerned. It does not address him, but the sonnets at either side do; and by doing so they make it even more improbable that he is, in the interval, forgotten. In Sonnets 117–20 a "trespass," an infidelity, is confessed by the sonneteer and he, repentant, seeks forgiveness of the offended beloved. The reconciliation sought must occur, for this crisis ends in Sonnet 120, the end authorizing the introduction of the new theme in Sonnet 121. The new theme, of course, pertains to the friend, as the contexts demand, and it vindicates, as the text of 121 makes plain, a form of sensuality that can only be sexuality with him. Once that is allowed, the poem becomes readily intelligible.

In the course of the argument directed against those who wrongly regard and reprove the poet as lasciviously "vile," he counters, in 121.3–4, by protesting the stifling effect such a charge has on sexual "pleasure," which is "just" rather than vile "by our feeling"—that is, according to our moral sensibilities and sense of propriety—if not "by others' seeing." "Our," the single use of the first-person pronoun, while conceivably equivalent to 'one's,' more feasibly, as contrasted with "others'" in 121.4, refers to 'my own and my beloved's,' who then are said to share the feeling that pleasure derived from their erotic interaction is blameless.

The second and third quatrains assail the reproachers. With "false adulterate eyes," or vision colored by their own licentiousness and adultery, they "give salutation to," or 'greet with knowing glances' (I/R), what they take to be "my 'sportive blood' [= habitual lust]," while those "frailer" in character and fleshly indulgence set themselves up as "spies . . . on my 'frailties,'" and "in their wills [= willfully or arbitrarily] count bad what I think good," thus adopting a moral criterion contrary to mine. The word "adulterate" in 121.5 takes the gloss 'adulterous' (Partridge) or, more precisely, 'affected by adultery,' and it establishes, what would anyway be evident, that the reproachers are heterosexual. They "level / At my 'abuses'" and thereby "reckon on their own"—their own vices of sexual profligacy; but since theirs are "normal" and they consider my homoerotic love unnatural, they feel superior and are complacently judgmental. Yet "I may be straight [= upright] though they themselves are bevel [= crooked, lacking rectitude]," and so "by their rank thoughts my [sexual] deeds must not be shown." "My abuses" should be understood as their judgments rather than the persona's admission of wrongdoing, and for that reason I have enclosed the noun in quotation marks, as also the words "sportive blood" and "frailties," which I also interpret to be their accusatory language, quoted in rebuttal.[37]

The most astonishing moment of the poem arrives at 121.9: "No, I am that I am." This ringing declaration of moral independence affirms the principle that the individual's conscience is the final arbiter of what is right or wrong for him, at least in the private realm of sexual mores.

Shakespeare goes beyond Freud, though they do agree that homosexuality "is nothing to be ashamed of, no vice, no degradation [or] illness." To be sure, such terms are used in the sequence to disparage love, but only in Part II, where it is lustful and heterosexual. Then it can be shameful (129.1–2), a vice (141, 142, 146, 151.1–6), a degradation (141, 144, 147, 150, 152), and an illness (147). The passionate attachment to the Master Mistress never comes in for such depreciation, nor is it ever viewed, with reservations like Freud's, as pathological or a symptom of arrested development. This love is decidedly advantageous (see, e.g., the couplets of Sonnets 29, 30, 66, 110) and supremely valued (see, e.g., 109.13–14).

In Sonnet 121 it is "our feeling," not what others think, that properly determines the rightness of our erotic "deeds." They are, to the detractors there combated, "vile," and, to the commentators, unbelievably vile—and hence to be explained away. Let Shakespeare finally be heard and understood; it is high time: "No, I am that I am."

6

"My Jealous Thought"

Jealousy is a salient theme and recurrent phenomenon in the Sonnets, emerging in a variety of situations and manifestations and inspiring some of the finest poems. It can come as no surprise that the author of *Othello* and *The Winter's Tale* chose this topic—or it chose him—for full and powerful treatment. If the protagonist, who proves to be habituated to jealousy, should be Shakespeare's alter ego, we would here meet with the kind of personal experience that served the dramatist so well in those and other plays. And the issue of jealousy is entwined with other major issues, some of which I have already raised, some not yet, such as the issue of the poet's homoerotic association with the fair friend, that of the play made for him by the dark woman and the rival poet, and that of the trustworthiness of the Quarto's arrangement. Finally, the congeniality between the Sonnets and Freudian psychology will become further evident.

The jealousy sonnets are listed below in the numerical order of Q, the reading order, and in chronological sequence except for the last group, Sonnets 133–44, which will be considered apart. They can be divided into seven categories, of which the first, second, fourth, and seventh cover single episodes and the sixth covers two episodes, while the third and fifth bracket sonnets that bear on the theme without being so episodically or circumstantially bound together.

1. Sonnets 33–35: The lover reacts bitterly to the friend's sexual relations with someone else, not further identified.

2. Sonnets 40–42: Addressed to the friend, these poems deal with his possible sexual intimacy with a woman, the one to whom the poet is attached, but nowhere else in the hundred twenty-six sonnets of Part I will any other reference to her or to this triangle be found.

3. Sonnets 48–49, 57–58, 61, 69: In this period anxieties about the loss of love and misgivings about the friend's conduct are intermittent and subjective.

4. Sonnets 78–86: Another triangle materializes, this one consist-

ing exclusively of males, the poet's competitor for the youth's favor here being another poet.

5. Sonnets 87–96: As in group 3 above, though more continuously and compulsively, the lover is haunted by fears of losing the beloved and speculations about sexual misdemeanors on his part.

6. Sonnets 109–12, 117–20: Now, toward the end of Part I, a dramatic reversal takes place, for it is the protagonist who is twice guilty of infidelities, which he confesses without particularizing, and it is his turn to repent and seek forgiveness, as the friend has done in Sonnet 34.

7. Sonnets from 133 to 144: These poems appear among those to and about the mistress, in Part II (and so the next chapter will take them up); the triangle here involves her, the poet, and the friend, and while it occupies more poems and elicits different attitudes, and while she is addressed rather than the friend, as before, it is demonstrably the same triangle as that of Sonnets 40–42.

I

A quarrel breaks out—the first between the lovers—at Sonnet 33, and even though they are soon reconciled, in 34–35, it proves unsettling to both; but it does not occur in a vacuum, having been prepared for in Sonnets 22 and 24.

The preparation consists of the older lover's distrust, twice entertained before, of the handsome youth. In the octave of Sonnet 22 the persona finds a way to stave off "death": by clothing his own "heart" in "*all* the beauty that doth *cover* thee," from head to toe, and this phrasing suggests at least a mental vision of the other's body nude. The remedy entails the exchange of hearts that generates the new anxiety of the sestet. How will his own heart fare in the exchange? The couplet introduces a fear of death once more, now not from age but from the loss of love, the plea of the third quatrain giving way to threat:

> Presume not on thy heart when mine is slain;
> Thou gav'st me thine not to give back again.

A similar "turn" of thought is met with at the end of Sonnet 24. That sonnet builds not only on the psychological process in which the fair "form" perceived by sight comes to reside in the heart; it also builds on the situation in which the lovers gaze so intently into each other's eyes that the friend can view his own image reflected on the eyeball of the poet (24.5–10). But the couplet avows that the "eyes," despite their painterly "art," are in "want" of this "cunning [= skill]": "They draw but what they see, know not the heart." The suspicions may arise from the insecurity of the elder, less attractive, and more dependent lover, or from his apprehension about the friend's unknown capacity for amorous constancy, or from both.

The friend offends, as anticipated, for the cause of the quarrel is a "trespass" (35.6), some "ill deed" (34.14), a "sensual fault" (35.9) of his. As to the word "fault," Coleman remarks "the frequent occurrence of a sexual flavour" in the word in "early modern English" (p. 7). The modifier "sensual" confirms that the fault is somehow sexual; how it is so can be, and *is*, divulged only by Sonnet 33. A soliloquy, for no listener is implied, it dramatizes a hurt reaction to a recent encounter between the youth and another:

> Full many a glorious morning have I seen
> Flatter the mountain tops with sovereign eye,
> Kissing with golden face the meadows green,
> Gilding pale streams with heavenly alchemy,
> Anon permit the basest clouds to ride
> With ugly rack on his celestial face,
> And from the forlorn world his visage hide,
> Stealing unseen to west with this disgrace:
> Even so my sun one early morn did shine
> With all triumphant splendour on my brow;
> But out alack, he was but one hour mine—
> The region cloud hath mask'd him from me now.
> Yet him for this my love no whit disdaineth:
> Suns of the world may stain, when heaven's sun staineth.

The octave describes a scene: the sky and landscape on the kind of morning that starts out bright and soon becomes overcast. While there are indications enough that the descriptive details imply meanings beyond themselves, it remains for the sestet to definitively establish their figurative status by interpreting those details, though it does so only partially, and by applying them to the lover's plight. Sun (33.14, to which "morning" in 33.1 is equivalent), earthly terrain, and clouds interact in the scene; the third quatrain provides tenors for the sun and the earth, as the friend and the poet, respectively; but the metaphor of "basest clouds" (33.5) is not explicated, so that its tenor must be inferred. Since the other two phenomena each represent a person, and since the plural "clouds" is converted to the singular "cloud" at 33.12, we can take "clouds"/"cloud" to stand also for someone who has come between the lover and the beloved. Hence the interaction among sun, cloud, and earth manifests a relationship among these three personages.

The same objects figuratively deployed in much the same way show up in another soliloquy, the one with which Prince Hal closes act 1, scene 2, of *1 Henry IV*. The similarities have often been noted; yet a comparison can prove useful, in ways that have gone unnoticed, for understanding the sonnet.

> Yet herein will I imitate the sun,
> Who doth permit the base contagious clouds
> To smother up his beauty from the world,
> That, when he please again to be himself,
> Being wanted he may be more wonder'd at
> By breaking through the foul and ugly mists
> Of vapours that did seem to strangle him.

Again the sun, the clouds, and the "world" (= this planet, as also at 33.7), and the interaction among them, are metaphorical and have human referents, the three entities standing, respectively, for Hal himself, for his "base" companions, Falstaff and the rest, and for the populace of the kingdom. One soliloquy is delivered from the point of view of the sun-prince, the other from that of the victim-world. The images are presented in opposite sequences, the sun in one case beclouded and then "breaking through," and in the other shining forth and then beclouded. The same verb, "permit," allows each sun the power to control the clouds, which are "base" in a dual sense in both passages: 'dark' with respect to the clouds, 'ignoble' with respect to the sun-person's associate(s), disapproved of by the reflective "I." Of the companions whom Hal intends to throw off, the principal one is old Falstaff; and the young friend in Sonnet 33 is accused of forsaking his older lover. Hal's planned repudiation befalls the unsuspecting Falstaff at the end of *2 Henry IV*; the sonneteer is never so rebuffed by his youthful friend, but he often expects to be, and he too can feel, as at 22.13, or in Sonnet 92, that he would not survive the abandonment.

My chief aim in juxtaposing the two texts is, however, to point out other and more telling contrasts than those just observed. The sun, though personified in both passages, has a face only in the sonnet. This point receives particular stress, with the "golden face" at 33.3, the "celestial face" at 33.6, the "eye" and a mouth implied by "kissing" at 33.2–3, the "visage" at 33.7, and with "mask'd" at 33.12. Thus the youth's face would seem somehow implicated in his "trespass." Moreover, the words "ride" and "rack" are absent from the sun/cloud interaction delineated by Hal. The "morning" sun of 33.1 does, at lines 5–6,

> Anon permit the basest clouds to ride
> With ugly rack on his celestial face, . . .

"To ride . . . on" = 'to pass across' in the description of the sky; but the verb also has a bawdy sense, and that makes the language transparent to the "sensual fault" committed by the sun-person with the cloud-person. Partridge glosses "ride" as '(Of a man) to mount sexually.'[1] The fault of the sun-friend, then, has been to "permit" the "basest" cloud-man to "ride on" his "face," and thus has consisted, as the gloss authorizes us to infer, of oral-genital carnality engaged in with some low type. The word "rack" at 33.6 is equivalent to the phrase "mists of vapour" in Hal's rendering of the skyscape; but a pun is likely, on 'wrack,' which = 'sexual dishonor' (Partridge; cf. Coleman). The Prince's soliloquy significantly differs from the poet's in its lack of bawdy diction, such as "ride" and "rack"/'wrack,' and of sexual allusion, such as that which demands the emphasis on the sun's facial features; for Hal does not conceive of any carnal interplay among those to whom he refers, since none exists, while the sonneteer does, for he is brooding on the friend's *sensual* betrayal.

The adjective "ugly," in modifying "rack," means 'unsightly'; but when it modifies 'wrack' in its sexual sense, it will take the meaning 'morally repulsive' (OED A, 4). The repugnant carnal indignity suggested by "ugly rack" accords with 33.8, which depicts the sun's "Stealing unseen [moving imperceptibly and also furtively] to west [westward, and also connoting, by likeness of sound, 'to rest'] with this disgrace [= 'disfigurement,' with reference to the sun; 'shame' with reference to the sun-person or friend—OED sb. 6, 3]." The word "forlorn" at 33.7 keeps the same sense, whether personifying the planet "world," when it is overcast and gloomy, or expressing the feeling of the "world"-designated poet when he is abandoned. The anguished lover's belief that the friend's "sensual fault" was fellatio with someone male and unworthy can be construed from the second quatrain.

The first and third quatrains adumbrate the former erotic commerce between the friend and the poet. He looks back at the brief auroral "hour" of their love from the darkened "now" of the aftermath (33.11–12) and in the first quatrain evokes the recurrent interplay of sky and earth figuratively, as analogous to the nonrecurrent and existential human situation defined in the third quatrain. However, the analogy is not fully spelled out, and by this I mean that the details in 33.1–2 serve as vehicle to the tenor supplied in 33.9–10, but the figurative details in 33.3–4, although they too are concerned with the previous amorous relations between the lovers, are not so supplied with a tenor, and their import is left tacit. The opening two verses of the octave,

Full many a glorious morning have I seen
Flatter the mountain tops with sovereign eye,

receive elucidation, and in language largely metaphorical, in the opening verses of the sestet:

Even so my sun one early morn did shine
With all triumphant splendour on my brow.

The "morning" of 33.1, made "glorious" by sunshine, corresponds to the "early morn" of the day of love, when "my sun," signifying 'my beloved,' in the full "splendor" of his physical beauty, looked on me. "Flatter . . . with eye" corresponds to "did shine"—implicitly, with the brightness of his eyes—and "the mountain tops" correspond to "my brow." Then 33.11–12 go on to elucidate not 33.3–4 but the second quatrain: "But out [light quenched, friend gone] alack [wordplay on 'a lack'?], he was but one hour mine [the love-possession was brief], / The region cloud [the rival] has mask'd him [by covering his face] from me now." The conundrum we are left with is what to make of 33.3–4.

The "mountain tops" stand for "my brow," and so the meadows and streams should refer to lower regions—campestral and anatomical. "Kissing" (33.3) surely intimates amorous play. The "meadows green" are richly suggestive. "Green," according to Partridge, "in Shakespeare and in many writers since, connotes 'vigour,' 'virility,' 'nubility,' especially with a sexual undercurrent of implication."[2] Shakespeare has Venus woo Adonis in these terms (lines 231–37):

I'll be a park, and thou shalt be my deer:
Feed where thou wilt, on mountain or in dale;
Grace on my lips, and if those hills be dry,
Stray lower, where the pleasant fountains lie.

Higher and lower terrain represent upper and lower parts of the body. The goddess proceeds:

Within this limit is relief enough,
Sweet bottom grass and high delightful plain,
Round rising hillocks, brakes obscure and rough . . .

The "bottom grass" in its literal sense = 'meadows, where "sweet" lush grass grows' (Coleman), and so, at that level, the term is exactly equivalent to "Meadows green." Partridge finds 'a *double entente*' in Venus's wording, the second sense being "(bottom = the human posterior) 'the hair growing in and about the crutch.'" For both glossarists "brakes" = 'pubic hair.' Farmer and Henley give 'green-groves = the pubes,' but this usage may not go farther back than the nineteenth century; even if so, it shows that the elements 'green' and 'groves' became fused, on the order of earlier fusions in Shakespeare, and among these I would include "meadows green" as having reference to the lower parts of the body and probably to 'the pubes.' In this context the "pale streams" of 33.4 suggest seminal fluid, and the line may be paraphrased 'enriching an orgasm with delectable magic.' The burden of 33.3–4, after all, is the remembrance of the way it briefly was while the youth was "one hour mine," and that way entailed sexual acts in three successive phrases: first, the sun-youth's beguiling eyeing of the "brow"—synecdoche here for 'countenance' (33.1–2, 9–10); second, his "kissing" of, oral contact with, the "meadows green" below (33.3); third, the world-lover's "pale streams," allusive to orgasmic flow. It may be that the friend performed the very same acts with the poet as he performed with the rival, but the sexual transaction in the first quatrain is kept more vague, the detail intimating that the lover's sexual enjoyment reached a climax but without the specificity that "ride" introduces in the second quatrain. In any case, it is not the form the sexual activity takes that makes the friend guilty of the "sensual fault" but rather his breaking of his love-commitment to the poet (implicit in the exchange of hearts in Sonnet 22) by being promiscuous.

After this betrayal the poet can hardly recall his sexual experience with simple pleasure. He looks back on it with mixed feelings, with doubts about the friend's original sincerity, and so he sees the "mountain tops" as "*flattered*" by the sun's "sovereign eye"; and this impression is reinforced when the sun is said to have shined "on my brow"—the site of the cuckold's horn's, for one connotation among many. Even "alchemy," though qualified as "heavenly," is not unambiguous, for it could connote fraud—as in *The Alchemist* or Donne's "Loves Alchemie"—as well as magical transmutation, and the practitioner of alchemy is the same as the one who has the flattering eye. The word "forlorn," which the speaker applies to the "world" representing him and so, indirectly, to himself, expresses the dominant emotion. He feels sadly forsaken but also vents related emotions. Although in the couplet he would strike an impeccable attitude—one compounded of persisting love, a denial of "disdain," and forbearance—the hurt and bitterness show through:

> Yet him for this my love no whit disdaineth:
> Suns of the world may stain, when heaven's sun staineth.

A degree of irony attaches to "no whit," for why would he bring up the notion of disdain at all if he intended simply to deny it? Patient acceptance is, if not outright parodied in 33.14, at least more aspired to then attained. The last turn of the analogy between the sun and the offender advances a patently specious justification of him: worldings can hardly be expected to excel heavenly beings. The verb "stain" = 'to lose luster' (OED 2); the world's "suns" (and 'sons') are dimmed figuratively, the "heaven's sun," when overclouded, literally. The figurative loss of luster, the dimming of the "all-triumphant splendour" in 33.10, is due to the friend's moral and sexual taint. The poet finds little solace in reflecting on universal imperfection—human and cosmic—as he closes his soliloquy, the form appropriate to one left in miserable isolation by a loved one who has strayed.

Besides disclosing the first serious altercation between the lovers, Sonnet 33 also makes the first disclosure of sexual interplay between them. Indications that they were moving in that direction were found in Sonnet 22, where the poet lays claim for his heart to "all" the bodily beauty of the youth, and in Sonnet 24, where they amorously peer into each other's eyes. The day of love is still young in Sonnet 33, and yet they have already engaged in lovemaking, which shows that the poet's program, enunciated at the end of Sonnet 20, to eschew orgastic relations with the Master Mistress despite the passion evoked by him, did not long withstand the erotic pressures.

Sonnet 34 returns to the incident treated in 33 but (a) somwhat later, after a certain lapse of time, and (b) with second-person address, the friends having now come together, and (c) in the form of a dramatic monologue rather than a soliloquy. Again the beloved is assigned the role of the sun, but implicitly, for the word is not used. The "base clouds" recur: they are still under the control of the sun, who "let" them "o'ertake me"; they conceal it, "Hiding thy bravery [= splendid appearance] in their rotten smoke [= pestilential mists]"; and they still stand for an intruder and are characterized in such a way as to imply loathing and his ignobleness and unwholesomeness. The poet, no longer under figurative guise as the "world," is now a man who "travels forth" on a "beauteous day"—similar to the "glorious morning" of 33.1—neither anticipating nor equipped for the foul weather ahead. And the "day" is that of love, love between the sun-friend and the human traveler, that promised to be so fine until the cloud-competitor intervened. However, in the second quatrain the sun reverses its prior mode of operation to break through the "cloud" (changed to singular once more, as at 33.12), which is to say that the friend banishes the rival; and just as solar heat evaporates rainfall, so the beloved returns to "dry up the rain," that is, to wipe away the tears, "on my storm-beaten face" (34.6), a countenance ravished with weeping. The consoling gesture is "not enough":

For no man well of such a salve can speak
That heals the wound and cures not the disgrace.

"Disgrace" occurred at precisely the same point in Sonnet 33, at the
end of 33.8 (where it also rhymed with "face"), and both times it
denotes a visible disfigurement—in 33 that of the sun befogged, in
34 that of a scar left by a wound. The next two lines—34.9–10—
apply the aphorism of the above verses to the present circumstances: "Nor can thy shame give physic [= medicine] to my grief
[the psychological 'wound']; / Though thou repent [the jilting], yet I
have still the loss," and 34.11–12 reiterate this idea, though in more
general and somewhat tougher language:

The offender's sorrow lends but weak relief
To him that bears the strong offence's loss.[3]

What is the offender then to do? His solacing the weeping poet
has not worked, and his remorse, in 34.9–10, has furnished but
"weak relief." He suddenly and spontaneously bursts into tears, between 34.12 and 13, and at this the lover relents:

Ah, but those tears are pearl which thy love sheds,
And they are rich, and ransom all ill deeds.

"Ah" signals the new reaction, one of tenderness and forgiveness,
and it comes about because the tears, as "pearl," are precious
enough in the beholder's view to "ransom," that is, 'expiate' and
'buy back,' any and "all ill deeds," and also because the tears are
construed as springing not simply from guilt or regret but precisely
from "thy love," and so they indicate that, despite the aberration,
the youth's commitment holds. The lovers are reconciled, and that
reconciliation is the theme of the sonnet.

Unable to bear the sight of the one he idolizes suffering pangs and
weeping, the poet, comforted, himself turns comforter in Sonnet 35:

No more be griev'd at that which thou hast done:
Roses have thorns, and silver fountains mud,
Clouds and eclipses stain both moon and sun,
And loathsome canker lives in sweetest bud.

He looks to the world of nature and the senses for his soothing examples of how normal it is for the odious to attend the fair. Neither
will perfection be found in human nature: "All men take faults."
But then the discourse takes an unexpected turn as 35.5 continues:
"and even I in this," where "this" is a fault not of the youth but of
the speaker, and it lies in his now "authorizing thy trespass [of in-
fidelity] with compare," i.e., with the comparisons of 35.2–4, above.

In 35.7–8 he feels himself corrupted in thus "salving thy amiss," having self-critical second thoughts about the propriety of his doing so and his method: "Excusing their sins more than their sins are." Here "their" refers to the natural phenomena of roses, fountains, etc., and "sins" to the thorns, mud, etc. In his eagerness to console and exonerate the grieving wrongdoer, he pushed the illogic of his analogies so far as to "excuse" the moon or buds of sinful eclipses or cankers. "For to thy sensual fault I bring in sense," and the exculpatory "sense" in 35.9, antithetical to "sensual," alludes to the 'sense perceptions' of 35.2–4 and to 'reason'; and, if there is word-play on 'bring incense,' the "fault" would be venerated as well as imagistically and intellectually rationalized. An uneasy yoking of affection and rankling, a combination of the wish to assuage and resentment in the lover, a "civil war . . . in my love and hate" persists from 35.5 to the end, and in the couplet he sees himself as both "an accessary" and victim of robbery by the "sweet thief," an oxymoron that condenses the ambivalence of feeling. Yet, however disquieted, he cannot but continue in love: "I an accessary *needs must be.* . . ."

In his edition of the Sonnets, Martin Seymour-Smith regards Sonnets 33–36 as a unit that depicts the "one occasion Shakespeare did have some kind of sexual relationship with the Friend" whom he blames, in Sonnet 34, for their sexual indulgence and forgives in Sonnet 35, and then, in Sonnet 36, acknowledges his own "responsibility" for the lapse.[4] But, first of all, Sonnet 36 is not integrated into the previous triad. While the poet in this sonnet advocates a permanent separation because of some undefined culpability in himself, it cannot be the "self-corrupting" of "salving thy amiss" in Sonnet 35, for that is private, occurring when the friends speak alone, and it is certainly not scandalous; but the "blots" and "bewailed guilt" of the persona in Sonnet 36 refer to something of a public and scandalous nature that "should do thee shame" and "take honour from thy name" if "thou with public kindness honour me." Besides going astray in several particulars, this reading of Sonnets 33–36 fails to notice the part played by a third party, the cloud-person. Yet it does have the merit of facing up to overt sexual relations between the male lovers, even if restricted to one occasion, and also of not dragging in the dark lady. In a later essay Seymour-Smith retreats from this position to the more conventional one, that "there is no evidence for more than a strong physical attraction."[5]

The episode treated in Sonnets 33–35—and definitely not in Sonnet 36—rehearses a reaction of jealousy on the poet's part, the components of which are these: (1) distress at the dismal turn of events just before Sonnet 33, when the youth was unfaithful in a sexual liaison with some male partner; (2) skepticism about the love that preceded the betrayal; (3) a "forlorn" feeling at being forsaken; (4) a hostile attitude toward the rival; (5) resentment of the friend, but muted, and tempered with a wish to somehow palliate his offense (especially at 33.13–14); (6) tears and recriminations; (7) reluctance to forgive, together with a desire to forgive, and vexation at succumbing too readily to that desire. In this case the jealousy is not misplaced, since, by his own admission, the beloved is guilty as charged.

2

Sonnets 40–42 handle the next occasion on which a rival enters the picture. The episode is unique in Part I because only here is the threatening intruder definitely female; but what adds weight to the otherwise brief and minor episode is that she is the woman who is the focus of attention in Part II, and there the same triangle will be taken up once again. It constitutes the only topical link between the longer first and shorter second part of the sequence. Sonnets 40–42 address the friend; the correlative sonnets that come later address the mistress, except for one, Sonnet 144, which is an interior monologue.

No feminine pronoun, however, comes into Sonnet 40, and it is not until afterwards that we discover the gender of the rival. The phrase repeated in the opening line—"Take all my loves, my love"—is a key one in the first half of the sonnet, where "my love(s)" appears first in the plural and then five times more in the singular, and with a range of meanings. Twice vocative, at 40.1 and 3—and it was not, remember, so used between men, apart from the Sonnets—it signifies 'my sweetheart' and is equivalent to 'you my Master Mistress.' The expression recurs three times in 40.5–6 and in senses that the following paraphrase brings out: if on account of ("for") "my love [= affection]" for you, "thou my love receivest [= accept my love-making]," I cannot blame you, because what then "thou useth [= sexually enjoy]" is the genuine ardor and devotion of "my love."[6] Thus does "all my loves" in 40.1 encompass 'my feelings of love' and 'my physical love,' if also something else, as yet unspecified.

That something else is the "more" queried in 40.2–4. The question "What hast thou then more than thou hadst before?" is answered negatively and cryptically, "No love, my love, that thou might true love call," since "All mine was thine before thou hadst this more." Only mine is true, and you have it totally, so that "this more" must be some kind of false love, though how so and where-from has yet to be disclosed and will not be fully until Sonnet 41. But Sonnet 40 does provide clues that a competitor is at hand, and we might further gather that this person is included among "my loves" in 40.1 and is therefore someone dear to the speaker and somehow available to the youth, offering him the probably sexual, "more" that is not more of love because it is that in no true sense.

A contrast occurs in 40.6 and 7: "I cannot blame thee" for x, "But yet be blamed" for y. The blameless x is your erotic receiving and using of my love, and the blameworthy y would happen

> if thou this self deceivest
> By wilful tasting of what thy self refusest.

The hypothetical "if" denotes a condition that does not obtain; "this self" is the self of the persona, "deceived" should the youth be sexually unfaithful to him, and the editorial custom of changing "this" to "thy," rightly rejected by I/R, is an arbitrary emendation that plays down the homoerotic factor; "By wilful tasting" = a headstrong carnal sampling of "what" you yourself would, given your sexual inclinations, normally find distasteful. Because the implied motivation is not so much instinctive attraction as a wish to hurt the lover, the tasting would be mischievous. Sex is reprehensible not when expressive of, but when divergent from, love, as 40.7–8 intimate, in anticipation of the theme of Part II.

The third quatrain proceeds—as though the "blame" had been incurred and the "if" of 40.7 had been forgotten—to grant forgiveness. But what is the crime? Figuratively, it is "robbery," the theft of "all my poverty" (= what little I own, amorously speaking), and this again indicates the rival's belonging to the speaker. Though the "robbery" metaphorically stands for carnal possession of the rival, this has not come about, or not yet, or not outside the fantasy of the persona; there are reasons for thinking that it has not, even aside from the "if" of 40.7, and they will subsequently emerge. The persona here "forgives" in a more lighthearted vein than he did in Sonnet 34; for besides being resolved not to break with the youth, he can engage in the playful laudatory-reproachful oxymorons of the vocatives "gentle thief" (40.9) and "Lascivious grace" and of the clause "in whom all ill well shows (40.12–13). This lenient tenderness and admiring indulgence give way to a more urgent note in 40.14:

> Kill me with spites, yet we must not be foes.

The word "spites" joins with "wilful taste" above to suggest naughty behavior; nonetheless, the objective of avoiding contention is fundamental and serious.

Only when we come to Sonnet 41 do we, the readers, realize (the youth addressed would, of course have known it all along) that this antagonist is a woman, and from this vantage point we may retrospectively construe 40.8 as follows: the "wilful taste" is of a female tidbit, and "what thy self refusest" is a likely reference to a self normally disinclined to heterosexual desire.

The "wrongs" at 41.1 are not the same as "love's wrong" at 40.12, for they do not advert specifically to "thy robbery" but are less definite; they are recurrent and are not restricted to the one example adduced, in 40.7 and after, which has to do with a seductive woman. These "wrongs" are "pretty," that is, 'trivial, fetching,' and possibly 'lusty,' and they are committed by the "liberty" (for which 'licentiousness' is too strong—'license,' perhaps, or 'impropriety'—and the sense of 'liberation') that is felt "When I am sometime absent from thy heart." Such peccadilloes—rather charming and conceivably entailing nothing more than flirtatiousness—would merely punctuate a continual allegiance to the poet, and he can understand that one of "thy beauty and thy years" may well be affected by the "temptation" that ever "follows where thou art":

> Gentle thou art, and therefore to be won;
> Beauteous thou art, therefore to be assail'd;
> And when a woman woos what woman's son
> Will sourly leave her till he have prevail'd?

Most editors, though not I/R and other more recent ones, substitute "she" for the "he" of Q in the verse above. If "she," then the allusion is purely and simply successful seduction by a female temptress. If "he" prevails, it may still be by sexual conquest; but the alternative remains, that he prevails by repudiating her advances, decisively rather than "sourly" slinking off to escape the predicament. Hence the "woman's son" (a fascinating phrase, with feasibly an oedipal implication that in the child's attachment to his mother lies the origin of his mature attraction to the opposite sex) either resists the wooing woman or else cooperates with her, but by taking charge. The wording of Q posits these alternatives and leaves them open. Yet, as I/R astutely point out, 70.9–10,

> Thou has pass'd by the ambush of young days,
> Either not assail'd, or victor being charg'd,

lend support to the alternative in which he rejects her.

Whereas the octave is permissive, the sestet appeals for restraint. A wistful exclamation "Ay me!" introduces the appeal, while "but yet" signals the "turn" to the major issue hitherto prologued. Yes, the "pretty wrongs" are allowable in one so captivating, "but yet thou might my seat forbear"—the noun alluding, as at *Othello* 2.2.290–91, to the 'genital part' of "my" woman. The youth, with amorous opportunities unlimited, is implored to refrain from sexual enjoyment of one person only, the poet's lady:

> And chide thy beauty and thy straying youth
> Who lead thee in their riot even there
> Where thou art forc'd to break a twofold truth. . . .

The "truth," which = 'troth' or 'faithfulness in love,' is owed the poet and is "twofold" because owed by two, his friend and his mistress (that the woman is such is confirmed in the sestet); and yet the friend would bear a responsibility of sorts for both betrayals:

> Hers, by thy beauty tempting her to thee;
> Thine, by thy beauty being false to me.

By "would," I mean that the dual infidelity has not yet been consummated, for the friend might still "my seat forbear," and "thy beauty and . . . youth" are still in the process of conducting "thee . . . there." And by "of sorts" I mean to qualify "responsibility," if that is the right word; for "thou art forc'd," and it is not yourself but "thy beauty" that would cause the duplicity; but then, again, "thou mightst . . . chide thy beauty and . . . youth," which suggests some measure of control over them. Line 13 seems to exonerate the mistress as a victim of temptation by male beauty, which is definitely *not* the position when the same triangular relationship is treated, and she is confronted on the same subject, in Part II. The closing phrase, "thy beauty being false to me," is arresting. How can "thy beauty" rather than *you* be "false," or, conversely, how could it be true? The beauty is that of the body and can be false only when carnally gratifying another and true when reserved for me. Moreover, this beauty would be no more "false to me" if granted to my mistress than if it erotically pleasured someone else, as Shakespeare is well aware. He suggests to the youth, and despite the tolerance of lapses in the octave part of the argument (an atypical tolerance, apparently withdrawn at the close), that his beauty is to be reserved for the sole delight of his lover.

The second quatrain of Sonnet 42—I will postpone consideration of the first—begins, "Loving offenders, thus will I excuse ye." This shift in 42.5 to plural address, as opposed to the singular address to the friend before and after, is odd. Another shift, to the future tense, suggests that the ensuing rationalization of the offense is prepared for some later occasion, seemingly because the objectionable conduct is no more than suspected now. The excuse, which runs through 42.6–8, is witty and sardonic: each of the two "for my sake" would make love with the other: he, for knowing that "I love her"; she, because he is "my friend."

Repetitious diction is a stylistic feature of the second half of the poem. Besides "for my sake" (three times) and "my friend" (three times), "loss"/"lose"/"losing" in the fourth quatrain furnish five words, accenting that notion as against the verbs "find" and "have found." The persona presents himself as the loser of the two he loves and them as finders of each other; but he does not appear to be excruciated on "this cross" that "both for my sake lay on me," for he concludes with a bit of whimsy, a mock consolation, not ill-humored, though with an edge of self-pity and a needling implication:

> But here's the joy, my friend and I are one,
> Sweet flattery, then she loves but me alone.

Although most editors put a semicolon at the end of 42.13, I retain the punctuation of Q in order to preserve the oscillating reference of "Sweet flattery," back to the idea of our being one and forward to that of her loving only me. The amorous sense of oneness with the beloved is felt with respect to the friend and not with respect to the lady. While the notion of 42.13 is conventional, Shakespeare waggishly draws from it the consciously sophistical inference that "she loves but me alone." This serves both to solace the speaker and taunt the friend; for she may love not only him but me too, since I am 'all-one' with him, and, taking "alone" as 'exclusively,' she may love just me. Ambivalent feelings are expressed in the couplet, which provides, as Shakespeare's couplets regularly do, the perfect finishing touch.

The initial quatrain of Sonnet 42 raises two issues of some consequence. The first, plainly resolved in 42.3, is that the poet's love for the friend takes priority in his mind over his love for the mistress, and so the loss of the former would be more grievous than the loss of the latter. Of her he says, in 42.2, "And yet it may be said I lov'd her dearly." But, while the attachment is not to be doubted, it is slightly qualified by the first six words, without which the statement would be more strongly positive, and "lov'd" is in the past tense, as if the attraction were over, though in what follows (42.5 ff.) it is spoken of as still viable.

The second issue is whether or not the mistress and the friend are thought to, and do, engage in physical relations. Their doing so is conceived of as a disagreeable possibility rather than stated as a fact in Sonnets 40 and 41. But then, in Sonnet 42, the two clauses "That thou hast her" (42.1) and "That she hast thee" (42.3), where the verb would be likely to carry the meaning of 'carnally possess,' suggest sexual consummation. However, this reciprocal *having* is in effect canceled out as one reads on; the conditional, futuristic clause of 42.9, "*If* I lose thee," indicates that the "loss of love" (42.4) that would result from the coupling has not been, and might not be, suffered. The "If" casts the whole third quatrain into a hypothetical mode, and so the three linked poems, Sonnets 40–42, close rather with a sense of uncertainty about what may be imminent than with a firm sense of what has happened. It would appear that the friend and the mistress, so far at least, have not made love. But this issue cannot be settled until the sonnets devoted to the same topic in Part II are examined in the next chapter.

Sonnets 40–42 can be contrasted with 33–35. Both triads are about a love triangle involving the poet, the friend, and someone else. The someone else in the earlier episode, evidently a male, is referred to only in figurative language and with detail—"base/basest clouds," "ugly rack," "rotten smoke"—that conveys an attitude of contempt, and nothing suggests that the poet knows him personally. The someone else in the later episode is the opposite in all these respects: a lady, she is referred to plainly and literally, and she is not only known to the poet but known carnally and "loved dearly." In the first triangle the youth's sex act with the cloud-person causes a breach between the lovers, which closes only after the one weeps and reproaches the other, who in turn weeps remorsefully. While Sonnets 40–42 are obsessed with thoughts of intercourse between the friend and the mistress, it almost surely has not taken place, and this triangle generates very different emotions from the prior one. Jealousy is quite restrained. A breach does not occur. The poet is more conciliatory than reproachful. He exhibits no bitterness, hostility, or anger, and, if he does exhibit some sadness, it elicits no tears and comes through as apprehension rather than the desolation of Sonnets 33–34. If the mistress and the friend do come together, he will excuse them, and, if he does so facetiously, the very humor of the projected rationalization at 42.5 ff. implies an equanimity that was lacking in the previous triangular predicament. When, in the soliloquy of Sonnet 144, however, he contemplates their coming-together, he does so with the utmost anguish, for there he views the possibility of the sexual union as more real and immediate than he does in Part I.

3

In Sonnet 78 we find out about a rival who is male and a poet and whose entry initiates an episode of jealousy that comes to a close only in Sonnet 86. For the space of nine sonnets—including the two that make no mention of him, 81 and 84—the protagonist must contend with his intrusive and threatening presence. The strategies of opposition show off Shakespeare's command of the art of disparagement, while the rivalry that is superficially a literary one is at bottom a sexual one.

The newcomer presumes to compose verse that is laudatory of the handsome youth, thus encroaching on the sonneteer's private domain. This is disturbing, in part because the subject is one that the persona has found erotically profitable, in part because the other poet may be superior in learning and style. At least he is said to be; but how seriously this is said is another matter, for the commendation appears for the most part to be ironic. Shakespeare (and I will now shift to using the proper name for the textual "I") is not at all concerned with a poetic triumph; he is vying only for the prize of the fair friend. The situation is somewhat analogous to that of a knight who does combat with an opponent not to prove which excels in feats of arms but to decide which one shall carry off the lovely damsel they both covet. However, the verbal combat is indirect, for the speaker never deigns to address his literary adversary; throughout, he addresses no one but the beloved.

It is the bawdy language in Sonnets 78 (the first in the series), 79, 80 (especially), and 84 that serves to convert the ostensible topic of letters into that of eroticism. Not surprisingly, wordplay on "pen" for the male appendage, or, as a Stein-cum-Joyce might say, "a pen is a penis a pen," is fully utilized. The poet remarks, at 78.4, "every alien pen hath got my use," where "alien" = 'of a stranger' and "use," besides 'literary practice,' can = 'carnal enjoyment.' At 79.5–6 he writes:

I grant, sweet love, thy lovely argument
Deserves the travail of a worthier pen.

The word "travail" was homonymic with 'travel,' and the pun was popular, employed, for example, by Donne in "The Indifferent," where, lecturing women, he asks (line 17), "Must I who came to travaile thorow you . . . ," that is, 'came to torment by means of you' and 'came to travel genitally through you.' Shakespeare effects a similar meaning: 'as matter for verse, you merit the work of an abler poet (= "pen," a metonym), and 'as your body is metaphorically a theme of loveliness, it deserves the exertion/travel within of a better (penile) pen.' Then later, at 84.5–6, he writes:

Lean penury within that pen doth dwell
That to his subject lends not some small glory.

I/R comment, "There may be not only the obvious pun ['penury/
pen'] but also a pun on each word," and let it go at that. The puns on
the individual words are surely phallic, and how are the lines to be
explicated when they are taken into account? I suggest the following: that male member has meager genital power that does not offer
its ("his") "subject" (= person to be acted upon—OED 12) the
"small glory" that consists of the tribute of an erection ("small"
because the penis erectus is a small part of the body relative to the
whole of it). "Lean penury" would then seem to allude to impotence
or at least to flaccidness, and "that pen," mocked as penurious in
Sonnet 84, is the rival's.

In Sonnets 78, 79, and 84 the sexual allusions are made in passing;
they are overtones, restricted to a line or two. But not so in Sonnet
80, the third poem of the series; there such allusions are pervasive,
and by then the "pen"-puns in the two previous sonnets have set
into motion the sexualization of poetic composition. The first quatrain of Sonnet 80 picks up the motif:

> O how I faint when I of you do write,
> Knowing a better spirit doth use your name,
> And in the praise thereof spends all his might,
> To make me tongue-tied speaking of your fame.

The surface sense, of the rival poet's lyric praise and its frustrating
effect on Shakespeare's own, camouflages an erotic sense that
comes through when the diction is afforded its bawdy potential. As
an adjective, *faint* can = 'timorous in lovemaking' or 'faint with
desire unsated,' and Partridge's gloss, plus the rest of the poem, authorizes a cognate sense for "faint" as a verb: 'to become shy or
enervated libidinously.' "Spirit" can = 'penis erectus' (Ellis); "use,"
'sexual employment'; and "spend," 'ejaculate.' Then, the "spirit
doth use your name" will bear the same meaning as the phallic
"flesh . . . rising at thy name," the woman's, at 151.8–9, in both
cases the name being genitally stimulating. In 80.1–4, writing verse
is the apparent subject, but it becomes less and less apparent from
here on—so much less that, if the remainder of the sonnet were
printed by itself, one would be hard put to guess that it was about
poetry at all:

> But since your worth, wide as the ocean is,
> The humble as the proudest sail doth bear,
> My saucy bark, inferior far to his,
> On your broad main doth wilfully appear,

Your shallowest help will hold me up afloat,
Whilst he upon your soundless deep doth ride,
Or, being wrack'd, I am a worthless boat,
He of tall building and of goodly pride.

The first thing to notice here is that words of bawdy import crop up thick and fast: "proudest" = 'most lascivious, lustful'; "bear" = 'to bear, support a superincumbent man' (Partridge); "saucy" = 'insolent in a bawdy or lascivious way' (Coleman); "wilfully" = 'sensually'; "ride" = 'mount sexually' (P); "wrack'd" = 'ruined by seduction, sexual abuse' (P); and "pride" = 'sexual desire, phallic turgidity' (C).

"Your worth" principally denotes 'your bodily beauty'; it is immensely complimented as oceanic, and "ocean" introduces the nautical conceit that dominates the second and third quatrains, in which the fetching youth is represented as the sea and the poets in conflict for his favors as sailing vessels that ply it. The ship was an established trope for the human person—e.g., in the first stanza of Herbert's "The Bag"—and it held particular appeal for amorous sonneteers, usually as figuring the poet-lover himself, in imitation of Petrarch's "Passa la nave mia colma d'oblio" (*Rime*, 189). Wyatt's "My galy," which is "charged with forgetfulness" in line 1 of his English version of that poem, refers to 'myself in the pangs of amorous misery,' and Spenser in no less than three of the *Amoretti* (34, 56, 63) adapts the Petrarchan conceit. Shakespeare adapts it, too, in Sonnet 116, where "love . . . is the star to every wandering bark." There the lover-bark is guided by the "star" on high of love, over against both metaphorical love boats in 80.5–12, imagined as contiguous with the "ocean" beneath. When my "humble sail" and "saucy bark" (the speaker's) "On your broad main doth wilfully [= desirously] appear," then "Your shallowest help will hold me up afloat"—which is to say, on the level of the vehicle, that 'this is a sailboat that can navigate shoals,' and, on the level of the tenor, that 'little on your part is needed to keep me carnally excited.' Conversely, the "proudest sail" of the rival, "he of tall building [large stature] and goodly pride [= magnificence, tumescence]," demands nothing less than "upon your soundless deep [to] ride."

The verb *to ride (on)* is a fascinating signifier in the Sonnets, where it occurs three times, and with the idea of penial insertion common to the signifieds. Nevertheless, the acts performed differ in each instance. In Sonnet 33, the cloud-man "rides on" the "face" of the sun-youth, to suggest fellatio. At 137.6, the mistress is the whorish "bay where all men ride," coitally, and again the image is one of watercraft on a body of water. And at 89.10 to "ride upon" the youth's "deep" refers to anal intercourse.[7]

Fear that the rival poet might possess him that way dictates the plaintive reaction of 80.11: "being wrack'd" (i.e., once ruined by seduction—only not mine but yours), "I am a worthless boat"; and this sentiment leads into the couplet:

> Then if he thrive and I be cast away,
> The worst is this—my love was my decay.

The "if"-clause of 80.13 informs us that the rival has not (or not yet, anyway, for the possibility is not foreclosed) sexually succeeded with the youth. But *if* he should "thrive," and if, as would then happen, I am discarded, what would the "worst" result be? The simple idea of ruination by love would furnish a rather lame conclusion. The closing clause may also contain a paradox. "Decay" can mean 'detumescence,' as the word does in verb form in lines 712–14 of *Lucrece*, where "The flesh being proud" alludes to the male member aroused, and "desire . . . revels" until "that decays [= becomes limp]." Although passionate love is wont to cause phallic turgidity, 80.14 says that my love, once repudiated by you, would, to the contrary, have a dispiriting phallic effect.

Is there a single rival poet, or are there others? There is only the one according to Sonnets 79, 80, and 86; but according to 78, 82, and 85 there are more, while in Sonnet 83 there is inconsistency between lines 11–12,

> For I impair not beauty, being mute,
> When *others* would give life and bring a tomb,

and the couplet,

> There lives more beauty in one of your fair eyes
> Than *both your poets* can in praise devise,

where Shakespeare is one of the two poets and the other one is the interloper. The "others" at 83.12 is clearly a slighting reference to him: 'others, imperceptive and misguided, take the wrong poetic tack—you and I know who does that.' All the plural allusions are to the rival alone and serve the same function: to derogate him by refusing to acknowledge him as a distinct person. Shakespeare resorts to this technique when condemning his art, both here and in Sonnet 82, or twitting it in Sonnet 85, or when first taking note, in Sonnet 78, that the rival is treading on his own territory of poetry and love.

Inconsistencies abound in this series, and the others have to do with poets, poetry, and poetics. Nowhere else in the Sonnets does

Shakespeare so persistently concentrate on these topics, but the far-thest thing from his thoughts is to render an account of his own critical theories or a serious evaluation of himself as a writer of verse. He assumes a variety of stances, often at odds with one an-other, and all of them for the purpose of dealing with a love rival who happens to be a poet.

Sometimes Shakespeare will depict himself, with mock humility, in the role of an inferior poet or one incapacitated by frustration: his "Muse" is "sick" in Sonnet 79 and his "gracious numbers are de-cay'd"; he is ignorant and inarticulate in Sonnets 78 and 85, and at 80.14 is "tongue-tied," as his Muse is at 85.1. This self-deprecation is undercut not only by the merit of the verse that expresses it but also by claims of superiority, as with the boast in the couplet of Sonnet 81, "such virtue has my pen" that it can make "you . . . live" forever. In lines 8–9 of this sonnet, "Your monument shall be my gentle verse," in which "you entombed in men's eyes shall lie." But in Sonnet 83 the "others" who metrically celebrate the youth's beauty "would give life but bring a tomb instead." The verbal tombs will either confer immortality or bury the subject; it all depends on who the maker is.

Again, the persona excels the rival by "silence," which in Sonnet 83 is better than to "impair beauty" with verse delineations and which in Sonnet 85 is more truly expressive of love than words, even though in Sonnet 82 the finest tribute is not silence but "true plain words by thy true-telling friend." Sonnet 84 explains how a poet ought to extol the youth: "Let him but copy what in you is writ," and that will make "his style admired everywhere." Yes, but when the rival followed that formula in Sonnet 79, he and his pro-cedure are jeered at:

> Yet what of thee thy poet doth invent
> He robs thee of, and pays it thee again.

Consistency is beside the point, except for the constant aim to move the beloved and, largely by means of derision, to remove the in-truder.

Shakespeare may seem to allow the other poet two advantages over himself: modernity and learning. The rival has a "modern quill" ("modern" also meant 'commonplace'), and his art is attuned to "the time-bettering days" of the present, while poor Shake-speare's verse is not so up-to-the-minute. The attitude taken toward literary progress and modernity in Sonnets 82 and 83 is, however, plainly facetious. This issue may cast an interesting sidelight on the date of composition. In what way could Shakespeare's verse be considered old-fashioned? One way might be that he was still writing love sonnets in a sequence after the vogue had subsided, by the last years of the '90s. The rival is never said to be a sonneteer. On the basis of this hint, the Sonnets would have been written around the turn of the century, the period to which most other evidence also points.

Since learning is stressed as an attribute of the rival, at 78.4–8 and in Sonnet 85, do we find here a confrontation between a poet of grammar-school education and another out of a university? In the seventeenth century, learning was not deemed one of Shakespeare's strong suits. Milton, or his "L'Allegro," gives Jonson a "learned sock" while having "sweet *Shakespear*" warbling "native Wood-notes wilde." Jonson tells of his "smalle *Latine* and less *Greeke*,"[8] but Shakespeare represents himself in Sonnet 85 as the "unletter'd clerk" who has *no* Latin and is illiterate to boot. He hyperbolizes the ignorance and inarticulateness of his persona with the intent of mocking the "erudite" rival. That, though, is as far as he goes; he neither lays claim to learning nor expressly denies that of his competitor. Yet Sonnet 86 does offer some curious and obscure revelations about the latter that may or may not bear on the question.

The rival has been "by spirits taught to write / Above a mortal pitch," has been aided by "his compeers by night," and has some sort of dealings with an "affable familiar ghost / Which nightly gulls [= dupes, and perhaps crams—I/R] him with intelligence [= information]." That the spirits are authors and the "familiar ghost" one in particular, whom he reads devotedly, is barely possible but unlikely. With the terms "spirits," nocturnal "compeers," and "ghosts" taken in their most obvious senses, we find that he believed himself to be in communion with preternatural collaborators who take part in his composition of verse. Shakespeare makes mention of this preposterous belief matter-of-factly, but it is so remote from, and foreign to, anything else in the Sonnets that he cannot but regard it skeptically. He may well report it in order finally to expose the rival's learning as outlandish and superstitious.

Sonnet 86 is written in the past tense, as distinct from the present tense of the eight previous sonnets, to signal the end of the episode. The rival poet disappears between Sonnets 85 and 86, whether by choice or dismissal, to be heard from no more, and the difficult situation is resolved in Shakespeare's favor. He looks back over it from the viewpoint of the terminal sonnet, and, even though the winner, he does not relent toward the vanquished opponent, derogatively adverting to "the proud full sail of his great verse" and underscoring his 'spiritual' composition, not to say his quackery. But that motif is

Chapter Six

subordinate to another intention, which is to define the issue that was at stake all along. "I was not sick with any fear" of the intruder for all his ghostly assistance, not until "your countenance fill'd up his line; / Then I lack'd matter, that enfeebl'd mine." Shakespeare finishes the episode by acknowledging what had long been evident, that the focus and cause of the contention were centered on the youth, not on literary laurels.

The poets compete for him, but not as a subject of verse, for both could praise him, if that were all, with no more difficulty than Donne and Jonson, say, found in their both praising the countess of Bedford. They compete for him as an object of desire. Sexual jealousy is what generates the antagonism, and, whether or not it was mutual, this jealousy is manifested one-sidedly, and most emphatically, in Shakespeare's continual and fecund derision of his antagonist. The episode is remarkable as a locus of poems of disparagement, which are well suited to the treatment of that kind of sexual jealousy whose foremost symptom is hostility toward a rival.

Some other elements of the protagonist's jealousy appear, but they are muted and isolated. Anxiety about his being "cast away," most notably in the couplet of Sonnet 80, is one. Another is mentioned in Sonnet 86: the detrimental effect of jealousy on his art. A third element is irritation with the beloved for being so avid of adulation that he vainly, and perhaps coyly, leads the other poet on, and this irritation breaks into reproach at the end of Sonnet 84:

> You to your beauteous blessings add a curse,
> Being fond on praise, which makes the praises worse.

But nowhere else in the series is the beloved criticized.

4

As many as sixteen additional sonnets in Part I—six of them distributed among Sonnets 48 to 69, ten in succession from 87 to 96—give utterance to thoughts and feelings of the protagonist that are connected with his habitual jealousy. The earlier six are placed between the intrusion of the mistress (40–42) and that of the rival poet (78–86), and, comprising two pairs, 48–49 and 57–58, plus 61 and 69, they are scattered, in order to make the envy, anxiety, or suspicion seem momentary and discrete. The later ten follow the rival-poet episode immediately and, it seems, consequentially, and they are contiguous, registering jealous apprehensions that take diverse forms but persist without letup. They are persistent during this stretch despite the other poet's leaving and the youth's having been culpable of no more than fondness for praise. The episode apparently left a residue of distrust in the suspectible mind of the lover.

These poems differ from the three sets of poems discussed earlier in that no particular corival is involved; no definite third party, such as the cloud-person, mistress, or meddling poet, threatens the friendship. The jealousy is more free-floating for not being tied into determinate episodes or confined to specific triangular situations, and yet the emotions expressed are in large measure the same.

Freud writes, in "Some Neurotic Mechanisms in Jealousy, Paranoia, and Homosexuality," a classic paper on sexual jealousy, principally in males, that this "affective state," if not "completely rational," is "normal," so much so that its absence is indicative of "severe repression." He distinguishes three "layers or grades" of jealousy: "(1) *competitive* or normal, (2) *projected*, and (3) *delusional*." Of the three grades, respectively deemed normal, neurotic, and psychotic, the first two are described as heterosexual, while the third is that of certain repressed homosexuals. In Freud's account of the first and second types, two men, one often the jealous husband, are rivals for a woman, usually the wife of one. This conventional triangle is not found in the Sonnets, where the triangles are extramarital and where either two men, one of whom is the jealous lover, or else the jealous lover and a woman are rivals for a young man. Freud says of competitive jealousy that "in some people it is experienced bisexually,"

> that is to say, a man will not only feel pain about the woman he loves and hatred of the man who is his rival, but also grief about the man, whom he loves unconsciously, and hatred of the woman as his rival.

What is here secondary and unconscious is primary and conscious in the sonneteer, for he loves the male in full awareness and above all else, never hates him as a rival for the woman's or anyone's love, and will consciously hate her, most vehemently in Sonnet 144, for her seeking to seduce his beloved. Freud is cognizant that "jealousy and rivalry play their part in homosexual love as well" as in heterosexual, love,[9] and the jealousy sonnets without exception bear this out; for in all of them, no matter what the sex of the rival, a male's sole or primary love object is male.

Only the first and second of Freud's three layers of jealousy have relevance for the Sonnets. The second includes the symptoms of the first, along with other symptoms of its own; the relevance of this projected level will be considered later. The first level, competitive jealousy, is

> essentially . . . compounded [1] of grief, the pain caused by the thought of losing the loved object, and [2] of the narcissistic wound, in so far as this is distinguishable from the other wound;

further [3] of feelings of enmity against the successful rival, and [4] of a greater or lesser amount of self-criticism which tries to hold the subject's own ego accountable for his loss.

All of these components, along with others, turn up in the jealousy sonnets.

1. *Grief at the thought of losing the beloved.* Shakespeare gives frequent expression to this painful prospect. He does so in triangular sonnets, as for example in Sonnet 34, with tearfulness and complaining of "the loss" of the other (an occasion later recalled in Sonnet 120), or in Sonnet 42, where the greater "loss in love" of the youth and the lesser loss of the mistress are looked upon with "grief" and "wailing." And the miserable anticipation of being forsaken is to be found in nontriangular sonnets too, as, recurrently, in Sonnets 90–93: in 90, "loss of thee" would be "the very worst" of all possible misfortunes and the greatest woe; in 91, "Thy love" is the persona's "general best," and only deprival of his supreme good would make him "wretched"; in 92 he consoles himself that "thou cannot vex me with inconstant mind," since he would not survive "the worst of wrongs," abandonment, but would die if it should occur.

2. *The "narcissistic wound."* This wound to the ego, this undermining of self-esteem, would be especially grievous when the homoerotic love is so rich in narcissistic gratification. In Sonnets 57 and 58 the lover bitterly feels himself reduced to the status of a slave by what "my jealous thought" perceives as the youth's high-handed treatment of him and suspicious behavior. Or, insecure in Sonnet 87, he bids "farewell" to the friend, who is "too dear for my possessing" and beyond "my deserving" and who, "on better judgment making," having come to his senses, will withdraw the "fair gift" of himself from one so unworthy as myself.

3. *Feelings of enmity against a successful rival.* The rancor toward the cloud-person is an obvious example. But rivals need not be successful to incur hostility; it is enough that they make advances toward the youth, as does the intrusive poet or the mistress. Animosity toward her, though soft-pedaled in Sonnets 40–42, is most pronounced in 144. Elsewhere the protagonist worries about anonymous persons in the company of the absent youth, but the attitudes he takes toward them may be neutral, as when he surmises that "where you are, how happy you make those" (57.12), or envious, as when he speaks of "others all too near [you]" (61.14), or even respectful, as he is when he expresses the fear, in the couplet of 48, that honest men may prove "thievish for a prize so dear."

4. *Self-criticism which tries to hold the subject's own ego accountable for the loss.* This component overlaps with the second, and the citation there from Sonnet 87 might just as well go here. So might the couplet of 49, which well illustrates this component, have gone there: "To leave poor me thou hast the strength of laws [= legalistic justification], / Since why to love I can allege no cause [= reason, legal case]." The unlovable "poor me" is both a narcissistically wounded me and the ego as cause of the looked-for loss. Shakespeare works a variation on this factor of taking responsibility for the anticipated loss in Sonnet 49 and again in Sonnets 88–89. The lover offers to support, to his own detriment, whatever charges the beloved may urge against him to rationalize a rejection of him, no matter how invalid these charges may be, and he admits to enough weaknesses and faults to make them appear not altogether invalid. This occurs in 88.5–7 and in the couplet:

> Such is my love, to thee I so belong,
> That for thy right myself will bear all wrong.

5. A component rather surprisingly missing from Freud's enumeration, which need not be taken as exhaustive, is anger at the loved one who is suspected. This factor is one that Shakespeare certainly made major use of in dramatizing the jealous passion suffered by Othello and Leontes toward their wives and by Hamlet when closeted with his mother. In Sonnet 35 the lyric "I" still rankles, even though the "sweet thief" is then pardoned, and is cross with himself for granting the pardon too readily: "Such civil war is in my love and *hate*" (35.12–14). The censure of the youth's behavior in Sonnets 58 and 59 is resentful and mistrustful. The most disapproving sonnet addressed to him, I think, is 69, which anticipates 94 and the sour stricture in its last four verses.

Sonnet 69 alludes to others who mark and praise the youth's exterior beauty and terms them "churls." They are not, however, rivals but critics of him, who, measuring "the beauty of thy mind" by "thy deeds," find it sullied. The speaker calls them churls ironically, for he cites them as witnesses and concurs in "their thoughts," which add "To thy fresh flower . . . the rank smell of weeds." His closing remark is,

> But why thy odor matcheth not thy show,
> The soil is this, that thou doth common grow—

where "soil" = 'ground' and 'stain,' and "common" = 'ordinary,' 'inferior,' or worse, for the youth is made "common" by licentious "deeds."

This sonnet is so reproachful that it might hardly seem out of place in Part II, where the mistress is regularly reprehended. In fact, Sonnet 131, directed to her, proceeds along similar lines. Again "some" are cited who find fault with her, but it is the opposite fault; for they are critical not of her character but of her appearance. The persona guardedly defends her as attractive; she is so to him, at any rate, if not to others. But he does not stop with that, for he goes on to consider the reason for "this slander" and decides that it stems not from her looks but from her "black deeds." Thus he ends as the one who charges her with licentiousness, finding her as common as, before, the friend was said to be. There are significant differences, however, between the two poems. She is denied objective beauty, but the first five lines of Sonnet 69 expatiate on the universally admired beauty of the friend. These lines make it unmistakably clear that this is a Part I rather than a Part II sonnet. Besides, the friend is wrongly accused and soon apologized to, while she is rightly accused and receives no apologies.

If, in Sonnet 69, the youth were blameworthy as charged, the closing dig would be justified and would betoken little, if any, jealousy. But he is exonerated in Sonnet 70—"thou present'st a pure unstained prime"—and the charges leveled at him before were "slander," whose "mark was ever yet the fair." The accusers, then, as slanderers, turn out to be churls after all. The poet, with a mind completely changed, now sees the beloved as a victim of defamation. But the same suspicions, and even vented in language reminiscent of 69.10–14, will reemerge in Sonnet 94.

The essential background of this famous and controverted sonnet is furnished by its immediate predecessors:

> Thou mayst be false and yet I know it not.
>
> (92.14)

> So shall I live, supposing thou art true,
> Like a deceived husband . . .
>
> (93.1–2)

> How like Eve's apple doth thy beauty grow
> If thy sweet virtue answer not thy show.
>
> (93.13–14)

The words "true," "false," and "deceived," along with the cuckold that the persona is afraid he might resemble, make it plain that sexual fidelity is at stake. Sonnet 93, while distinguished for its opening and closing verses, rather sags in between, where it repetitiously insists on the friend's being singularly privileged in that whatever falsehood lurks in his heart never appears on his face. Then the couplet harks back to lines 1–2, for if "thy sweet virtue" of constancy in love does not correspond to "thy show [= looks]," then "thy beauty" becomes "like Eve's apple," which was "pleasant to the eye" (Gen. 3:6, and cf. *Paradise Lost*, 9.776–77, 996) but had "power to hurt," to harm all mankind, and, of more immediate pertinence, to harm herself and her husband, Adam.

Read in this context, Sonnet 94 will be seen as the kind of speech a suspicious husband might make for the benefit of a wife he has come to mistrust. The poet lauds those who are chaste, "Unmoved, cold, and to temptation slow," and berates those who "hurt," that is, inflict mental anguish upon, the man to whom they have pledged fidelity. Blessed are the nondoers (94.1–10) and shame on the doers (94.11–14) of promiscuous deeds.

> They that have power to hurt and will do none,
> That do not do the thing they most do show,
> Who moving others are themselves as stone,
> Unmoved, cold, and to temptation slow—
> They rightly do inherit heaven's graces
> And husband nature's riches from expense;
> They are the lords and owners of their faces,
> Others but stewards of their excellence.
> The summer's flower is to the summer sweet,
> Though to itself it only live and die;
> But if that flower with base infection meet,
> The bravest weed outbraves his dignity:
> > For sweetest things turn sourest by their deeds;
> > Lilies that fester smell far worse than weeds.

"They" are exemplary types, bodily and morally. They have the "power to hurt," which they choose not to wield, and it is "the thing they most do show," what their appearance suggests they might readily do, and that is because they are "beauteous" and "therefore to be assailed" (41.6). They constantly move others to temptation simply by being beautiful, but they themselves are not reciprocally moved, and they are, properly in these circumstances, "as stone . . . cold." But whom might they "hurt"? The moved admirers, left unrequited, might appear to be the victims; but that cannot be the answer, for then the movers would in fact be exercising the "power," however effortlessly, that 94.1–2 approve them for eschewing. The answer is not to be found in this text at all but in the adjacent sonnets. From them we learn that the one who would be hurt—and by being deceived—is a lover, a husband (cf. 93.1–2), or somebody to whom the splendid mover is bound by a vow of love, exactly as the Master Mistress (for whom, though he is not addressed, the lecture is intended) is bound to the author. Once that is granted, the details fall into place. For example, to be "as stone / Unmoved, cold" is not the disagreeable personality trait some readers have thought it to be; instead, it is the posture of one true in love toward outsiders drawn to him, and his being "hot as embers, easily moved, and quick to temptation" with respect to them would be distasteful. The high tribute paid to the "cold" movers in the second quatrain is fitting and straightforward, not ironic. The two phrases "heaven's graces" and "nature's riches" share the meaning 'physical perfections,' but each has an additional meaning. The first, "heaven's graces," refers also to inward moral qualities (OED 11e), the "sweet virtue" of 93.14. The second, "nature's riches," is equivalent to "beauty's treasure" of seed at 6.4 ("nature" can = 'semen' [OED 7a]), and to "husband" these riches "from expense" can connote 'prudently conserve them from orgasmic squandering.' That construction implies that Shakespeare had male movers in mind, and of course he did.

These male movers are, in 94.7, "the lords and owners of their [own] faces," in distinction from "others," who in line 3 are moved and in line 8 are "but stewards [= custodial servants] of their [the movers'] excellence." These enthralled subordinates minister, with wonder and attraction, to the physical and moral excellences of the self-possessed owners and "Lords" (capitalized in Q) but never gain sexual possession of their persons, for which "faces" is apparently a synechdoche.

The octave is cast, except for "as stone" and "riches," in nonmetaphorical language, whereas the sestet speaks, except for 94.13, in floral conceits. The account of the "summer's flower" in 94.9–10 is a figurative recapitulation of 3–8. This flower is "to the summer sweet," by reason of its loveliness and fragrance, "Though to itself it only live and die." That autonomy alone will suffice for its success—though there is a faint intimation that something better is possible—just as the movers do well to be autonomous in relation to the moved, for both they and the flower will thereby escape contamination.

"But" at 94.11 signals the critical turn in the argument and divides the sonnet into sections of ten and four lines on top of the octave-sestet division. Until now a positive ideal has been advanced, but now a caveat is injected. The "base infection," a plant disease, with which "that flower" might meet would degrade it below the "basest weed"; just so, by implication, would the sublime mover, if morally and sexually corrupted—with a suggestion here of venereal infection—sink below the level of the vilest human creature, who would then "outbrave" him (= show up better) in "dignity [= worth]." The underlying idea often adduced by annotators, *corruptio optimi pessima*, is then translated into the couplet, where each of two statements convey it, the first more abstract, the second imagistic and gnomic.

The "sweetest things" in 94.13 that "turn sourest by their deeds" can hardly be flowers, which admit of "sweet" and "sour" but not of "deeds." The verse is laden with sexual innuendo. Since "sweet" can = 'sensually delectable,' "deeds" can = 'coital' and probably other 'sexual acts,' and "things" can = 'genital organs,' the things that do the deeds would seem to be rather phallic than floral, and, though I think the line has a more general reference, this meaning is comprehended. I think that the line in another way was a particular reference: that the poet may use broader terms but has the youth's "thing" (20.12) very much in mind.

The flower imagery of the third quatrain returns in 94.14, with one species specified. Why lilies? They rot malodorously; also, they are emblems of purity. The festering of the lilies stands for the stink of corruption in the movers, and the worst deterioration is that of the brightest and the purest (cf. 110.14).

Intense and irascible feelings are voiced at the close, and, although the discourse purports to be a character of moving young men, good-looking and good when unmoved though in danger of depravity by being seduced, and although the friend is not addressed, as he is in the neighboring poems, it·is evident that Sonnet 94 is a message for him, an admonition, and that that fact accounts for the fervor of the conclusion. In the sestet of Sonnet 69 the lover, prompted then, as now, by jealous suspicions, and there speaking directly to him, used pharasing strikingly similar to that in 94.11–14; and while those suspicions were conceded in Sonnet 70 to be unfounded, precisely because they were unfounded they would most likely resurface. They do in Sonnet 94, where the tacit source and motive of irritation is distrust of the beloved.

Sonnets 95 and 96, companion pieces, resume direct address to the friend and have affinities with the poems before them. For example, the "gazers" at 96.11–12, whom he might "lead astray" if he so chose, correspond to the moved "others" at 94.3 and 8, who are responsive to the movers in the same erotic way. Like Sonnet 94, 95 ends with a one-line aphoristic and figurative generalization: "The hardest knife ill us'd doth lose his edge." This cautions the youth against lustful misuse of his beauty, and, as befits the sexual topicality of the poem, plainly has phallic implications. Not only does "knife" belong among the objects of penetrative acuity, such as "sword," "tool," or "pen," that Shakespeare frequently adduced to represent the male organ (Partridge, p. 23), but both "hard" and "edge" can have reference to tumescence and "used" can refer to 'carnal employment.' The verse is akin to 94.13, which also carries a warning against phallic profligacy, only there the "things" do "deeds," just as the genetalic "flesh" does in Sonnet 151, whereas the knife is conceived of rather as a wielded thing.

Sonnets 95 and 96 reintroduce, from 69–70, the subject of scandal spread about the friend. Two possibilities—that he is guilty of faults as rumored and so to be reproved, or he is not guilty and yet is to be advised to safeguard his "budding name" from detraction—are held in suspense through most of the paired texts. The first possibility is generally entertained in the sestet of Sonnet 95 and the octave of 96, the second in the octave of 95 and the sestet of 96, where finally the matter is settled. The beloved, as in Sonnet 70 and as usual, turns out to be blameless: "*If* thou wouldst use the strength of all thy state," that is, exercise the full power at your command, though as yet you have not done so; "But do not so," that is, continue *not* to take advantage of your sensual opportunities, and refrain because "I love thee in such sort / As, thou being mine, mine is thy good report" (96.12–14).

The couplet of 96 exactly repeats the couplet of 36. There the persona announces that "we two must be twain," even though united in "loves," because of some "blot" in himself, a "bewailed guilt" that "should do thee shame" if "thou with public kindness honour me." "But do not so," for "thou being mine," so is everything of yours, and "mine is thy good report"; hence I gain something as well as you by *my* not besmirching your name. "But do not so" in Sonnet 96 means 'do not abuse the amatory strength attaching to your beauty,' and once again, by love-possession, "mine is thy good report"; hence I too have a stake in *your* not besmirching it. The lover demonstrates his devotion in Sonnet 36 by a selfless resolve to remove himself rather than dishonor the beloved; the verbal repetition in Sonnet 96 may remind him of that resolve and thereby dissuade him from a shameful course that would be harmful to them both.[10]

If Sonnets 95 and 96 were read out of context, they might be construed as expressive more of one friend's concern with the reputability and demeanor of the other than with jealous sentiments. But when the prior context has so firmly established jealous doubting as a character trait of the persona, and when allusions to "vices," "sins," and "faults" are so loosely predicated, now of the youth and now of gossip about him, until the resolution of the second sestet, at least a residue of suspiciousness can be detected in these sonnets. Never again after Sonnet 96, however—neither in the rest of Part I nor in the chronological scheme of the sequence—does the protagonist manifest any jealous suspicions of the Master Mistress. Why he does not will be considered later.

All of the elements of which normal or competitive jealousy are compounded, according to Freud, who had heterosexual men in mind, enter into the sonneteer's homoerotic jealousy. Then Sonnet 61 offers another perspective on the affect—one not in Freud's treatise—by regarding it as a desideratum, a concomitant and sign of the most ardent passion.

The scene, as in Sonnets 27–28 and 43, is at night in some unfamiliar room where the lover is lying in his lonely bed and an "image" of the beloved, or "shadows like to thee," so impinge on his mind as to keep him awake. Three questions in the octave entertain the illusion that the image is under the other's control and that he wills and desires to send it forth and hinder sleep, and the second quatrain conjectures a motive for him—jealousy:

> Is it thy spirit that thou send'st from thee
> So far from home into my deeds to pry,
> To find out shames and idle hours in me,
> The scope and tenor of thy jealousy?

This fantasy of the friend's spirit's spying, the 'mark' and 'purport' of which is to find out what lascivious acts the lover may be about in his spare time, might come across as paranoia until one reads on and discovers at once that this is not a dread but wishful thinking. Unable or refusing to sustain the fantasy, the poet snaps back to disappointing reality in 61.9: "Oh no, thy love though much is not so great"—not so great as to generate such suspicions or so great as "mine own true love," which does generate them, and which "doth my rest defeat, / To play the watchman ever for thy sake." His own jealousy comes through in the couplet: "For thee watch I [= stay awake], whilst thou doest wake elsewhere, / From me far off, with others *all too near.*" Those envied and troubling "others," be they definite or fanciful rivals, are envisaged as physically in touch with the youth. From the sestet we learn that the jealousy wistfully ascribed to him was a projection of the persona's own jealousy, that he is the one who seeks to pry into the lascivious misdeeds perchance being done by the distant beloved, and that the cause of the lover's sleeplessness is his own envy and mistrust. Although he measures the quantity of love by the presence or absence of jealousy, another inference might be drawn from 61.9–14 and from data throughout Shakespeare's sequence: that the friend is far less prone to be jealous than the protagonist is.

5

Eight more sonnets of Part I have a bearing on jealousy. They consist of two groups of four, separated by four others: Sonnets 109–12 and 117–20. They present novel situations and the reverse of those imagined beforehand, for the protagonist is now the confessed wrongdoer, shamed by infidelities, and the friend is now the one who has cause to be jealous. To what extent he is cannot be known directly; it can only be inferred from the apologetic and solacing words of the sonneteer, who monologizes throughout. These words imply that the friend does feel affronted, and they grant his right to be. He may not be much given to jealousy, but that does not mean that he is invulnerable to amorous disloyalty. Yet the uppermost concern in what follows is not with his reactions but, as always, with the psychology of the persona as disclosed by his conduct and emotional life. Accordingly, two questions might be asked of the text at this juncture: why does he breach his love commitment, and not merely once (in Sonnets 109–12) but soon again (in 117–20), and is there some kind of connection between this inconstancy and the inconstancy he compulsively used to suspect in the youth?

There is a connection, to be sure, and to understand it requires extratextual help, once again from Freud, here from his exposition of *projected jealousy,* which is

> derived in both men and women either from their own actual unfaithfulness in real life or from impulses towards it which have succumbed to repression. It is a matter of everyday experience that fidelity, especially that degree of it required in marriage, is only maintained in the face of continual temptations. Anyone who denies these temptations in himself will nevertheless feel their pressure so strongly that he will be glad enough to make use of an unconscious mechanism to alleviate the situation. He can obtain this alleviation—and, indeed, acquittal by his conscience—if he projects his own impulses to faithlessness on to the partner to whom he owes faith. This strong motive can then make use of the perceptual material which betrays unconscious impulses of the same kind in the partner, and the subject can justify himself with the reflection that the other is probably not much better than he is himself.

The "unconscious impulses" noted in the other, though "inevitable," are not inconsistent with loyalty, and they take the form of "little excursions in the direction of unfaithfulness," such as wishes to attract or make conquests, or being tempted, or mild flirting. But the jealous lover cannot tolerate these impulses or believe that they are aborted.

The poet proves to be such a lover. True, the beloved once was unfaithful, as Sonnet 34, where he tearfully owns up to his culpability, reveals; and Sonnet 120 will show that the poet long retains a memory of that incident. Yet that early and repented misdemeanor at best accounts only partially for the continual uneasiness over inconstancy and abandonment. The protagonist expects one so young and fetching to meet with frequent temptations (41.1–6; 48.7–8, 13; 96.11–12) and perceives him as flirtatious with the mistress (40.13, 41.1–4) and with the rival poet (82.5–9) or occasionally as relishing his erotic powers and their commendation (84.13–14, 96.1–4). This is the "perceptual material" that betrays the same kind of unconscious impulses in the friend as those lodged in the mind of the lover. The lover exhibits the elements of Freud's projected jealousy: he alleviates guilt by suspecting the other of a falsity that is really the projection of an unconscious urge to be false to him, for the allegations of sexual deception are, with the one exception, unwarranted, as he himself comes to recognize; and he finally does deceive the other, in the way he had suspected that he was being deceived, on the two occasions treated late in Part I. He is contrite after each, and he never again misdoubts the youth. While his jealousy has abated since Sonnet 96, it had sometimes abated before, only to return. Now it does not return; and although several factors will be seen to contribute to its cessation, his own infidelity, in which his own repressed wishes are consciously acted out, is a pertinent factor. The aspect of the mechanism of jealous projection by which the subject of jealousy capriciously fancies the absent loved one engaging in licentious activity is exemplified in Sonnet 61, discussed above.

In *delusional* jealousy, Freud's third and deepest layer, the male subject is a repressed homosexual who can deal with his carnal impulses only by projecting them onto his wife or paramour. Shakespeare was aware of such jealousy, for he depicted it in Iago.[11] This type is of course missing from the Sonnets, where the poet's homoerotic love for the Master Mistress is conscious, expressed verbally and actively, and never displaced onto anyone else.

An exchange in *Othello* between Desdemona and Emilia has elucidative value for the theme of projected jealousy in the Sonnets:

DESDEMONA: Alas the day, I never gave him cause!
EMILIA: But jealous souls will not be answer'd so;

They are not ever jealous for the cause,
But jealous for they are jealous; 'tis a monster,
Begot upon itself, born on itself.

(3.4.156–60)

Although the friend did once give cause, subsequent doubt of his devotedness is mostly self-begot by the jealous soul. The monster is finally exorcised, paradoxically, by the doubter's own infidelities. The purgation of jealousy both foreshadows the demise of his passion and concurs with its diminution.

In Sonnets 109–12 Shakespeare depicts himself (or the persona, if one prefers) as a committer of recent infidelities (109.5–8, 110.1–6); but he is now repentant (109.8, 111.9–12), has come to his senses (110.5–6), has recollected the preciousness of the love he has jeopardized, and has weighed the meanness of lustful gratification against the forfeiture of long-standing mutuality (109.11–14, 110.8–11). Now he seeks—by offering apologies (110.5–8), excuses (110.10–11, 111.1–7), appeals for "pity" (111.8, 13–14), pledges of amendment (110.10–12), and declarations of the utmost devotion (109.4–5, 12–13, 110.12–14, 112.5, 13–14)—the forgiveness (111.8) and approbation (112.3–4) of the friend and reconciliation with him (110.13–14). The excuses tendered are not consistent among themselves, comprising now the "impression" of being cuckolded, which "vulgar scandal stamp'd *upon my brow*" (112.2), now the motivation of testing accustomed love by the "newer proof [= experiments, experience]" of wantonness (110.9–12), and now the misfortune of a life that entails "public means which public manners breeds" (111.1–7). One cannot tell from the Sonnets what Shakespeare alludes to here. To surmise that he alludes to his career in the public theater is to import biographical information from outside. It may be legitimate to do so, and that would explain 111.4 ff. as connoting manners coarsened by the relentless pressure on player and playwright to cater to public taste. But the sonneteer is not expressly associated with the theater, and this interpretation would assume a strong autobiographical current in the cycle.

The reconciliation sought at the end of Sonnet 110 is with

A god in love, to whom I am confin'd.
Then give me welcome, next my heaven the best,
Even to thy pure and most most loving breast.

When Shakespeare writes at 109.4–5 of "my soul, which in thy breast doth lie— / That is my home of love," he is· thinking of the interior bosom ("*in* thy breast"). In the couplet above, the breast is again interior, as pure and loving, but also exterior ("*to* thy . . .

breast"); and "next" denotes 'nearest to' (OED 14). Then "my heaven," a metaphor whose explicit tenor is "thy breast," is the place where the devotee and the god come together physically, and "the best" of welcomes would consist of being clasped by the friend in a gesture of forgiveness and love. The reconciliation does occur, following Sonnet 111; for that the "pity" there requested is bestowed we learn from the opening lines of 112. And perhaps the most effectual steps, as they are certainly the most moving steps, taken to bring about the reunion are the cogent expressions of love that punctuate this set of sonnets.

It does seem as if the "worse essays prov'd thee my best of love" (110.8) when the sonnets of the next group, 113–16, bear out this optimistic sentiment. Here love is voiced as powerfully and persuasively as anywhere in the sequence. In 113–14 consciousness of the beloved is visually and mentally all-absorbing. The poet discovers in 115 that "Love is a babe," in that it keeps on increasing without ever attaining the limit of "full growth," and he confidently proclaims in 116 that "Love alters not." It is as if the summer of love has been regained; but this is an Indian summer, for what does 117 tell us but that the protagonist has once again lapsed into sexual waywardness? And this second "transgression," committed between 116 and 117, supplies the subject matter through 120.

Sonnet 117 opens, "Accuse me thus," and then, in the octave, lists these four charges: first, ingratitude:

> that I have scanted all
> Wherein I should your great deserts repay;

second, forgetfulness:

> Forgot upon your dearest love to call,
> Whereto all bonds do tie me day by day;

third, consorting with bad company:

> That I have frequent ['familiar'] been with unknown minds
> ['strangers']
> And given to time your own dear-purchas'd right [spent time
> with them that should have been devoted to you];

and fourth, choosing to avoid you:

> That I have hoisted sails to all the winds
> Which should transport me farthest from your sight.

And the latter two verses, 7–8, reverse the corresponding 7–8 in Sonnet 116 by saying, in effect, "I am a bark that has deliberately wandered away from my love." The fourth quatrain presupposes the validity of the four accusations.

We are further made privy to the poet's "trespass" (120.13–14) in the confessional conceit, drawn from alchemy, that opens Sonnet 119:

> What potions have I drunk of siren tears
> Distill'd from limbecks foul as hell within, . . .

"Potions" are 'drinks administered, either medicinal or poisonous' (Schmidt), and this sense connects the word with the "drugs" that "poison" of the preceding line, 118.14. A "limbeck" is an alembic or retort, designed for distillation. "Siren," though capitalized and italicized in Q, is an adjective modifying "tears" and *not*, as is sometimes thought, the possessive noun "syren's" or "syrens.'" The "potions . . . drunk" are composed of "tears" of a "syren" quality from dirty "limbecks." These metaphorical details adumbrate "the wretched errors" that "my heart committed" (119.5), and the plural nouns—"errors," "potions," and "limbecks"—imply that the speaker has transgressed more than once and with more than one partner. That the partners are morally base is suggested by "foul as hell within," this detail alluding to the depraved inwardness of the human objects of lust and also, though less aptly, to the filth of the limbecks. The sexual acts perpetrated may be construed as oral-genital. The "potions" are "drunk," and "distill'd" is a word that imports male orgasmic emissions at 6.2. The "tears" secreted from eyes stand for genital secretions, and they are "siren" because, like the mythic sea nymphs the word evokes, they are enticing and destructive—destructive to true love if not also in other ways. For Booth "the suggestions of male homosexual fellatio" are "at least as strong as those of cunnilingus."

Perhaps so, but in my deciphering of the lines the latter is the more likely alternative. I take "limbecks" to be a female rather than a phallic symbol. In 6.2–3 the youth is to be sexually "distill'd" *into* a "vial" that images the womb, whereas here the "potions" are distilled *out of* vessels that are more feasibly vulval than penial. "Tears" in 119.1 connote the eye, and Partridge finds a Shakespearean association of the eye with the pudendum; and, in 119.2 they are "syren," which connotes femininity. In "Loves Alchemie" Donne employs the conceit of the "pregnant pot" from which the "chemique [= alchemist]" might obtain "Some odoriferous thing, or med'cinall" with reference to women as sexual objects, and Shakespeare proceeds in like manner with the conceit of "limbecks" that yield gustative "potions." The women so figured, for being "foul as hell within" and equatable with the "unknown minds" at 117.5, might well be prostitutes.

Sonnet 118 combines two tropes, of which the shorter first one is based on eating (1–2, 5–6), the longer second one on evacuation (3–4, 7 ff.). These tropes make the use of tart appetizers to sharpen the palate and the use of purgatives as preventive medicine analogous to the dissolute comportment of the lover. He tried the "bitter sauces" of dissipation as a way to make his carnal "appetites more keen," even while "being full of your ne'er cloying sweetness." The savory "sweetness" stands for the 'erotic delight' found in the youth; and, if it never cloys, why the need for spicing it up salaciously, and why, if "full," did he seek the additional morsels? With the more elaborated, witty, and unromantic second trope he presents himself as an amorous hypochondriac. The ills he suffers are those anticipated when "sick of welfare" (= surfeited with fine fare/happiness—I/R) and those induced with precautionary cathartics, whereby the medicament becomes the disease. The "healthful state" of love was, paradoxically, "rank [= foul, sick] of goodness," and "would by ill be cured," which is to say that the goodness required remediation, and by evil. The "policy of love" adopted was to "anticipate / The ills that were not" and to try the purge of debauchery, thus making nonexisting ills grow "to faults assured"; but he has now learned the "lesson" that "Drugs poison him [= infidelities are pernicious to the one] that so *fell sick of you*" (118.13–14). The peccavi ends on an unexpectedly chilling note, however it is modified by the overall argument and intent. The poet grew tired of the beloved and their smooth-going friendship and sought relief from monotony in venery. Things had come to a pretty pass, and his ardor for the youth is transparently cooling.

And yet, at 119.13, "I return rebuked to my content." The clause includes the senses 'I regain my contentment (in true love),' 'I derive satisfaction from being rebuked,' and 'I am back after an absence.' The absence was both temporal and psychological. Temporally it occurred during an indefinite interval between Sonnets 116 and 117. The reader becomes aware of this extended interval only retrospectively, once he finds out how much has meanwhile transpired. But as he goes through the sequence, he is first struck by the dramatic juxtaposition of Sonnet 116, "Let me not to the marriage," with Sonnet 117, "Accuse me thus." The effect is analogous to that produced in some of the plays, and notably in *Othello*, by the contrast between the dramatized onstage time, highly compressed, and the lengthier offstage time implicit in the events of the plot. The psychological absence that precedes the return consisted of a vacation from, even a vacating of, love; and one learns with some surprise how much it had deteriorated, to the extent of being a "ruin'd love" that had to be "built anew" (119.11).

Still, the lover now wishes to repair the broken friendship, and so he makes various attempts to mitigate his misconduct. The first is in the couplet of Sonnet 117, where "my [legalistic] appeal says I did strive to prove / The constancy and virtue of thy love." To justify infidelity as a test of the other's devotion is rather forbidding. In the sestet of Sonnet 119 he exclaims, "O benefit of ill," and claims to have discovered that evil can ameliorate the good, that decayed love renewed is "fairer . . . more strong, far greater" than before, and that the investment in lechery is therefore paying rich dividends. That may be so; but we might recall that he said something similar at 110.6–9, following his previous lapse.

Sonnet 120, the last of this set of four, the last of the eight sonnets 109–12 and 117–20 that treat of sensual faults committed by the protagonist, and the last of the numerous poems in Part I that touch on the theme of jealousy, serves an epiphanic function that befits its position of finality. Now the poet undertakes a new tactic of conciliation by recalling two earlier confrontations between himself and the friend, one recent and not otherwise recorded in the sonnet sequence, the other remote and depicted in Sonnets 33–35, the very first poems to touch on the theme of jealousy. Thus Sonnet 120 will prove illuminative of that overarching theme from its inception to its termination.

The persona refers to the recent confrontation as "our night of woe" (120.9), and what happened on that unhappy night can be gathered only from hints in the sonnet. Apparently the youth reproachfully spoke of his being troubled by the lascivious behavior of his lover, who all the while remained unsympathetic and unyielding. The lover has since had a change of heart and regrets responding as he did. He now wishes he had "remember'd," from his own past experience, his "deepest sense how hard true sorrow hits," had conceded his guilt, and had "tender'd / The *humble salve which wounded bosoms fits*" as "soon to you as you to me" on another occasion (120.9–12).

When was that? It was in Sonnet 34, when the youth was quick to acknowledge his offense of sexual disloyalty and to tender "a *salve . . . That heals the wound*," however incompletely, of the distraught protagonist (34.7–8). That the confrontation remembered in Sonnet 120 is the selfsame one treated of in Sonnets 33–35—a connection observed by a number of expositors—is made manifest by the verbal echo that I have italicized above and by other echoes as well. The word "trespass" in the couplet of Sonnet 120, where "mine" matches "yours," harks back to "thy trespass," also a "sensual fault," at 35.6 and 9; and the speaker's "faults" are sensual too at 118.10. The verb "ransom," which reappears twice in the last line of Sonnet 120, where the ransoming agent of one transgression is another, had appeared in the last line of Sonnet 34, where "tears . . . ransom all ill deeds." Then, "ills" and "ill," again alluding to infidelities, though this time the poet's, crop up at 118.10 and 12 and at 119.9—poems adjacent to Sonnet 120 and on the same topic. "Sorrow" as the "offender's" and, again, as tearful "rain" on the face of the sufferer at 34.11 and 6 resonates in "that sorrow that I then did feel" and in the recollection of "how hard true sorrow hits" the sufferer at 120.2 and 10.

This striking dictional repetition reinforces the correspondence between the two situations. With the phrases "That you were *once* unkind," "how *once* I suffer'd in your crime," and "you to me *then* tender'd," where "once" signifies both 'in the past' and 'one time only,' and "then" means 'on that occasion,' Shakespeare informs us that he has a particular prior incident in mind. It is one whose circumstances reflect and reverse those in which the friends now find themselves. Then the youth would have been the guilty party, would have consoled the anguished poet, and would, contrite, have sought a reconciliation. Sonnet 34, along with 33 and 35, exactly fits the bill.

The thesis of Sonnet 120 is presented at the outset: "That you were once unkind befriends me now." Your single unkindness in the past 'works to my present advantage' in two ways, in making me able to empathize with your hurt, the same as mine then, and in supplying a "fee" by which "your trespass now . . . must ransom me" as, at long last, "mine ransoms yours" (120.13–14).

Sonnet 120, in itself and in connection with its forerunners, Sonnets 117–19 and the suite 109–12, puts all the sonnets on jealousy into perspective. This poem winds up the last rift between the lovers, which is due to the recent inconstancy of the one, and it patently reverts to Sonnet 34 and its companions, 33 and 35, where the first rift took place on account of the inconstancy of the other and where, also, the persona's jealousy initially came into view. And the quarrel of more than three years before is not just recalled in Sonnet 120 but is here finally resolved to the poet's satisfaction. Hence this text shapes and rounds out the jealousy sonnets with a circular design that ties the end to the beginning.

This large artistic design is fraught with psychological implications. The sonneteer's jealous suspicions and accusations do not reemerge after Sonnet 96. In part they do not because of a gradual though unsteady attenuation of his passion for the youth, erotic jealousy being, as Sonnet 61 intimates, commensurate with erotic passion. If that fully explained the jealousy and its cessation, it would simply be jealousy of the competitive type; and without his two excursions into promiscuity, and the two sets of sonnets that deal with them, we would never learn that the jealousy is of the projective type. The persona's lapse and relapse into infidelities are signs and results of a slackening of ardor, and the confession of infidelities affords him and us glimpses into the dynamics of his projected jealousy.

Sonnet 120 lets us realize something unstated before: that, aside from that single slip into licentiousness, immediately repented and long past, the youth was innocent of the sensual looseness with which he was forever being taxed. The inconstancy he was suspected of was projected *onto* him, and the projections had their source in the disturbing desires that were being repressed in the psyche of his lover. We discover that the lover had harbored such desires only when he expresses them, or when we come to the sonnets, from 109 to 120, in which he tells of his fault. He experiments with inconstancy not only because of these unconscious wishes, and not only when and because his passion for the youth is diminishing, but for a third reason as well, if, as I hold, he satisfies his lustful urges with female partners. The heterosexual side of his bisexual nature would then exert part of the pressure.

Freud writes that projected jealousy differs from that "belonging to the third layer, the true delusional type," in being amenable to analytic treatment. The analyst "must refrain from disputing [with the analysand] the material on which he bases his suspicions" and "can only aim at bringing him to regard the matter in a different light," which is to be done "by exposing the unconscious phantasies of the subject's own infidelity." Shakespeare shows that the therapeutic goal might be achieved by other means than psychoanalysis. By acting on his formerly repressed impulses toward unfaithfulness, the sonneteer gains such insight into the unconscious origins of his prior suspicions that he is able to exonerate the youth and, finally, to fully cure himself of projected jealousy.

In their overall organization the jealousy sonnets lend solid support to my thesis that the order of poems in Thorpe's Quarto is *demonstrably* correct, and, in their delineation of the psychology of jealousy, they support my argument that the love between the male friends is consciously and actively sexual. But other conclusions reached in this chapter are likewise departures from the standard commentary, which tends on the whole to look down on the friend, to view him as unworthy of Shakespeare—a view diametrically opposed to that of the Sonnets themselves. They do not depict a Shakespeare so smitten with a self-absorbed young nobleman, or else so compelled by the idea of love or a need to worship that devolves on him, as to be blind—though *we*, of course, are not—to his short-comings. To the contrary, the poet is so passionately in love with the youth as to idealize him on the one hand and, on the other, to suspect him, wrongly, of faults out of erotic jealousy; and when the passion and its concomitant, distorting projected jealousy, subside, the youth is absolved of all misdemeanors but one. From Sonnet 120, as elsewhere, we learn that he did not have sexual relations with the mistress or the rival poet or anyone else after that escapade with the cloud-person, reported in Sonnet 33, and that he has since been loyal in love. He is the one who is finally hurt and rejected. But just the fact that he was Shakespeare's chosen beloved for a number of years and could be a begetter of such sonnets should be enough to make him a figure to be admired.

The rearrangers among the commentators usually jam together the separate groups 109–12 and 117–20. By doing so, they eliminate the effective juxtaposition of Sonnets 116 and 117, which includes the contrast I have pointed out between 116.7–8 and 117.7–8. They conflate the two separate episodes of the poet's infidelities into a single episode, even though it is highly significant that there are two and that the second is a relapse, occurring despite the persona's vigorous repentance of the first and the consequent renewal of his love. Such conflation obscures a telling distinction between the two runs of sonnets: in Sonnets 109–12 some of the most fervent expressions of amorous commitment in the entire sequence will be found, but expressions of the same kind and intensity are missing from Sonnets 117–20.

7

The Wills of the Mistress

Within Part II, Sonnets 127–54, to be studied in this chapter and the next, the poet again suffers jealousy, most excruciatingly in Sonnet 144, at the thought of a sexual liaison between the friend whom he passionately adores and the woman to whom he is powerfully attracted. Though his thoughts and feelings continue to constitute the subject matter, the shift of their focus at Sonnet 127 from the original male object of love to a second, female, object introduces what amounts to a new subject, the poet's affair with his mistress. The shift introduces a peculiar feature of Shakespeare's sequence and one of its major departures from Renaissance precedents in the genre.

The woman who displaces the Master Mistress through all of Part II is alluded to as "my mistress" at 127.9 and 130.1. Never named, she is popularly known as the "dark lady," even though Shakespeare never refers to her as a lady and only once as "dark"—savagely at 147.14: "[Thou] are as black as hell, as *dark* as night." He ordinarily employs the former adjective, and an appellation more textually apposite would be "black mistress," but that term has racial and racialist connotations that make it unusable. She is black in senses both commendatory and disparaging. Partly it is a matter of coloration, for she is a brunette (130.4) and has "eyes . . . raven black" (127.9); and though traditionally such features were not "counted fair" (sonneteers, like other gentlemen, preferred blondes), in the poet's "judgment" her "black" is beautiful (127, 131.12, 132.13–14). The judgment is one that will change, for she is "a woman colour'd ill" at 144.4 (and see again the couplet of Sonnet 147). But early on her blackness is conceived of in another way: "In nothing art thou black save in thy deeds" (131.13). Here the adjective figuratively and pejoratively qualifies her deeds as licentious.

Her licentiousness comes up frequently, as in Sonnet 135, where it stimulates elaborate wordplay on "will." This word appears as a noun thirteen times—seven times capitalized and italicized in Q— and it takes one or more of the following senses: (1) carnal desire,

(2) volition, (3) the male genitals, (4) the female genitals, and (5) the familiar form of William, the meaning that is always applicable, if not exclusively so, when the term is put in italics.

> Whoever hath her wish, thou hast thy *Will*,
> And *Will* to boot, and *Will* in overplus;
> More than enough am I that vex thee still,
> To thy sweet will making addition thus.
> Wilt thou whose will is large and spacious
> Not once vouchsafe to hide my will in thine?
> Shall will in others seem right gracious,
> And in my will no fair acceptance shine?
> The sea, all water, yet receives rain still,
> And in abundance addeth to his store:
> So thou being rich in *Will* add to thy *Will*
> One will of mine to make thy large *Will* more.
>   Let no unkind "no" fair beseechers kill;
>   Think all but one, and me in that one *Will*.

In 135.1–2 three men named William are under the amorous sway of the woman being beseeched. One, the "I," is Shakespeare, who refers to himself by the familiar form of his given name; and while the self-reference is obvious, it is confirmed in 135.14 and again by the couplet of 136:

> Make but my name thy love, and love that still,
> And then thou lov'st me, for my name is *Will*.

Another William is the friend, the preceding sonnets, 133–34, making the identification clear; and 143.13, where Will is again italicized and names the "feather'd creature" that stands for him, furnishes corroboration. The third William is often and reasonably assumed to be a husband. A sonneteer's mistress may, like her courtly-love counterpart, be married, as Stella is to Lord Rich (*Astrophel and Stella*, 24, 35.11, 37), and the marital status of the woman is intimated at 152.3 with the reproach "In act thy bed-vow broke," which "certainly *suggests*," to Ingram and Redpath, and to me as well, "that she has a husband." Which "Will" is which in 135.1–2 is a question. I would surmise the first to be the friend, on the basis of the two previous sonnets, and particularly because "thou hast both him and me," in 134.13, is echoed right afterwards (135.1–2) by "thou hast thy *Will*, / And *Will* . . . and *Will*. . . ." The third one should be the poet, for 135.3–4 make that pretty clear, and that leaves the second to be the spousal Will. The attraction of the woman to three men called Will need not be mere coincidence; a name can play a major part in erotic fantasy life, and, for her, a lover by any other name might smell less sweet. Shakespeare is fully aware of this psychological principle at 136.13: "Make but my name thy love, and love that still." That the friend should bear the same name as his lover has other implications, reinforcing the narcissism that, as we saw before, is so salient a factor in their psychoerotic economy.

The five pertinent glosses of "will" enumerated above are distributed through the rest of Sonnet 135, from line 3 on, as follows:

Line 4	Glosses 1 and 4
Line 5	Glosses 1 and 4
Line 6	Gloss 3
Line 7	Glosses 1 and 3
Line 8	Glosses 2 and 1
Line 11 (first use)	Glosses 1 and 5
Line 11 (second)	Glosses 1, 2, 4, and 5
Line 12 (first)	Glosses 3 and 1?
Line 12 (second)	Glosses 1, 4, and 5
Line 14	Glosses 1, 2, 4, and 5

The nickname occurs in line 11 twice and once in lines 12 and 14; in three of these instances "*Will*" is used collectively, to refer to all three men; but at the end of line 11 only one is alluded to, and he may be either the youth or the husband, though more likely he is the former.

Jealousy is at least muted in Sonnet 135. The persona is perfectly willing to allow the lady her other two Wills. He does not seek to oust them; his plea is simply that he not be ousted, that she grant her sexual favors to him as well. She may be promiscuous, but never mind, so long as he gets his share. He does not demand fidelity of her, as he normally does of the friend, and he even tolerates (as at 135.9–12 or 136.3–10) insatiability on her part. In courting her, he employs unmistakable bawdy (a strategy of arousal?) and exhibits the combination of desire and disrespect that is the hallmark of lust in Part II.

Inquiring into the complex of emotional transactions among the mistress, Will the Speaker (hereafter W. S.) and Will the Handsome Youth (hereafter W. H.), I will dwell on the four sonnets in Part II that are most germane, Sonnets 133–34 and 143–44, and will raise these three questions: (1) How does the triangle treated in these four poems relate to the triangle in Sonnets 40–42? (2) How are the events of Part II to be correlated chronologically with those of Part I? (3) How well founded and to what extent confirmed are W. S.'s jealous suspicions of the mistress and W. H.?

The answers I find to the questions are these:

1. Most readers agree (a minority of dissenters notwithstanding) that Shakespeare is speaking of the same set of circumstances and the same cast of characters—W. H., the mistress, and W. S.—in Sonnets 40–42 as in 133–34, 143–44.

2. If that is so, then Sonnets 133 through 144 would be synchronous with 40–42, and the affair with the mistress would take place not subsequently to Part I but concurrently with it and at an early stage. This concurrence is sometimes noticed in the commentary.

3. The evidence is mixed and inconsistent, but when it is collected, sifted, and, above all, examined in the order of its presentation in the sonnet sequence, the conclusion can be drawn that the mistress and the friend, despite her seductive efforts and the poet's suspicions, do not have carnal relations. This hypothesis is new.

The above theses will be severally argued below.

I

If we read Sonnets 133–34, which are linked sonnets and the seventh and eighth in the second division, with a sense of *déjà vu*, that is because we encounter a situation exactly like that in Sonnets 40–42, and the similarities are not only situational but verbal, emotional, and attitudinal. But there is one conspicuous difference: although in both sets of sonnets the jealous lover entertains suspicions of the friend and the mistress, the first set is addressed to him, the later set to her.

Sonnet 134 is full of verbal echoes of 42. The clauses "That thou hast her" and "That she hast thee" appear in 42.1 and 3, while in 134.13, addressed to the woman, we read, "thou hast both him and me." In Sonnet 42, the forms "loss," "lose," and "losing" occur six times, while the verb and the past participle "lost," though with reference to the loss of the male alone and not both of them, as before, occur at 134.12 and 13. The phrase "for my sake," though given more prominent play in Sonnet 42, recurs at 134.11, along with "for me" at 134.7. The phrase "my unkind abuse" at 134.12, that is, 'mine of him' in having him underwrite my amorous "bond," may recall 42.7, "even so does she abuse me." The shrewd poet complains to the friend, not to the mistress, of his own abuse by her, and he confesses to the mistress, but not to the friend, his own abuse of him. The repetitions of diction attest that the two widely separated sonnets deal with one and the same incident.

Confirmation will be found by juxtaposing 133.7–8,

> Of him, my self, and thee I am forsaken,
> A torment thrice threefold thus to be crossed,

with 42.11–12,

> Both find each other and I lose both twain,
> And both for my sake lay on me this cross.

Both passages express a painful sense of being abandoned by the other two, though "this cross" is that of a twofold loss, while the "torment" is "threefold"—"thrice" intensifies rather than multiplies the three—by reason of the added notion of being "crossed" (= thwarted) by losing "self"-possession.

Certain attitudes of the protagonist toward the other two, and his estimate of their characters, remain constant through Sonnets 40–42 and 133–34. He prefers the male beloved, as he explicitly states at 42.3–4, and feels protective toward him, esteems him, and loves him more deeply, while directing virtually all his hostility toward the mistress. These feelings are most forcefully vented in Sonnet 144, "Two loves I have." In Sonnets 133–34 "my sweet'st friend" is "kind" in contrast to the "covetous" female. The friend is, moreover, "my next self" and, synonymously, "that other mine"; his heart lies, as hers does not, in the heart of the lover. These sentiments accord with that of 42.13, where "my friend and I are one." The idea of selves united and hearts interchanged is repeatedly adduced to define the masculine mutuality (e.g., at 22.5–7, 48.10–11, 109.3–5, 110.13–14) and is never adduced with regard to the poet's attachment to the mistress. The nearest approach to the idea—and it is not very near—comes with the jail conceit in the sestet of Sonnet 133, where "my heart" is imprisoned in "thy steel bosom's ward," to connote that the persona is involuntarily under her erotic enthrallment; but he does not enjoy that condition, finding it rather repellent and coercive: "I . . . *perforce* am thine." His chief concern in the poem is to safeguard the youth from being a "slave" to such "slavery."

The lady makes the initial advances toward the friend. We first learn at 41.7 that she "woos" him; and at 134.11 she is said to "sue" him, the verb bearing its legal sense figuratively—on which level she is cast in the role of a Shylock—and on the literal level importing 'pursue, woo.' Her sexual aggressiveness is disclosed again at 142.9–10:

> Be it lawful I love thee as thou love those
> Whom thine eyes woo as mine importune thee.

Among those whom she fancies and ogles, the youth should be one, for she is the same seductress who assailed him earlier (41.6) and who, in the next two sonnets, 143 and 144, is bent on having him.

There is no reason for doubting that Sonnets 40–42 in Part I and, in Part II, Sonnets 133, 134, and other sonnets, through 144, have to do with one and the same episode, in which the same young man, the same woman, and the same poet interact in the same triangular way.

2

The episode holds both structural and temporal implications for the Sonnets. It is singular in the sense that it alone is staged twice, at points far apart, and it alone comes into both Part I and Part II. Brief and minor in Part I, where it occupies but three adjacent sonnets a third of the way through, it commands the central segment of Part II, occupying, though intermittently, the seventh to the eighteenth of the twenty-eight sonnets. Because it is common to both, it functions as the jointure that holds the two divisions together. Without it, they could have appeared to be distinct sonnet cycles, though printed and numbered as if one and sharing a single persona; he would have been seen as engaged with the friend and the mistress in distinct and successive relationships that never impinged on each other. But Sonnets 40–42 together with 133 to 144 require us to apprehend the structure of the sequence as far less disjointed and more fully holistic. The same groups of sonnets also provide the essential clue to the chronological relationship of Parts I and II.

The affair with the mistress, while of indefinite duration, appears to be brief, and on grounds other than simply the smaller number of sonnets in Part II (twenty-eight) than in I (one hundred twenty-six). No time span is indicated in Part II, while Sonnet 104 informs us that the male friendship has already lasted three years. In Part II there are no poems about absence, composed when the poet is on one of his periodic journeys, no mention of gaps of silence, as in Sonnets 100–102, no allusions to the changing seasons, as in Sonnets 98–100 or 104, and no thought given to Time, or aging, or death, which are continual concerns in Part I, as in the many treatments of the theme of immortalizing verse between Sonnets 15 and 107, a theme never brought into Part II. It may be inferred that the entire amour lasts no longer than a matter of months.

That period would include the triangular episode that coincides in Sonnets 40–42 and 133–44. Hence the two sets of sonnets serve to synchronize the series of events represented in Parts I and II. Then Part II as a whole might be conceived of as appendage to Sonnets 40–42 or as a kind of footnote to them, as indicated by the asterisk in the following rough diagram:

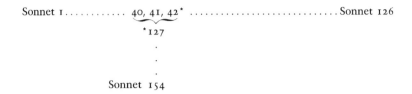

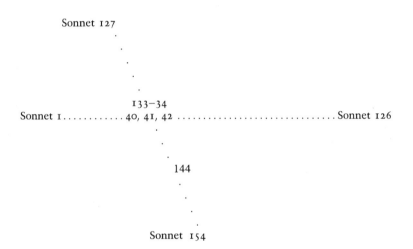

Alternatively, Part II might be conceived of as an underplot that features the lady, who would otherwise have so small a part to play. In this scheme, the one episode belonging to the main and secondary plots takes place at the juncture where the two lines of action intersect. It might be diagrammed thus:

Even if Sonnets 127–54 violate chronology by reverting to an amour long since over by the end of Part I, a more fitting location for them can hardly be imagined than the one they occupy in the Quarto. Shakespeare was right in deciding to keep each part intact and each distinct from the other. True, this design does impose a burden on the reader to backtrack, to recognize the concurrence of these sonnets with sonnets that come temporally and numerically much earlier. The alternative would have been to seriously interrupt the continuity of Part I, and its fixed focus on the friend, with an insertion, in the early 40s, of a run of twenty-eight sonnets on the affair with the mistress. As the next chapter will show, the bipartite organization yields rich dividends, consisting of thematic and other contrasts, which far outweigh any disadvantages.

3

The jealous lover, who is bisexual, enjoys both the mistress, who is heterosexual, and the young man desired by both, who is, very likely, homosexual.

The young man is, first of all, homosexually linked in Part I with three specific men: with the poet in their ongoing intimacy; with the cloud-person in the sexual incident prior to Sonnet 33; and with the rival poet, whose amorous attentions and tributes elicit his fascinated response. He proved unresponsive to the poet's persuasions to breed. He is explicitly pictured in the company of women only in the handful of sonnets that connect him with the mistress. That connection is crucial, the test case of his sexual orientation.

The poet does at times seem to believe that his friend and his mistress make love. He thinks so in Sonnet 144 and is devastated by the thought. He says so, though wittily, with greater equanimity, and addressing her, in the couplet of Sonnet 134: "Him have I lost; thou hast . . . him," where the meaning must be bawdy, for "He pays the whole," with a probable pun on 'hole.' His attitude is more detached than in Sonnet 144, and one wonders why. Is it because he knows better and is soft-soaping the lady with what she wants to hear? In any case, we have seen that he is much given to jealous fantasies where the friend is concerned. He sometimes speaks in Sonnets 40–42 also as if the other two were sexually intimate; however, as I have argued in chapter 6, that set of sonnets leaves the question up in the air. Still, if Sonnets 133–34 were read out of context, or if they provided the last word on the subject, the idea that the lady has her way with the youth could hardly be doubted.

But the last word is provided instead by Sonnets 143–44, and these poems put the matter in quite another light. Sonnet 143 depicts the poet's seeking the woman, her pursuing the youth, and the youth fleeing her: "So runn'st thou after that which flies from thee, / Whilst I . . . chase thee." The conceit calls forth a barnyard setting for the three figures—the lady in the role of "housewife" and "mother," the poet in that of "her babe," and the youth as an escaping fowl—and puts them through comic paces. The persona is hardly made wretched over the deportment of the other two, even though the "babe" cries for its mother at 143.6 and 14 and to be erotically "mothered" at 143.12; for he expects her, "if thou catch thy hope," to "turn back to me," and at the end he is willing to "pray that thou mayst have thy *Will*." The prayer petitions that she may (1) enjoy W. H., (2) gratify her carnal desire, (3) do as she likes, and —since "will" also = 'the male member,' along with "thing" at 143.4, where the word refers to the "feather'd creature" pursued— (4) catch the cock/get young Will's organ. In this, the penultimate sonnet on the rivalry for the youth, W. H. is no more than a "hope" for the mistress, and, though she is attracted to him, he is repelled by her. We might be reminded of 41.7–8: "when a woman woos, what woman's son / Will sourly leave her till he have prevailed?" Maybe not "sourly" but seemingly more in revulsion or fright, W. H., for one, "will leave her." Or we might be reminded of 40.7–8: "But yet be blam'd, if thou this self deceivest / By wilful taste of what thy self refusest." The phrasing is hypothetical: the blameworthy deed may or may not be done by the youth; but 40.8 can be paraphrased, 'what you normally disdain but now with an effort of will may take,' and that is a female sexual partner. "What thy self refusest"—and who—becomes very clear in Sonnet 143. W. H., certainly so far, looks to be a homosexual.

In the soliloquy of Sonnet 144 Shakespeare dramatizes the workings of the jealous imagination. The protagonist projects, somewhat voyeuristically, the most dreaded of scenes, in which his "two loves" may truly be sexually engaged, with the male angelic one being currently debauched by the female diabolic one. The lover of both is extremely distraught, which is curious, since he could joke about this union at the end of Sonnet 134 and pray for it at the end of Sonnet 143. Before, he seems not to have seriously expected that it would come about. Now, insanely jealous—or almost insanely—he surmises otherwise. Yet it is far from certain that the other two *are* together. He himself is not convinced that they are: "suspect I may, but not directly tell." Why he should now be so overwhelmed by suspicion is left unexplained, except that "jealous souls . . . are never jealous for the cause, / But jealous for they are jealous."

The jealous soul in Sonnet 144, as is his wont, exonerates and idealizes the friend and focuses his wrath and hostility upon the female. She has demonic designs on both males: to "win me soon to hell"—a psychological hell of jealousy, anger, and isolation—and to draw the youth into the fiery and morbid hell of her pudendum. The poet is suffering his hell, though not fully, since his state lacks one infernal element: he has not quite abandoned hope.

> I guess one angel in another's hell.
> Yet this shall I ne'er know but live in doubt,
> Till my bad angel fire my good one out.

Since "fire . . . out" means 'to infect with venereal disease,' the seduction of the friend cannot be confirmed until he is thus infected.

But he never is. Therefore, by the logic of the sonnet's argument, he did not have intercourse with the mistress: Q.E.D.

But the logic is really illogic. The syphilis test is bizarre, a device of invective, invented by the frustrated lover to vent his rage. The lady herself is not infected, for he himself copulates with her both before and afterward without contracting the disease. And the whole ludicrous idea is forgotten as suddenly as it is obtruded. The crisis of Sonnet 144 is not resolved but simply disappears, leaving not a trace behind.

The very next sonnet, 145, while the most trivial and inane of all, makes the point that the lady does not hate the persona, and he, in a lighthearted mood, bears no grudge against her. Not only is the topic of venereal disease dropped after Sonnet 144, but so is the notion of a sexual entanglement between the she-devil and male angel. Indeed, he is never alluded to in terms of jealousy in the next ten sonnets of Part II (145–54), and she, after Sonnet 42, is never alluded to at all in the remaining eighty-four sonnets of Part I.

I conclude that she never does have the youth, and a later sonnet in each part of the cycle reinforces this finding. In Sonnet 120 the poet recalls the single former occasion upon which the friend betrayed him; that occasion was the one recorded in Sonnets 33–34, where the infidelity was with a male and was committed and confessed to before the advent of the mistress. In Sonnet 152 she is reprimanded for being "twice forsworn" in "to me love swearing." "Twice" because (1) "In act thy bed-vow broke," that is, she violated her marital oath by adultery with the poet, and (2) she broke the "new faith" sworn to him by soon turning against him in hostility and "vowing new hate after new love bearing." Hence she is guilty of two breaches of promise, one made to her husband, the other to her accusing lover, and the friend is not a party to either of these breaches. If he is of concern here, it is because of the persona's admission in 152.1, "I am forsworn," which may advert to maltreatment of him.

Of course W. H. would derive gratification from his participation in the triangle, in which both his lover and his lover's lady dote on him. He might not, either, be averse to causing his lover some distress for being so impassioned of her. Even in the unlikely event that W. H. had, "by wilful taste of what" he habitually repudiates, succumbed to her advances—as local statements more than the total picture allow for—the impression of his homosexuality need hardly be modified. His being seduced by the mistress would then be anomalous—a deviation, under these special conditions, from his basic sexual adaptation.

Commentators on the Sonnets are very much in agreement that the poet and the friend do not have sexual relations and that the friend and the dark lady do. The conclusions I reach, largely on the basis of my experiment in reading the Sonnets as they sequentially occur in the original edition, are exactly the reverse.

To sum up these conclusions in Shakespeare's bawdy terms of Sonnets 135 and 136: although the mistress fulfills her lustful will by filling her vaginal will with the phallic will of the bisexual Will, W. S., she fails to do so with that of homosexual Will, W. H.

8

The Action of Lust

Possibly no single poem in Shakespeare's sonnet sequence is more imperative for understanding it holistically than Sonnet 129, "The expense of spirit." This key sonnet defines the central theme of Part II as lust, sheds light on its arrangement of sonnets, and, as we shall see later on, serves as a critical point of reference when the basic antitheses between Parts I and II are investigated. This sonnet is the third one of Part II, and the first two—127 and 128—prepare the way for it in the course of introducing the secondary subject of the Sonnets, the liaison with the mistress.

The protagonist is already infatuated with her in Sonnet 127. Nothing is said about how or when they met. He does not address her directly here but launches into that stock-in-trade of the amorist, praise of her beauty. It is not of the type normally admired, being "black," and so he must defend it while eulogizing it. That gives a mildly unconventional twist to the opening poem, though it barely hints at the unconventionalities to follow. The first quatrain points out that, in the past, "black," in the sense of the dark coloring of a brunette as opposed to the light coloring of a blonde, "was not counted fair [= comely, with a play on 'blonde']," and the same prejudice exists today. The long-standing vogue of blondeness proves, according to the second quatrain, corruptive: it promotes widespread use of cosmetic "art" for "fairing the foul," with the consequence that "sweet" and natural "beauty" is, if brunette, deprived of its proper designation. Gentlemen may prefer blondes, but the blondes often have bleached hair; "black" is truly beautiful and more likely to be genuine. In the octave the poet comes on, with his historical and moral observations, more as a social critic than as a lover. In the sestet he turns from generalizations to particularized application to the lady:

> Therefore my mistress' eyes are raven black,
> Her eyes so suited, and they mourners seem. . . .

The single feature of the mistress noted is her eyes, the color of ravens and mourning apparel. Such eyes may metonymically imply dark hair and skin, and Shakespeare may have had in mind her total appearance; in any case, we soon learn that her hair (130.4) and "complexion" (132.12–14) are also "black." The ocular "mourners" seem sad because of the prevalent "false esteem" of feminine pulchritude:

> Yet so they mourn becoming of their woe,
> That every tongue says beauty should look so.

The verb "looks so" takes the two meanings 'appear so' and 'look in the way her woeful eyes do.' Only now is praise of the lady made overt. Commendation of her is not restricted to the one admirer, for everyone agrees, and her "becoming" sadness may be bringing about new and better standards of taste.

Sonnet 128 is the first poem to address the mistress directly. The persona recounts his sensations upon listening to her playing the virginals and watching her fingers move across the keyboard, "that blessed wood." In the second and third quatrains he explains amusingly why "I envy those jacks," and the noun is at once a misnomer and a metaphor for the keys: a misnomer because, though a spinet has jacks, they do not touch the player's hands but are operated by the keys and hold the quills that pluck the strings; a metaphor because a "jack" can denote, and does here, 'ill-mannered fellow' or "knave' (OED 2). Shakespeare opts for the figurative sense, and never mind the literal exactitude. The wooden "jacks" are personified as rivals of the envious wooer's personified lips. Those rascals "leap / To kiss the inward tender of thy hand, / Whilst my poor lips," which covet that pleasure, "At the wood's boldness by thee blushing stand" (128.5–8). The language becomes more sensual when the lips, yearning to be "tickled" by her fingers walking across them, would change places with the "dancing chips." Then the couplet proposes a compromise, designed to satisfy both parties:

> Since saucy jacks so happy are in this,
> Give them thy fingers, me thy lips to kiss.

And so the close reveals the motive of the speech. Something is sought, in contrast to Sonnet 127, and it is to kiss the lady, and not, after all, her hand but her mouth.

The reader may feel a bit of a letdown at the finish. In a speech so charged with libido, is nothing more sought than a kiss? Well, yes, *kissing* is, and that it will be passionate is guaranteed by the erotic excitement evident in the wooer. The suit, with its nice blend of humor and ardor, obviously succeeds, for we next learn that the lady has granted him, and not necessarily beyond his design, her lips and

more, herself. They have sexual relations, in all likelihood for the
first time, in the period following Sonnet 128 and shortly before the
opening of 129.

Once desire for the woman has been sated, revulsion sets in. In
that frame of mind the protagonist delivers the monologue of Sonnet 129, which anatomizes "lust" while dramatizing his struggle to
come to terms with it.

> Th' expense of spirit in a waste of shame
> Is lust in action, and till action, lust
> Is perjur'd, murderous, bloody, full of blame,
> Savage, extreme, rude, cruel, not to trust;
> Enjoy'd no sooner but despised straight;
> Past reason hunted, and no sooner had,
> Past reason hated as a swallow'd bait,
> On purpose laid to make the taker mad—
> Made in pursuit and in possession so,
> Had, having, in quest to have extreme;
> A bliss in proof, and prov'd a very woe,
> Before a joy propos'd, behind a dream.
>   All this the world well knows, yet none knows well
>   To shun the heaven that leads men to this hell.

The experience is described as divisible into three successive
phases: (A) carnal desire, or lust "till action"; (B) consummation, or
"lust in action"; and (C) the aftermath. These phases, of which only
the first two are textually and properly denominated "lust," are
taken up not in a fixed but in a fluctuating order. The order is tabu-
lated below, with each of the capital letters designating an experiential phase and the small letters, a and b, indicating the first or second
half of the line:

First quatrain:
Lines 1–2a: (B)   (A) 2-1/2 lines; (B) 1-1/2 lines;
Lines 2b–4: (A)   (C) Indirectly in line 1
Second quatrain:
Line 5: (B), (C)   (A) 1/2 line; (B) 1 line [1/2 + 1/2]
Line 6: (A), (B)   (C) 2-1/2 lines [1/2 + 2]
Lines 7–8: (C)
Third quatrain:
Line 9: (A), (B)   (A), (B), (C) are allotted equal
Line 10 (C), (B), (A)   space in three references, each
Line 11: (B), (C)   of a half-line or less
Line 12: (A), (C)
Couplet:
Line 14a: (B, A)   (B, A) balances (C)
Line 14b: (C)

From the table one can see at a glance that earlier in the poem the mind of the speaker tends to linger over one or another phase; then, in the third quatrain, it moves more nimbly among the three. This freer play of mind helps suggest a more detached attitude toward the experience and a reevaluation of it; so, too, does the increased use of balance and antithesis as the sonnet proceeds. The first phrase of 129.6a is parallel with that of 7a, and at 9, 11, and 12 the two halves of the verse counterbalance. As the stages of lust, preliminary to and during its indulgence, and then the aftertaste are each in turn surveyed below, it will be seen that revulsion gradually slackens, doing so to the very end, when, at 129.14b, "this hell" intrudes a problematic detail.

PHASE A: LUST "TILL ACTION"

Lines 2b–4: "... and till action [= before coitus], lust / Is perjur'd [= swears falsely, will tell any lie], murderous [brings a killer instinct to pursuit of its goal], bloody [= bloodthirsty; probably also pertinent to sperm, thought of as composed of blood, and perhaps sensually passionate],[1] full of blame [of censure for whoever opposes the quest], / Savage [wild, feral], extreme ['violent'—I/R, OED 4e], rude [uncouth, uncivil], cruel [willing to cause pain, sadistic], not to trust [= be trusted, untrustworthy]." These characterizing terms are highly pejorative, are poured forth randomly, and have meanings that often overlap ("murderous" and "bloody"; "savage" and "rude"; "perjur'd" and "not to trust").

Line 6a: "Past reason hunted. ..." This predication of irrationality, while not incompatible with what goes before, is a milder indictment. The locution may appear curious, since one might expect lust to be the hunter and its object to be the "hunted"; but since "lust" includes two stages, the second, "lust in action," is "hunted," in the first, "till action."

Line 9: "Made in pursuit ... so"—i.e., made "mad."[2] Since to be "mad" is to be "past reason," this seems to be repetitious of line 6a, but there is a difference. The madness here is produced by a "bait" inadvertently "swallow'd" by the unsuspecting "taker" (lines 7–8), so that he is the victim as if of a trap "On purpose laid" by someone else.

Line 10b: " ... in quest to have, extreme." The adjective was used before, at line 4. The context then dictated the gloss 'violent'; now the different context elicits another gloss, 'immoderate.'

Line 12a: "Before a joy propos'd. ..." Yes, the initial stage of lust is looked upon here as no more reprehensible than the proposal of a "joy." The carnal desire so vehemently stigmatized in lines 2b–4 comes to be countenanced almost wistfully and finally is exalted when the word "heaven" is applied to both the anticipation and the consummation of lust in line 14a.

PHASE B: "LUST IN ACTION"

Lines 1–2a: "Th' expense of spirit in a waste of shame / Is lust in action, . . ." Ordinary syntax is here reversed, with "lust in action" (= copulation) the subject, of which line 1 is the predicate. "Expense" (= expenditure), along with "waste," calls up, figuratively, the squandering of monetary or other material resources. The resources literally squandered are physiological and psychological. The "spirit" spent is both, for the body's 'vital energy' (I/R) as well as the 'spirit generative' is lost 'in the act of sex' (Cruttwell),[3] or, possibly, the " 'spirituality' [is] thought of as dissipated in the grossness of sensuality" (I/R). The "shame" is of course psychological only, and the "expense of spirit" may be conceived of 'within' a 'wasteland of shame' or 'into' a 'shameful waste.' A latent implication, that "shame" itself is "a waste," seems excludable for going counter to the tenor of the passage, but later and retrospectively this meaning may come to assume relevance, once the shame wanes.

Line 5a: "Enjoy'd no sooner but. . . ." However fleetingly, it is admitted, and for the first time, that the sensuality does entail pleasure—a notion heretofore obscured by the sense of shame but one that will come forward more and more as that shame recedes and a perspective of greater distance and objectivity is gained.

Line 6b: " . . . and no sooner had." The phrasing surprises, for while "had" can = 'sexually possessed," it is normally someone that is thus "had" and not, as here, "lust" (line 2). The unusual idiom, "to have lust," reintroduced at line 10, is rather like the colloquial expression "to have sex" and must signify 'the orgastic sating of lustful desire.'

Line 9b: " . . . and in possession so"—i.e., "mad." Here the predication of madness, after "enjoy'd" in line 5 and the more neutral "had" in line 6, is the first negative estimate of this indulgent phase of lust since line 1, although, as remarked above, the madness might be extenuated by being induced by "a swallow'd bait."

Line 10: "having . . . extreme" = 'immoderate,' a less deprecating estimate.

Line 11a: "a bliss in proof [= experience]. . . ." Here is the most positive appraisal yet of the sexual activity, and to term it blissful represents a striking turnabout from the opening repugnance. The "heaven" in line 14a, alluding to this and the yearning stage, reinforces and enhances the notion of "bliss."

Phase C: The Aftermath

Line 5b: ". . . but despised straight." After sexual enjoyment abhorrence sets in 'immediately,' so that the persona is reacting to a carnal act just now performed. The opening line reveals that he is in a state of revulsion from the outset, even though he makes express reference to the third phase only now.

Lines 7–8: "Past reason hated, as a swallow'd bait / On purpose laid to make the taker mad." "Hated" may seem to be synonymous with "despised" in line 5b but is not, for the qualification "Past reason" suggests that the hatred itself is judged adversely, as unreasonable, irrational. Lust, having been "hunted" "till action" and "had" "in action," is then "hated" in the same way as "a swallow'd bait" designed to engender madness (somewhat like the "insane root" in *Macbeth* 1.3.84) should be hated by its "taker." This "taker" corresponds, no doubt, to the speaker; and whereas he was—or at least the lust driving him was—a ruthless victimizer in lines 3–4, he now becomes a victim, somehow the swallower of maddening "bait / On purpose laid." The word "purpose" intimates intention and personality, but whose "purpose"? Possibly no one in particular is meant, but, if someone is, who could it be but the human and female object of desire? Possibly she, "on purpose," drives her lusting lover crazy. Either way, he is crazed, and not only in the aftermath but "in pursuit" and "in possession"—all three phases being affected by the "bait" so "laid."

Line 10b: "Had . . . extreme," that is to say, merely 'intemperate.'

Line 11b: ". . . and prov'd, a very woe," with "woe," if still disagreeable, less acute than "despised" before.

Line 12b: ". . . behind a dream." The aftertaste here is not unpleasant, and from its vantage point lust comes to seem illusory and remote but not disagreeable.

Line 14b: ". . . this hell." Just what "hell" is "this"? Is it the hell within, of shame and repugnance—the feelings vented at the outset? Has nothing changed after all, and is the speaker still harboring these same emotions at the close? Certainly lines 11–14a have led us to believe that his initial nausea has subsided. But the "hell" of line 14b can be understood in a rather different way, as one that is evidently and inextricably, *though but passingly,* connected with lust. This construction not only draws the final judgment into unison with the rest of the sestet but gains corroboration from the couplet as a whole: "All this [i.e., all that has been said in lines 1–12] the world [= everybody] well knows"—it is common knowledge—

and "yet none [= no one] knows well [how] / To shun the heaven [of sexual desire and gratification] that leads men to this [consequent and inevitable] hell [described supra]."

The couplet holds surprises. It suddenly and cunningly universalizes lust: everyone knows about it, but no one knows how to escape it. The generalization interjects the familiar vindication that "everybody does it." This conclusion is at odds with the outcome that lines 1–9 had disposed the reader to anticipate. He might there have contemplated a resolve or admonition to shun lust. The actual closure, however unexpected, is by no means illogical, the grounds for it having been carefully prepared.

As lust "till" and "in" action ebbs in memory, antipathy wanes and the assessment undergoes retrospective alteration. The persona comes to survey the phases of his sexual venture with a more balanced mind, from a more detached viewpoint, and in more controlled language. He recollects, finally, the erotic "heaven" consisting of "a joy propos'd" and "bliss in proof." This recollection, representing a marked change in attitude, also foreshadows the revival of carnal desire. Postcoital depression not only fades but shades into anticipation of the next act of lust, and the couplet provides rationalization for the *volte-face*.

However, the argument of Sonnet 129 is yet more complex. The initial revulsion does exhibit a steady diminution—from lust as "despised," then "extreme," then "a woe," then, in line 12, "a dream"—until, in the terminal note of the sonnet, the process is arrested with "this hell." Thus does the end glance back at the beginning to tighten the internal organization. The couplet astonishes in two ways: by extenuating lust when its repudiation had seemed, as late as line 10, inevitable, and then by a partial reversal of this revised estimate of lust at the close. The speaker has not, after all, forgotten his initial torment and may still be suffering it to some extent. If he is, it is far less acute than at first, as can be inferred from the context of "this hell." The term is counterpoised and qualified in line 14 by "the heaven," for one thing, and, for another, it occurs in the sestet, where the condemnation of lust is transmuted into unreluctant resignation. The momentum toward the resuscitation of desire is too firmly established to be undermined simply by the recall of "this hell." That much is clear enough, it seems to me, from a perusal of Sonnet 129 alone, but further confirmation is forthcoming in 130.

Sonnet 129 is intrapsychic, since the feelings connected with a memory of the speaker are kept inside his mind. The three-stage process connected with lust is conceived of in the soliloquy as condensed and circular. It is condensed because the experience that is dramatized, lying between a recent and a likely forthcoming sexual act, progresses from disgust full-blown to its recession and then to the tinges of returning appetite, so that a course that would require a longer period is compressed into the space of fourteen lines. The process is circular because, as the phases follow, one upon the other, the third mutates into the first, as may be illustrated by this diagram:

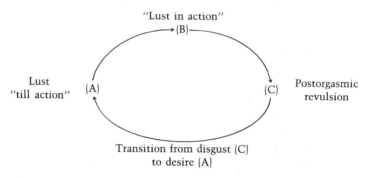

Thus does lust "course it in a ring," and in a manner akin to "Sinnes round" in Herbert's poem of that name; however, the word "sin" is not used of lust in Sonnet 129.

The sonnet has been elucidated with fine insight not once but twice—first, and seminally, by Richard Levin, second by Helen Vendler, who concurs with his analysis and enlarges it with fuller explorations of the verbal detail. My own reading is largely indebted to Levin's. He shows, by attending especially to the diction and syntax, that the sonnet "dramatizes the internal 'action' that the speaker is undergoing" and that the couplet is "an 'unexpected and probable' denouement."

> It is unexpected since the ideas and feelings expressed in the opening lines would lead us to predict that the speaker (if not all the world) would henceforward know well to shun this heaven; but upon looking back we realize that this change in attitude . . . has been carefully prepared for by the development up to this point, by the gradual dissipation of the man's disgust in the body of the sonnet. This dissipation has itself been made probable, both on general psychological grounds—as what might be expected when anyone has freely given vent to his painful emotions, and their immediate cause has receded into the background—and also in terms of the specific situation here, the insidious power of sexual desire and the speaker's weakness with respect to it.[4]

In a "recapitulation" toward the end of her article, Vendler writes that "the course of the feeling enacted in the sonnet seems common enough" and includes

> a recognition that we are so constituted that we cannot have foreknowledge of endings, that sexual desire makes us pursue its object as the keenest joy, even if afterwards it seems all woe and illusion. And, finally, that we will do it all over again if the occasion arises, that desire is unteachable.[5]

As is evident from these excerpts, my own reading in the main accords with theirs—though more fully with Levin's; but it also differs from theirs in some notable respects.

Both Levin and Vendler examine Sonnet 129 as an autonomous poem, independent of the sequence. So viewed, it has nothing to do with the mistress, though she not only is the focus of attention through the whole of Part II but is directly addressed in both of the immediately adjacent sonnets, 128 and 130. Hence the light that these might cast on 129, and it on them, is overlooked. The seductive argument of 128 leads up, as I have shown, to the very "lust in action" that elicits such vehement repugnance at the opening of 129. The situation in 129, then, is more specifically defined than these critics have allowed. I might add that the wooer in 128 turns out to have harbored, by his own subsequent testimony, more frenzied and violent feelings than his courting speech let on. The testimony comes at 129.2b–4, where his "lust" is said to be, "till action, . . . perjur'd, murderous, bloody, etc.," this passage now providing a kind of retrospective subtext to 128. In Sonnet 130 the poet, recovered from his shame, is once more engaged in the wooing that the couplet of 129 implicitly anticipates.

Levin and Vendler alike suppose that the aftermath of lust as represented by Shakespeare is nothing out of the ordinary. But do such anguished and repudiative reactions, far in excess of *tristitia post coitum*, normally attend sexual gratification? Perhaps so under certain conditions, which must be specified; certainly not under other conditions, and not for the protagonist himself when he engages in carnal intimacy with the male beloved. Then he feels no wasteful "shame" and experiences no "painful emotions" of disgust and self-loathing. A distinction is called for, and it will depend on just what Shakespeare means by "lust."

The word is used pejoratively, and it appears only twice in the Sonnets, both times in a single line, 129.2. But the line is in Part II, and that is enough to tell us that the lust is heterosexually oriented. This, though it is everywhere assumed in the commentary—and rightly so, if only by default—cannot be inferred from the sonnet itself but can be from its contexts. By itself Sonnet 129 tells us nothing about the gender of the other participant. Transgressions of marriage vows or of the divine will might make for a guilty conscience, but neither the issue of adultery nor that of sin is expressly raised. Christian morals will not help us to the definition sought, for according to them the homoerotic commerce between the lovers, which is never termed lustful, is "unnatural" and therefore much more heinous than "natural" adultery. The sexual ethic of the Sonnets, which radically diverges from the Christian, is conceived of in psychological rather than religious terms, and Freud offers something to the point.

He does so in "Being in Love and Hypnosis," which is chapter 8 of *Group Psychology and the Analysis of the Ego* (1921). There he defines "what is called common sensual love," *which is precisely the same as the "lust" in Sonnet 129*, as "nothing more than object-cathexis on the part of the sexual instincts with a view to direct sexual satisfaction, a cathexis which expires, moreover, when this aim has been reached." He later adds that

> sexual impulsions which are uninhibited [by affection for the other participant] in their aims suffer an extraordinary reduction through the discharge of energy every time the sexual aim is attained. It is the fate of sensual love to become extinguished when it is satisfied.

Just so does the lust in Sonnet 129 suffer expiration upon orgasmic climax. Freud remarks the "certainty" with which it is "possible to calculate upon the revival of the need which had just expired." The certainty is confirmed in the sestet of the sonnet. Freud further points out that, from factors operative in the development of the personality, "a sensual current" may "remain separate" from "'affectionate' trends of feeling," in which case a man may be sexually aroused by a woman "whom he does not 'love' and thinks little of or even despises."[6] The speaker of Sonnet 129 indeed thinks little of the female object of his lust; in fact, he does not think of her at all, unless—and this is ambiguous—she should be regarded as the setter of the madding "bait." Otherwise she is not a presence, and his disgust is directed toward himself and toward the libidinal enterprise. Elsewhere, though, he repeatedly reviles her. Her "deeds" are "black" (131.13); she is "the bay where all men ride" (137.6); her "heart" is "proud" (140.14, 141.12); she is "my female evil" and "my bad angel" (144), and "as black as hell, as dark as night" (147.14). Freud remarks on subjects of "sensual love" who "will only be potent" with despised women, and the persona tells his mistress at 150.13 that "thy unworthiness rais'd love in me." Not only is her character faulted, but even the physical attractiveness ascribed to her in Sonnet 127 comes to be denied. In Sonnet 141 she appeals neither to sight nor to any of the other "five senses," however enticing to "one foolish heart"; and the couplet of Sonnet 152 disavows her beauty: "For I have sworn thee fair—more perjur'd eye [and 'I'], / To swear against the truth so foul a lie."

Lust, then, as represented in Sonnet 129 is sheer and remittent carnal passion, devoid of the sustaining effects of respect, admiration, and affection for its object. She—and it could just as well be a he—might not appear attractive to the aroused suitor; but, if she did, the attractiveness would not outlive the passion, which dies with satiety, leaving nothing, or an emptiness, behind. Emotion, like nature, abhors a vacuum, and so repugnance rushes in. Its intensity then lessens in inverse proportion to the rejuvenation of desire.

The protagonist's entire response to the mistress is properly termed "lust," and it is the term that I shall use. This terminology attests to the weight my reading of Part II places on Sonnet 129, the only place in which the word appears. Elsewhere Shakespeare calls the feeling for her "love." But it is a love fundamentally different from that for the youth. Freud distinguishes between "common sensual love," which is equivalent to Shakespeare's "love" in Part II and "lust" in Sonnet 129, and a second type, a "synthesis" of "unsensual, heavenly love and sensual, earthly love," an "interaction of uninhibited instincts" of "purely sensual desire" with "instincts of affection,"[7] which is equivalent to Shakespearean love in Part I. This is a point I will expand on later, but here let me add that the devotion to the friend is affectionate, respectful, and admiring as well as passionate—a fact that goes far toward explaining why the sexual experience with him is antithetical to that with the woman.

The libidinal process delineated in Sonnet 129 is cyclic, and this cycle—moving from desire to gratification, then to abeyance of desire and aversion, then to the renewal of desire—is operative throughout Part II and, I submit, gives intelligible form to the arrangement of the sonnets in it. Again and again we come upon two juxtaposed poems, one of which vents loathing for the mistress and the passion she stimulates, while the other exhibits a predilection for her, expressed in the form of a commendation or supplication, and for the attraction, now accepted without qualms. For illustration we need look no farther afield than the sonnet next after 129.

A light and amusing bouquet for "My mistress" could hardly be anticipated in 129.1–10, where the persona is seized by sexual revulsion. But the next four lines, which presage the revival of his sexual appetite, do prepare the way for Sonnet 130, "My Mistress' eyes are nothing like the sun." This first verse initiates the spoof of the Petrarchan sonneteer's blazon of his lady's sensate delights—delights visual (eyes like the sun, lips red as coral, hair golden wires, breasts white as snow, cheeks of roses red and white), olfactory (a perfumed breath), auditory (her speech is music), and kinetic (she walks like a goddess). Shakespeare produces the comic effect by simple means. He catalogues the overfamiliar tropes while denying their applicability to his own mistress in 130.1–12 and, in the couplet, to all mistresses, since *"any* she" so depicted is *"belied* with *false* compare [= comparison]." The poem has two distinct aspects, that of extended literary travesty and that of compliment; the latter is succinctly expressed, being limited to the clauses "I love to hear her speak" in 130.8, and, at the conclusion, "I think my love [= beloved] as rare [= excellent] as . . ." those women are in themselves who have been flattered with falsehoods by amorists. His praise, even tempered in this way, may not altogether jibe with his mocking of the Petrarchan tropes. In mocking them Shakespeare obliquely rejects stale artifice and, by doing so, lays claim to a more sincere and convincing commendation. Entertaining to the reader, the travesty may be designed to entertain the mistress as well. But would it, necessarily? The descriptive conventions of the Petrarchists had not yet lost viability. For evidence of that, one need not go outside the Sonnets themselves, where some of these conventions are elsewhere adopted for praising the Master Mistress. He has, at 20.5, "an eye more bright than" women's. "Music to hear" at 8.1, he is, in Sonnet 99, the archetype of beauty and fragrance, with flowers the ectypes. His breath gives off the perfumes of violets and roses, and the hues of roses, red, white, and pink, tint his countenance. He has, moreover, a lily-white hand, hair like "the buds of marjoram," and veins of subtler purple than the violet. With respect to physical beauty alone, apart from other qualities, he is esteemed not only far beyond the lady but in the Petrarchan terms denied her. The parody in Sonnet 130 may be rather less compatible with the compliments than is generally assumed. Still, after the hiatus of Sonnet 129, courtship is definitely, and in a playful vein, resumed.

Sonnet 131 opens, surprisingly after 130, with two lines of Petrarchan rhetoric: "Thou are as *tyrannous* . . . / As those whose beauties *proudly* make them *cruel."* Having made fun of the laudatory blazon, Shakespeare straightway appropriates the accusatory language of the same sonneteers, who habitually charge an unyielding mistress with tyranny, pride, and cruelty. He then differentiates between his own subjective response to the lady and the more disinterested opinions of other beholders: "Thy black is fairest in my judgement's place" (131.12); and yet, in 131.5–8,

> Yet in good faith some say that thee behold,
> Thy face hath not the power to make love groan;
> To say they err, I dare not be so bold,
> Although I swear it to myself alone.

Without renouncing the counterview, he yet protests his own passion, confessing to "A thousand groans but thinking on thy face" (131.10), and the couplet attempts to adjust the disparate reactions:

> In nothing art thou black save in thy deeds,
> And thence this slander as I think proceeds.

"Black" as a noun in 131.12 has reference only to appearance, which may or may not be judged "fair," and, as an adjective in 131.13, it denotes only morally 'foul.' The "deeds" so labeled either stem from her haughtiness in 131.1–2 or else are unspecified. Her sexual laxity has yet to be mentioned. But the couplet is the harshest thing said *to her* so far and is supposed to account for the "slander" of her physical unattractiveness. The blackness that ought to repel is not that of her looks but that of her character. In this sonnet the ambivalence barely intimated in the jocularity of Sonnet 130 comes into the open, but a strategy of wooing is still being pursued, one that combines intimidation with declarations of passion.

Then Sonnet 132 woos her more simply—without ambivalence or intimidation. "Thine eyes I love," the opening clause, sets the motif of the long first section, lines 5–9 of which praise their beauty, while lines 1–4 account for their "black." It was "put on" as though "pitying me, / Knowing thy heart torments me with disdain," and the conceit of the eyes as "mourners" (132.3, 9) repeats the conceit in the sestet of Sonnet 127—only there they mourn for the fashionable blonding of brunettes, here for the speaker in amorous torment. The second section, from the volta in 127.10 through 12, focuses on the heart, which she should "let . . . mourn for me" likewise, thus to "suit [= clothe and harmonize] thy pity like in every part," the heart as well as eyes. The couplet promises her a reward for complying:

> Then will I swear Beauty herself is black,
> And all they foul that thy complexion lack,

where "complexion" = facial skin-color. Sonnet 132 so vividly recalls 128, not only with the reiterated conceit but with verbal repetitions as well (including "suited/suit," "face," "black," "mourners/mourn/mourning," "becoming/become"), as to imply that the protagonist has come full circle, returning to the point at which he began, thus proving that he does not "know well [how] / To shun the heaven" that leads to the "hell" of 129.1–9.

Sonnets 144–47 reveal similar fluctuations in the course of lust. When Sonnet 144, "two loves I have," vents vehement contempt toward the she-devil, who would anticipate the levity of the very next lyric? The totally altered and relenting attitude toward her in Sonnet 145 shows not only that the jealous rage has passed but that desire has reemerged. This sonnet is unique in at least two ways: in its tetrameter measures and in recording the only words spoken by anyone other than the persona. Four words are attributed to the lady, and they constitute the "punch line": "I hate . . . not you." Well, she had seemed to hate him in Sonnet 144 (attempting "to win me soon to hell") and he to hate her, while now her hatred would, according to 145.14, kill him. No longer "my female evil," she has "lips that Love's own hand did make" (145.1), a "tongue . . . ever sweet" (145.6), and a "heart" receptive to "mercy" (145.5); and when, in the third quatrain, "'I hate' she alter'd with an end"—that of "'not you'" in 145.14—the end is said to follow "as gentle day / Doth follow night, who like a fiend / From heaven to hell is flown away." The simile descriptive of "night" calls up details from Sonnet 144. There she was the hellish fiend; now she wields the verbal power to exorcise a figurative fiend—that of night and of woe.[8]

The poet jests in Sonnet 145 about the lady's erotic power over him because he is at the moment under its control. But Sonnet 146, "Poor soul," finds him in a radically different frame of mind. He gives her no thought and, out of a sense of dissatisfaction with his life, takes stock of himself and resolves to reform by henceforth subduing the flesh. It is not unreasonable, on the basis of Sonnet 129, to surmise that an unrecorded experience of "lust in action," which would account for the change of mood, intervenes between Sonnets 145 and 146.

The persona's self-admonition in Sonnet 146 opens with a salutation to "Poor soul," his own, the object of address throughout and characterized in 146.1–2 as follows:

> the center of my sinful earth,
> [My sinful earth] the rebel powers that thee array.

The phrase in brackets, which repeats the end of line 1 and adds an undue metric foot, is clearly a misprint. Two syllables have been lost, and irretrievably lost, but the sense they bore can be deduced

from the overall poetic design, as will be shown. The design comprises a profusion of metaphors. Here are the others of the octave
(146.3–8):

> Why dost thou pine within and suffer dearth,
> Painting thy outward walls so costly gay?
> Why so large cost, having so short a lease,
> Doth thou upon thy fading mansion spend?
> Shall worms, inheritors of this excess,
> Eat up thy charge? Is this thy body's end?

It is the metaphorical vehicles that are richly diversified, for there
are but two tenors and they never change. One is the "soul," designated vocatively in 146.1 and 9; the other is the body, specified in
146.8; and these are the polar terms on which the introspection
turns. The body is represented as "sinful earth" (the 'dust' of Genesis and the origin of 'sins of the flesh'); as "rebel powers" (sensual
forces in insurrection) which "array" (= afflict)[9] the soul; as its
"outward walls" and "fading mansion" (an edifice); and as its
"charge" (= burden, expense, trust). The soul, correspondingly, is
represented as "the center" (both 'inward' and in the privileged position); as "?" in 146.2; as a householder who starves and otherwise
deprives himself for the upkeep of his house; as a lessee who spends
lavishly on a decaying "mansion" when his lease is soon to expire;
and as one immoderately concerned about an estate destined for
greedy and unsavory heirs—the grave-worms of 146.7. The "soul" is
reproved for its perverse "excess" in inverting means (an abode) and
ends (the occupant), in its asinine wasting of its resources (as lessee),
and for the misguided providence of its bequest to the maggots.

The octave—in an interrogative mode, for it is composed of four
questions—renders the regrettable moral condition of the persona
as it now is; the sestet, in an imperative mode, directs the soul toward the opposite moral condition: the one aspired to, the one that
should obtain (146.9–14):

> Then, soul, live thou upon thy servant's loss,
> And let that pine to aggravate thy store;
> Buy terms divine in selling hours of dross;
> Within be fed, without be rich no more:
> So shalt thou feed on Death, that feeds on men,
> And death once dead, there's no more dying then.

These metaphors, in conveying instructions to the soul to set right its
relations with the body, methodically evoke and reverse the metaphors of the octave—or do so at least after 146.9. In this line soul is
implicitly the master; for the body is "thy servant," and the trope

carries over into 146.10, where the servant/body should "pine" in order to 'increase the wealth' of the master/soul; this is the obverse of 146.3, where it is the soul that "dost . . . pine" and "suffer dearth." A profitable financial transaction is proposed in 146.11, as opposed to the unprofitable investment in real estate in 5–6. Precious time ("terms divine") is to be bought at the price of wasted time ("hours of dross"). In 146.12, "Within be fed" again recalls, and reverses, 146.3, where the "dearth" (= famine) is the soul's; and so too does "without [in body] be rich no more" recall and reverse the bodily "walls so costly gay" of 146.4; and the "within" and "without" may hark back to the soul's inner centrality in 146.1 and the body's circumferential outerness. The most complex affinities of all are those between the last two lines of the octave (7–8) and the last two of the sestet (13–14); but for now I will simply point to notions of death and eating as common features and to the body as fed on by worms, the soul as feeder on death. This system of metaphorical transpositions may be summed up as follows: there are reversals in line 10 of line 3; in line 11 of lines 5–6; in line 12 of lines 3–4; and in lines 13–14 of lines 7–8. Line 1, although it may have a connection with line 12, really lies outside the scheme. What is missing within it is a correlative for lines 2 and 9, and this suggests that these two lines might be meant to correlate with each other.

Two principles can be perceived to operate in the figurative pattern. The first, in the octave, is that of perversion, by which the proper order of things is turned upside down. The same device is used by the Fool in criticizing Lear: "thou bor'st thine ass on thy back o'er the dirt" (*Lear* 1.4.168–69). So, here, the dweller is for the sake of the dwelling rather than vice versa. The second principle, in the sestet, is that of restoration. Both principles will serve as guides to the drift of the missing syllables in 146.2. The bodily "rebel powers" there must somehow hold their legitimate ruler in subjection, and this political inversion should be reformed in the sestet, and probably in its first verse, 146.9. Both of these requirements would be satisfied with such emendations in 146.2 as these: "Rul'd by," "Sway'd by," or "Slav'd by"—participles modifying "Soul" in 146.1; or "Slave to," "Thrall to"[10]—nouns in apposition to "Poor soul." Then 146.2 gives us an implicit ruler (poor prince!) under the control of mutinous subjects, while 146.9 urges the soul, implicitly conceived of now as a master, to reassert his position of privilege over an exploitative, insubordinate servant. The political and domestic situations alike entail a relationship of power and authority, with the relationship deemed wrongful in line 2 and corrective in line 9. The idea of the soul as governor or lord of the body is of

course highly traditional. These considerations all lead to the conclusion that the purport, though not the precise wording, of the foot
displaced by the misprint of 146.2 is ascertainable.

The couplet poses interpretative problems. Does it posit the
soul's immortality, and does it thereby make the poem Christian?
The two questions are more disjoined than is often realized, for
Christianity neither originated nor holds a monopoly on that belief.[11] However, a negation of it would be un-Christian. In 146.13,
"So [= in this manner] shalt [whether expressive of simple futurity
and parallel to 146.7 or of obligation] thou feed on death, that feeds
on men, . . ." The feeding will be, or ought to be, twofold and simul-
taneous, the soul's on death and death's on "men," a word that does
not denote the body only but human beings in their body-soul complex. The body is for the worms; in 146.7–8 they "eat up" corpses.
Death's food, however, is the living, who are in plentiful and continuous supply; so death will last as long as its provisions do, and they
will last as long as the human race. Hence the persona must needs
expire before death does. What then could 146.14, "And death once
dead, there's no more dying then," mean? In Christian terms the
meaning would have to be eschatological, for death will come to an
end only with the Second Coming and the resurrection of the body.
This doctrine could be foisted on 146.14 only implausibly; but the
line admits of another construction, one more consonant not only
with its own phrasing and with the rest of the sonnet but with other
sonnets too: "And death once dead" = 'when death ceases to exist,'
not universally (as from Christ's sacrifice, never alluded to) but for
each individual whom it devours and for whom, consequently,
"there's no more dying then" in the sense that 'once you're dead,
you're dead'; then 'all, including the fear and process of dying itself,
will be over and done with, period.'[12]

It remains to be seen just how, in that case, the soul should "feed
on death" and in what way that will work the hardships on the body
set forth in 146.9–12. The counsel to the soul in line 13 augments
"Within be fed" in line 12, the verbs "be fed" and "feed on" both
connoting 'nourishment' in contrast to the verb "eat up" in line 8—
the action of the graveworms upon the body—which = 'consume.'
The soul will be nourished and strengthened by an awareness of the
limits of mortality. Soul can redeem time, "buy terms divine,"
while the lusting body only wastes time—the "hours of dross." The
two halves of line 11 exhibit contrast in the verb and verbal "Buy"
and "selling," in the temporal nouns "terms" and "hours," and in
the epithets "divine" and "of dross." The word "terms" may denote
a longer stretch of time than "hours"—one that can encompass

months, such as a scholastic term, or years, a lease's term, or the entire "term of life" (92.2)—but yet denote a fixed period, 'a limit of time' (OED 4). With this meaning, the opposite of 'eternity,' the word in fact excludes that idea, and annotations to the contrary are misleading. The "hours," those through which lust runs its short course, are "of dross"—'refuse' (Schmidt)—while the "terms" are oppositely characterized as "divine," which in this context has to be glossed as 'extraordinarily good or great' (OED 5b). Hence the "terms divine" to be purchased by the soul must refer not to an everlasting heaven but to the relatively extended yet finite span of terrestrial time that the soul may command. It may do so by its own proper activities: of loving in the best sense, in a "marriage of *true minds*" that "alters not with . . . brief hours" (Sonnet 116), and of the "creative intuition" that comprises the knowing and making that are coordinated in poetry.[13]

For elucidation of Sonnet 146 one would do well to turn back to Sonnet 74. There, just as here, the body is "the prey of worms," and it is also "earth," which "can have but earth," the grave, as its "due." Yet another and "better part of me," namely, "my spirit" (= soul—Schmidt 6), is "thine" (the friend's, therein addressed), and will ever remain so; for, in the couplet of Sonnet 74, "The worth of that [the body] is that which it contains [the spirit], / And that is this [poem], and this with thee remains"—i.e., after my death. The soul does survive, but it survives here on earth, not in an otherworldly hereafter, and it survives with the beloved and by means of its own product, verse. Two mental powers, those of love and poetic composition, unite to create the poet's "memorial": in 74.3–4, "this line [of verse] . . . for memorial still [= always] with thee shall stay." The "terms divine" in 146.11, then, are those given to loving truly and to composing enduring and immortalizing poetry: the operations of the soul that make possible its personal but not supernatural preservation.

The soul and the body are pictured in a state of conflict throughout Sonnet 146. The good of each demands that the good of the other be sacrificed. If the soul is to "live," it can do so only with "loss" for the body. The soul's "store," its "terms divine," and its proper nourishment require, in the third quatrain, that the body "pine" (languish in appetitive frustration), that "hours of dross" (misspent on concupiscence) be relinquished, and that corporal impoverishment (as carnal neediness) be imposed. Mortification, or disciplining of the flesh, is necessary for subduing the sensuality that impedes the nobler activities of the mind and spirit.

The body is "sinful earth"—sinful in contributing the root and coercion of lust. The membership of Sonnet 146 in Part II establishes that. If the sonnet were torn from this mooring, one might think of other flaws that can be associated with the flesh, such as gluttony or sloth, or vanity, with "walls so costly gay" suggesting cosmetic and tonsorial adornment; and vanity may be glanced at as a concomitant of lust. Lust is of the flesh, fleshly, expensive of spirit (129.1), and deplored as dehumanizing, wasteful, and short. Love, on the contrary, is conceived of in the Sonnets as moral, creative, and long-lasting, and what makes the difference between it and lust is not the absence of passion for the Master Mistress (20.2) but the soul's participation in the attachment to him. Thus the poet can speak of "my home of love" that is "thy breast" wherein "my *soul* . . . doth lie" (109.4–5), and this is a love productive of poetic immortalization for both participants: "Death to me subscribes / Since spite of him I'll live in this poor rhyme," while "thou in this shall find thy monument" (107.10–11, 13). The fullness of erotic devotion that the protagonist knows himself capable of provides a standard by which his carnal lust is judged intolerable. Freud's "earthly sensual love" is Shakespeare's "sinful earth's" sensuality.

The self-criticism undertaken in Sonnet 146 leads the persona to a powerful resolution to amend his ways, but any hope of his doing so—on his part or the reader's—is dashed in the very next sonnet, where love for the mistress is elaborately analogized to a sickness, one whose remedy is rejected by the victim. As against the metaphorical diversity of Sonnet 146, a single conceit is dominant in 147. The vehicle traces out the progress of a fever, which entails a constant yearning "For that which longer nurseth [= fosters] the disease." Here "that" is food medically proscribed but eaten anyway, whereupon the physician quits the case in disgust; the patient then realizes that his feeding is proving deadly, and, in despair, he lapses into delirious ravings. The tenor and import of the conceit are as follows: the "fever" stands for "my love" (147.1); the fever's "longing" for unwholesome edibles (1–3) and the "uncertain sickly appetite" (4) correspond to sexual "desire" (8); "that which" is yearned for and fed on is the object of desire, the mistress (though references to her are only implicit before 13, when she is addressed); "the physician to my love" is "my reason," who "Hath left me" because "angry that his prescriptions" to curb desire are not followed (5–7); and, finally, the patient, obstinate, self-destructive, restless, and expiring, is the lover himself, bereft of reason and become "desperate" and "frantic mad" (7, 10). He now knows from experience (= "approves") that "Desire is death, which physic [= medical treatment] did except [= exclude]." This line, 147.8, merits attention. "Which"

modifies "desire," and "desire," in urging "that which doth preserve" the mortal "ill" / illness of lust, is, if indulged, destructive of
spirit and thus equatable with "death." Since the verb "except" is
transitive, and since "which," whose antecedent is "desire," can be
either nominative or accusative, the subordinate clause can be construed either as "desire" excluded "physic" (reason's remedy) or
vice versa. Both readings are pertinent; they complement each other
to present a compressed version of the old antipathy between sensual desire and right reason, either of which may be said to debar the
other.

In Sonnet 147 the conflict between body and soul in Sonnet 146 is
reenacted, but with the opposite outcome. There soul was in-
structed, and expected, to subjugate the flesh; here soul's reason re-
tires and fleshly appetite prevails. Some of the diction of Sonnet 146
is redeployed. There the soul can be "fed within" and can "feed on
death" by restraining desire, while here carnal love does the "feeding," on its female object, whether by enjoying her or by anticipating enjoying her, and sensual "desire" is spiritual "death." The
juxtaposition is dramatic and follows the curve outlined in Sonnet
129. The protagonist's moral scruples and determination to reorder
his life quickly fail as passion resurges. He may be wretched at his
backsliding, but he abandons hope: "Past cure I am now reason is
past care" (147.9). He is also "frantic mad with evermore unrest"—
the restlessness of passion, as in Dante's Second Circle—and his
"thoughts and discourse" are "as madmen's" (147.10–11). That lust
is "mad," both "in pursuit and in possession," and maddening was
observed at 129.7–9.

Crazed with lust, the persona's "thoughts and discourse" are, in
147.12–14,

> At random from the truth, vainly express'd:
> For I have sworn thee fair, and thought thee bright,
> Who art as black as hell, as dark as night.

Whether the woman is addressed all along or the lover, distraught by
a return of passion, ends by irately apostrophizing her in fantasy, the
outburst of contempt for her in the couplet is part and parcel of the
deprecated, though irresistible, longing for her rehearsed in the
quatrains.

Sonnets 151–53 again illuminate the fluctuations of lust. At
151.7–8, "My soul doth tell the body that he may / Triumph in
love." This dramatically reverses the resolve taken in Sonnet 146,
where the soul is rather to restrain than to license carnality. And
151.5–6, "I do betray [= give up—OED 1b] / My nobler part to my

gross body's treason," recall the bodily "rebel powers" of 146.2. Consequently, at 151.8–10, the "flesh [penile] stays [= waits for] no farther reason [none beyond the soul's consent], / But rising [in tumescence] at thy name doth point out thee [the mistress] / As his triumphant prize." The phallus, "proud of this pride [= sexual turgidity]," is "contented thy poor drudge to be." To triumph into drudgery, even if contentedly, interjects a note of paradoxical levity, in keeping with the sonnet's carefree mood; the point of view and sentiments in 151.8–12 are those of the personified penis, pleased rather to be under the sway of the paramour than to be ruled by reason or conscience.

The question of conscience is raised at the opening and close, only to be discounted. "Love [Cupid] is too young [since he is a child] to know what conscience [the inner moral sense] is," and "Yet who knows not that conscience is born of love [the passion, not Cupid]?" Love does not give birth to conscience or consciousness in the sense of causing either to exist, as if both did not antedate erotic fixation; it does so rather in the sense of bringing conscience forth, into the external world, from within. The puzzle of 151.1–2 is solved in 3–4: "Then [= therefore], gentle cheater, urge not my amiss [= do not charge me with an offense], / Lest guilty of my [sensual] faults thy sweet self prove" in "betraying me [= leading me astray—OED 4]." Thus is "conscience . . . born," as translated from inside the lover and to the mistress, moral responsibility being transferred outwardly to her. The betrayal of his "nobler part" to his "gross body" does but follow her lead and example (151.5). The couplet produces this clever, facile self-justification: "No want [= lack] of conscience [should she or anyone] hold it that I call / Her [by the term of endearment] 'love' for whose dear love [hers for me, mine for her] I rise and fall"—genitally, and not unconscionably when he does so for the sake of her who has become keeper and embodiment of his conscience.

Not only is the poet in Sonnet 151 primed for "lust in action"; more than that, he seems to allude to repeated sexual experiences with the mistress in the final clause: "I rise and fall." The presumption that he "falls" after orgasms is reinforced in 151.12 by the phrase "fall by thy side." That phrase denotes his being in bed with her and is otherwise suggestive: of detumescence in withdrawal after emission? of *coitus interruptus* (perhaps as a method of birth control)? or of some noncopulative form of sex?

The reactions that come after such gratification are those that the paradigm of lust in Sonnet 129 has prepared us to anticipate. Sonnet 152 erupts into anger, the speaker reviling the mistress and also himself. He begins, "In loving [= pledging love to] thee thou know'st I am forsworn" (we have yet to be told how); then, in 152.2, he remarks, "But thou art twice forsworn to me love swearing," the "twice" being as follows: you (1) "In act [that of adultery] thy [matrimonial] bed-vow broke"; and (2) the "new faith" you vowed to me was soon "torn / in [your] vowing new hate [to me] after new love [carnally] bearing [me]." Incidentally, the repetition of "new" (three times in 152.3–4) gives a hint of the brevity of the affair. If she is guilty of "two oaths' breach," yet "I am perjur'd most," for "I break twenty." This "twenty" is hardly an exact figure, the idea being that 'I am much more culpable of the same offense—by a ratio, say, of ten to one.' In fact, five false oaths are listed in 152.9– 13, each multiply sworn, and they are oaths (1) "of thy deep kindness," (2) of "thy love" (believed genuine), (3) of "thy truth [= uprightness, trustworthiness]," (4) of "thy constancy [= fidelity]," and (5) of "thee fair [physically]." All these "oaths" pertain to qualities she was avouched to possess; they have been sworn to others, perhaps, and certainly to her. These qualities—and especially the last, her physical beauty—are negated in the recantation: "more perjur'd eye [and 'I'], / To swear against the truth [= objective fact] so foul a lie." The instability of lust recounted in Sonnet 129 is once again dramatized, and we are specifically reminded of 129.2–3, where lust, "till action," is "perjur'd, . . . not to trust." Just so does the persona now divulge that his own "oaths" were "but to misuse [= maltreat, deceive] thee" for his own appetitive purposes. Moreover, the lady's "vowing new hate after new love bearing" is appalling in any case but becomes more intensely so when carnal satiety makes lust itself "despised straight" and "past reason hated" (129.4, 6). The rancor toward the mistress in Sonnet 152 is thus the reaction of a lover not only scorned but undergoing "a waste of shame." The entire thrust of the sonnet is denuciatory of her, so that the confession of perjury, though not to be brushed aside, is subordinate.

Two developments, observable earlier in Part II, terminate in Sonnet 152. The first is the increasingly abusive language delivered to the mistress. She has been viewed with disfavor often enough before, though frequently in soliloquy, as notably in Sonnet 144. She has also been insulted in second-person address, as in the couplets of Sonnets 131, 137, 141, 147 (if this is indeed spoken to her), 148, and 150. The second development is the poet's sense of being personally corrupted by his affair with her. This motif begins with the wasteful "shame" described in 129.1–9, and it includes the octave of Sonnet 146 ("Poor soul") and such admissions as "past cure I am now reason is past care" (147.9), "thy unworthiness rais'd love in me"

(150.13), "I do betray / My nobler part to my gross body's treason" (151.5–6), and, finally, in Sonnet 152: "more perjur'd [I]," "all my vows are oaths but to misuse thee," and, at 152.8, "all my [capacity for] honest faith [= fidelity and honesty]" is "in [my dealings with] thee . . . lost [= gone, vanished]." Indulgence of lust with her brings about moral degeneration; love for the Master Mistress produces no such effect.

In sharp contrast with Sonnet 152 and all its predecessors in Part II, Sonnet 153 introduces mythology. The myth is postclassical and ultimately derives from an epigram of six Greek lines composed in the fifth century by the Byzantine poet Marianus Scholasticus. The octave recounts a story of Cupid asleep and of the "maid of Dian," who seized his "love-kindling" torch and submerged it in a cold stream nearby, which thereupon became a "seething bath" that yet proves curative of men's "strange maladies." The sestet continues the narrative by assigning a part in it to the sonneteer and his lady. The quenched "brand" was reignited by Love "at my mistress' eye," and, to test the flame, the "boy" touched it to "my breast." Then "I, sick withal, the help of bath desir'd, / And thither hied," but to no avail: "the bath for my help lies / Where Cupid got new fire—my mistress' eyes."

The rhyme words of this couplet repeat the "eye/lie" rhyme of the couplet of Sonnet 152 and thus provide a link between the two sonnets that otherwise stand in opposition. They do so stylistically, for the first sonnet is nonmythic, nonnarrative, and written in a language that is vituperative, plain, colloquial, and, aside from 152.11, wholly literal. They do so also as regards the psychological state of the protagonist. In Sonnet 152 he is irascible, holds the woman in the strictest contempt, and denounces her. Sonnet 153 finds his mood altogether changed. He is "sick," as in Sonnet 147—and apparently again with a fever, since fire is the cause, and bathing might help—sick with infatuation. We have been conditioned to expect, whenever lust and the mistress are repudiated, that desire will presently reassert itself. Sonnet 153 does not disappoint. The poet has another erotic seizure, inflicted by Cupid in line 10, and the only cure for it rests in "my mistress' eyes."

This final phrase of 153.14 has previously occurred three times: at line 9 of Sonnet 127, the *first* poem of Part II; at 130.1; and once before in Sonnet 153 (which I believe, on grounds soon to be adduced, was intended as the *last* poem of Part II)—at line 9, where it occurs as "my mistress' *eye*." It is at this singular "eye" that "Love's brand" was "new fir'd." According to Partridge, the eye may connote the female organ. Hence the "eye" that alone holds relief for the persona's amorous ailment stands for the 'presence,' the 'prettiness,' and perhaps the 'pudendum' of the mistress.

Shakespeare relates the same legend of Cupid in both of the two final sonnets, 153 and 154. The reduplication is puzzling and pointless. It muddies the waters, obfuscating whatever effect the myth was meant to have. One version would do, and one would do much better than the other.

In an informative study of analogues of the two sonnets, James Hutton criticizes the first two lines of 154,

> The little Love-God lying once asleep
> Laid by his side his heart-inflaming brand,

as "deficient in sense" because the god is made "in his sleep" to "perform the act of laying aside his brand." The deficiency is corrected in 153.1. For this and other reasons Hutton postulates the prior composition of Sonnet 154 and, implicitly, its artistic inferiority. He sees "mainly padding" in its lines 3–4 and 7–8, and he notes the greater "compression" of Sonnet 153.[14]

I concur in these judgments and find much else in the texts to reinforce them. For example, the aphorism that concludes Sonnet 154, "Love's fire heats water, water cools not love," is neat and effective—until closely examined. In 154.11–13 "I, my mistress' thrall," went to the "bath" hoping "for cure." Not surprisingly, he found none. Bathing may help sickness—and at 153.11 he *is* sick, with yearning—but it is hardly a sensible way to go about seeking relief from *thralldom*; and, more obviously illogical, heated water can hardly be expected to "cool" love or anything else. The single "maid of Dian" in Sonnet 153 more efficiently and quickly accomplishes in three lines (2–4) the task that the nymphs in Sonnet 154 take five lines (3–5, 7–8) to perform. The eleven and a half verses devoted to the received account of how Cupid's torch came to convert a cold fountain into a hot and remedial one in Sonnet 154 are reduced to eight in 153. This revision improves and regularizes the internal organization. The volta, signaled by "But," is placed more normally, at the beginning of 153.9 rather than inside 154.12. Thus Sonnet 153 divides into an octave and a contrasting sestet that tells how Cupid, awake, rekindled his brand and then introduces, and more expansively, the application of the myth to the speaker and mistress. Hutton remarks the "original conceit"[15]—found in none of the analogues—of 153.9–14. The originality is readily explainable. Shakespeare recast his earlier poem not only to better it but also to make it more adaptable to the design and exigencies of Part II. The phrases "my mistress' eye(s)," and the other details, noted above, that establish connections between Sonnet 153 and earlier sonnets in Part II all show up in the sestet.

Shakespeare, whose authorship of these two sonnets has frequently been doubted, surely composed both;[16] he wrote Sonnet 154 first and then rewrote it for incorporation into his sequence, where it appears as 153. Hence Sonnet 153 properly belongs in the Sonnets, and 154 does not.[17]

How this earlier and inferior version got included will forever remain a mystery. Those who hold that Shakespeare did not see his sonnets through the press would have done well to cite this piece of evidence had they been aware of it. Although Sonnet 154 contributes nothing and may even be considered a blemish on the work, we do not wish it away; for we have here, as nowhere else, a Shakespearean sonnet at two separate stages of development. Ben Jonson's players were wrong: more than blotting a line, the bard reworked an entire lyric, and here we are treated to a rare glimpse of his revisionary process.

Part II of the Sonnets, which depicts lust as circulating through the phases discriminated in Sonnet 129, stops with the sonneteer in a phase of erotic anticipation, in Sonnet 153, and could just as well have stopped when he felt the bitterness and disgust with himself and the woman recorded in Sonnet 152. The terminal point will necessarily be arbitrary, for lust's round does not admit of a resolution. Whatever happens later—whether the passion subsides, or the lover summons the willpower to quit the unsatisfactory amour, or both—has not yet happened by Sonnet 153, and transactions between him and the mistress will go on for a while, though without further poetic communications and, to judge from Part I (where she is heard of no more after Sonnet 42), not for long.

A few further facets of the design of Part II should be noted. While the dominant organizational principle has the sonnets arranged around the orbit traversed by lust "till action," "in action," and thereafter, they are generally aligned with the first and third of these phases, and some of the sonnets that deal with the suspicions of a liaison between the friend and the mistress lie outside the scheme. Sonnets 127 and 128, though subsumed into it, do constitute a kind of beginning, since in them the persona seems not yet to have had sexual intercourse with the woman. The only concession made to closure is Shakespeare's sudden shift in Sonnet 153 to mythologically oriented discourse and to the new, more "literary," less personal way of speaking about the lady. If a change of feeling toward her is implicit, it would be one tending toward detachment.

Even though the affair with her in Sonnets 127 through 153(154)

is concurrent with Sonnets 40–42 and is over when the male friendship still has a long way to go, the Sonnets do terminate, when read
through in the Quarto arrangement, with the fable of Cupid. This
terminal idea may have been suggested by Spenser. The four anacreontics he placed at the end of *Amoretti*, between the sonnet sequence and *Epithalamion*, in the volume published in 1595, likewise render fables of Cupid, the second even having some resemblance to 153.1–8. The likelihood is that Shakespeare found in
these pieces a hint and example for the finishing touch to his own
sequence, and, if he did, it would bear an implication for the dating
of his composition. A Spenserean influence would indicate at least
that the Sonnets were not completed before the second half of the
1590s.

Shakespeare's sonneteering is extraordinarily innovative. His innovations comprise, beyond his choosing sexually consummated relationships with the Master Mistress and the lesser mistress for in-
depth psychological treatment, the invention, as a vehicle for this
bisexual subject matter, of the bipartite but unified sonnet sequence. Its two parts, which hinge, as we have seen, on the love
triangles common to both, collaborate by means of the imitation of
loving in the first and of lusting in the second so that the very antithesis serves as a principal means of integrating the subcycles.
    This pervasive and all-encompassing antithesis finds localized
manifestations in certain interdivisional pairs or small groups of
sonnets of contrastive ideas and attitudes. No two sonnets better
illustrate this feature, or more call out to be compared, than Sonnet
129 in Part II, on lust's "expense of spirit," and Sonnet 116 in Part I,
on love's "marriage of true minds."

> Let me not to the marriage of true minds
> Admit impediments; love is not love
> Which alters when it alteration finds,
> Or bends with the remover to remove.
> O no, it is an ever-fixed mark
> That looks on tempests and is never shaken;
> It is the star to every wandering bark,
> Whose worth's unknown, although his height be taken.
> Love's not Time's fool, though rosy lips and cheeks
> Within his bending sickle's compass come;
> Love alters not with his brief hours and weeks,
> But bears it out even to the edge of doom.
>   If this be error and upon me prov'd,
>   I never writ, nor no man ever lov'd.

This poem begins, just as Sonnet 129 does, with an arresting proposition of a line and a half; but the thesis, that it is of the essence of
love to be lifelong and unalterable, is expounded in more restrained
and orderly discourse. Negative assertions alternate with affirma-
tive ones in 116.2b–12: "love is not . . ." (line 2); "O, no, it is . . ."
(line 5); "It is . . ." (line 7); "Love's not . . ." (line 9); "Love alters
not . . . / But bears it out . . ." (lines 11–12). Symmetries are pronounced. That "is *not love* / Which *alters*" in lines 2–3, and "*Love
alters not*" in line 11. Self-reference frames and personalizes the
generalizations with "Let *me* not" in line 1 and "upon *me* prov'd"
and "*I* never writ" in the couplet. The language is figurative between lines 5–10 and not so before and obscurely so afterwards. The
inadmissible "impediments" are those of time and space: time,
which effects corporal decay in line 3 and as the personified scythe-
wielder in lines 9–10; space, which separates the lovers when one of
them, "the remover" in line 4 or a "wandering bark" (= sailing ves-
sel) in the Petrarchan trope of line 7, is absent from the other. The
images of a sea "mark" and a navigational "star" declare love "ever-
fixed" through any and all external variabilities. The assertions
from line 2b through line 12 are doctrinaire and made in absolute
confidence, as the speaker indicates in the couplet: "If this be error
and upon me prov'd" (= 'proved against me' / 'proved by citing my
own case in evidence'—I/R), then "I never writ [a patent absurdity],
nor no man ever lov'd," that is, even though no one may have realized such love, its nature remains as described, *and*, if I myself have
not, why then "no man ever lov'd."

If a definition of love is tendered, it is formulated in 116.1 as "the
marriage of true minds," and marriage serves as the definitional
model. Commentators forever remark, seldom bothering with the
implications, that 116.1–2 echo the portion of the marriage service
in the Book of Common Prayer where the minister inquires of the
groom and bride "if either of you do know any impediment why ye
may not be lawfully joined together in matrimony. . . ." The "impediments" there are canonical, not those of spatial separation and
temporal decline alluded to in the sonnet. Nevertheless, a verbal
echo may well be audible. If so, why should Shakespeare introduce
it, unless to indicate that the friends are joined in marriage, the essential features of which are these: (1) constancy, mutually pledged
by "minds" that are steadfast in love; (2) permanence, the union
lasting until either lover reaches the brink of death, which = "the
edge of doom" at 116.12; and (3) sexuality, one sense in which the
minds are "true" being that they choose sexual fidelity.

The flesh plays an essential part in this marriage as in others.

This one admits of *no* impediments, and one expressly excluded is the impairment of the body as it ages, which is what "alteration" signifies in 116.3, and the idea is underscored in 116.9–10. There, within the "compass" of time's "sickle," lie "rosy lips and cheeks," which by synecdoche stand for youthful beauty. If "Love's not" the "fool" (= dependent, servile jester) of "Time," not subject to it as the passing rose-like loveliness of the countenance is, that is not to say that love is independent of, or disconnected from, physical beauty. On the contrary, such beauty engenders love (and this point has been established long before Sonnet 116 in the sequence, and long before the sequence); but, once so engendered, love will last as long as the lover lives and will survive the fading of the other's fairness.

The way of being in love described in Sonnet 116 and realized through most of Part I is one that entails an interaction of "affectionate" emotions with the sexual instinct, or, as Freud puts it, a "synthesis between the unsensual, heavenly love and the sensual, earthly love," of which the characteristics are these: "a lasting cathexis upon the sexual object," so that it may be loved "in the passionless intervals" between the gratification of erotic desire and its return, "the phenomenon of sexual overvaluation," and a narcissistic relation to the subject's ego. Sexual overvaluation, or the "tendency" toward "idealization," means that "the loved object enjoys a certain amount of freedom from criticism," that "its characteristics are valued more highly than those of people not loved," and that, "if the sensual impulsions are more or less repressed or set aside, the illusion is produced that the object has come to be loved on account of its spiritual merits," whereas the converse may be true, that these merits have rather been "lent to it by its sensual charm." Moreover, the lover treats the loved object just as he does himself, so that "a considerable amount of narcissistic libido overflows" onto it, and "in many forms of love-choice," among which the sonneteer's homosexual form would certainly be included, "the object serves as a substitute for some unattained ego ideal," being loved "on account of perfections" that the subject has wanted and can now acquire by being in love, a "roundabout" means of "satisfying his narcissism."[18]

All of these characteristics, it hardly needs saying at this point, belong to the poet's love for the friend. It is a love that pays handsome narcissistic dividends, is steady, and is, as the "star" at 116.7, heavenly; it is advantageous also for the friend, who is praised and prized for personal qualities that would likely pass unnoticed were the poet not under the spell of his beauty. The mistress, on the other hand, offers no narcissistic advantages; she is disesteemed, with vice but never virtue ascribed to her; even her physical attractiveness is more and more impugned as the affair proceeds; and she arouses lust that comes and goes.

When Sonnets 116 and 129 are read in place in Q, additional contrasts between them appear. The friend is not addressed in 116 but is addressed in the adjacent sonnets, and the same is true of the mistress in 129, who is not addressed there but is addressed immediately before and after. Sonnet 116 is undoubtedly intended for the eyes of the friend, for why should so eloquent a disquisition on the "marriage" in which he participates be kept from him? Besides, Sonnet 115, which does speak directly to him, likewise expresses the continuousness of love. Sonnet 129 can hardly be intended for the eyes of the mistress, for she could only be appalled by its contents. Besides, the theme is sharply at odds with that of Sonnet 128, which woos her, and of 130, which pays her a compliment—one she would hardly be receptive to after seeing 129. Text and context indicate that in Sonnet 116 the poet is mindful of the other "true mind" espoused to his and that in Sonnet 129 the personality of the lady, his accessory in lust, is remote from his consciousness.

Sonnet 129 appears early in its division (it is the third one), and it is critical, for it introduces and spells out the psychology of lust that contributes the semantic and architectonic dimensions of Part II. Sonnet 116 turns up late in its division and is not crucial, for the theme and structure of Part I have been established before it arrives and could be viewed in much the same way without its contribution. In fact, the theme of the poem is qualified by the poems around it. Marriage-of-true-mind love supposedly "looks on tempests and is never shaken." It did look on a tempest quite recently, in Sonnets 109–12, where the poet confesses his infidelities, and he will immediately do so again in Sonnets 117–20. His love does seem to be shaken by these tempests, particularly the second one, and there are various indications that love is on the wane. Nevertheless, his powerful faith in the conjugal permanence of the loverly devotion that informs Sonnet 116 is indubitably in earnest.

Because Sonnets 116 and 129 are interdivisional—one located in Part I, which ends with Sonnet 126, the other in Part II, which begins with Sonnet 127—and because they offset each other thematically and in other respects, they typify what I would call *antithetical sonnets*. Shakespeare has written a number of sets of these into the sequence, of which I have selected three—Sonnets 130 vs. 106, 141 vs. 46–47, and 115 vs. 152—to serve as examples.

Sonnet 130 (Part II) vs. 106 (Part I). Both sonnets assess pulchritude, that of "my mistress" and that of the youth, by criteria taken from poetry, but taken from different genres. One is the Petrarchan love sonnet, and it, or its blazon, which praises the beauty of the lady with a set simile for each of her bodily parts, comes in for a spoofing as the poet methodically and comically runs through each comparison to deny it to the mistress. He does pronounce her "rare" in the couplet, but she is truly no more so than the numerous women "belied with false compare," and neither she nor they measure up to the hyperbolic if humdrum rhetoric of Petrarchan compliment.

The other genre, medieval romance, is not made fun of; rather, it is much admired in Sonnet 106, for the "old rime" is "beautiful," made so by the "descriptions of the fairest wights" of both genders and the "praise of ladies dead and lovely knights." Then, in the second quatrain, the poet apprehends "in the blazon [= description, inventory] of sweet beauty's best, / Of hand, of foot, of lip, of eye, of brow," indifferently male or female, just what the "antique pen" of the romancers strove to give expression to, namely, "Even such beauty as you master now" (106.8). The splendor of the Master Mistress is, once again, a bewitching blend of the comeliness of both sexes. This androgynous quality is wanting in the woman.

The sestet of Sonnet 106 evokes another book, namely, The Book; for the conceit it contains is based on biblical hermeneutics. The chivalric poets serve the function of Old Testament prophets, for "all their praises are but prophesies / Of this our time," and "they look'd but with divining eyes"; the knights and ladies of their imaginations are shadowy types of the friend, "all you prefiguring"; and he is the Christ, the theophany of beauty finally come forth in "these present days." Even "we," who now behold him "with eyes to wonder," must do so dumbly, for lacking "tongues to praise." The lyric could hardly be more lavishly laudatory, and yet the adoring lover ends by protesting the deficiency of the tribute. If the romancers "had not skill enough" to feign "your worth" as a beauty, neither can the Petrarchan sonneteers properly praise the likes of "my mistress"; but whereas the latter poets overshoot the mark, the former fall short of it.

Sonnet 141 (in Part II) vs. the double sonnet 46–47 (in Part I). The antithesis here is between the poet's divided sensibility in responding lustfully to the woman and his unified sensibility in responding lovingly to the man. Sonnet 141 starts, "In faith I do not love thee with mine eyes, . . . But 'tis my heart that loves what they despise" (141.1, 3), and Sonnet 46 opens on a similar note, "Mine eye and heart are at a mortal war." The two arguments proceed, however, along very different lines. According to Sonnet 141, the mistress is not only visually unattractive; she is as unappealing to the other four senses as to sight, so that the speaker has no "desire to be invited / To any sensual feast" with her "alone," and, further, his "five wits" are put off by her as well. In this intrapsychic conflict the "heart," conceived of as the seat of passion, alone opposes and can override all the other faculties, sensory and mental, and it is adjudged "foolish."

But in Sonnets 46–47 the eye and heart do not pull in opposite directions, for both alike dote on the beloved "you." The issue in contention between them is that each claims that the other is encroaching on its domain or usurping its function in the love experience; and a portrait of the youth occasions the quarrel. The eye, holding that "in him thy fair appearance lies," would keep the picture from the heart, which "doth plead that thou in him doth lie." Then the jury of "thoughts," to whom the case is submitted for arbitration in the sestet of Sonnet 46, delivers a "verdict" that defines each complainant's right, the eye's being "thy outward part" and the heart's "thy inward love of heart." Thereafter, in Sonnet 47, the reconciled eye and heart assist each other in performing their proper offices of love, with the initial competition giving way to alliance and full cooperation. The eye, for example, will "feast" with "my love's picture" and invite the heart, smothering with amorous sighs, to the "painted banquet." The banquet yields visual and heartfelt "delight" (47.14) and may be contrasted with the "sensual feast" that the mistress presents at 141.8—a feast that elicits aversion.

These texts prominently feature the heart. The "heart in love" (47.4)—which harbors the image of the beloved and an awareness of the reciprocated "inward love" abiding in *his* heart (46.5, 14), as well as "thoughts of love" (47.8)—is wholly approved, over against the "foolish heart," which is disapproved, because, through the "plague" of lust, it dehumanizes the poet and enslaves him to the woman's "proud heart" (141.10–13).

Sonnet 115 (in Part I) vs. 152 (in Part II). The first begins, "Those lines that I before have writ do lie." The second ends, ". . . more perjur'd eye [I], / To swear against the truth so foul a lie." In this pair of antitheticals the protagonist acknowledges and retracts false assertions he has previously made. His misstatements, however, were of very different kinds. Those he confesses to in Sonnet 152 were oral, in the form of lover's oaths, and "foul" because perjuries, for he had sworn that the mistress had virtues and beauty that he knew very well she lacked. Those he admits to in Sonnet 115 were written, in lines of verse, and innocent—statements erroneous but made in good faith. He really believed it when he said of the friend, "I could not love you dearer," and he really "knew no reason why / My most full flame [of passion] should afterwards burn clearer." He even explains what led him to make such a mistake; it was anxiety about the vagaries of the future: "Why, fearing Time's tyranny, / Might I not then say, 'Now I love you best'?" But he has since come to realize why he was wrong to say it:

> Love is a babe; then might I not say so,
> To give full growth to that which still [= always] doth grow.

Love, he has learned from experience, has the remarkable capacity, like that of an infant, for pure, continuous growth without any tincture of decay. Here, as in Sonnet 152, the poet must unsay—but gladly rather than bitterly, and from a fresh intuition rather than in guilt and anger—what he said before. The truth about love in Sonnet 115 is better than it was thought to be; the "truth" in Sonnet 152, about the female object of lust, is worse than, and the opposite of, what it was sworn to be.

Fundamental and pervasive in Shakespeare's two-part sequence is the contrast between "two loves" in two senses of the word: two 'loved ones,' the sense at 144.1, the male and the female; and 'two types of love,' the homoerotic true love and the heterosexual lust. The antithetical sonnets serve to etch the contrast more sharply and, in doing so, to interlink Parts I and II. The reader does not begin to perceive the antitheses until he reaches Part II with Part I in mind, and so they lend semantic resonance especially to Part II. The effect is similar to that of reading Milton's companion pieces "L'Allegro" and "Il Penseroso," for there, too, it is only when we reach the second that the systematic contrasts between them emerge.

Of love in the sense of erotic response, that for the woman, but never that for the man, is termed a "sin" (142.1–2, 141.14) and a "disease," a "fever" that engenders madness (147.1–2, 10–12). In Sonnet 119 the poet also suffers "this madding fever," but the illness there is not his erotic love for the friend but, to the contrary, the "wretched errors" he himself committed in sexual acts when unfaithful to him. "Desire" for him is made "of perfect'st love" (51.10), "desire" for her is "death" (147.8). His "being had" is reason "to triumph" (52.14). She is a "triumphant prize" also, but of the excited male member (151.8–10); and she is prized only until had, for having her leads to a "waste of shame" and recriminations.

Of the two loves in the sense of persons beloved, the woman is allowed beauty only at the outset, never beyond Sonnet 134, and she is never allowed virtue. Moreover, her physical and moral blemishes are increasingly stressed; but the man is never anything other than awesomely beautiful, and he is continually admired for his concomitant moral attributes: "truth [= virtue, rectitude] and beauty on my love [= beloved] depends" (101.3); "'Fair, kind, and true' is all my argument . . . Which three till now never kept seat in one" (105.9, 14). The friend is often enough reprehended, to be sure, but almost always out of motives of jealousy.

The protagonist might well react differently to personalities of such different makeup, even apart from the oppositeness of their sex. Lust as characterized in Sonnet 129 is so unscrupulous and violent that he might find it difficult to indulge it with a lady fair and virtuous. But he does have the capacity to be deeply in love, as Part I makes amply clear. He can combine romantic sentiment and esteem with sexual desire and its passionate fulfillment, though he does so not with a woman but with a man. Only psychoanalysis could fathom the reasons why. Still, factors contributing to the more sustained and exalted love of the Master Mistress as compared with that of the mistress, such as his excelling beauty, his superior character, and his seemingly more congenial personality, are not to be discounted.

Some of the most affecting, most familiar, most often anthologized love lyrics in all of English poetry come from Shakespeare's Sonnets, and virtually all of them belong in Part I. The best-known poems in Part II, such as Sonnets 129, 144, and 146, are nonamatory, treating such matters as lust anatomized, a jealous crisis, and self-examination with reformatory intent. The amatory verse to and concerning the mistress is low-keyed; it is also comic (Sonnets 128, 130, 151), lascivious (Sonnets 128, 135–36, 138, 151), or an ambivalent compound of denunciation and courtship (as in Sonnets 131, 142, 150). But whoever would "read what silent love hath writ" (23.13) in the most eloquent and ardent accents must turn to the poems that express homoerotic responses to the fair friend.

A number of motifs presented in Part I and absent from Part II constitute a further contrast between them. The motifs include those of "breed," of absence due to journeys, of nocturnal visions in dreams or wakefulness of the beloved (Sonnets 27, 28, 43, 61), of compensations gained through him for misfortunes and past losses (Sonnets 29–31), of the poet's anticipations of his own death (Sonnets 71–74), of the dread of destructive time, and of the power of "rhyme" to confer immortality. The persona in Part II does not, unless tacitly in Sonnet 130 and obliquely in 153–54, depict himself in the conscious role of a poet, and no reflections on the nature and power of poetry appear in this division. Part I exhibits a greater diversity, encompasses a broader range of issues, and touches more bases, and it does so not only because it is lengthier and renders a longer-lasting relationship. Part II more narrowly converges on the feelings generated by the affair and creates the impression that lust is more confining than love, more compulsive, and less able to make contact with other interests.

Finally, an organizational distinction is observable between the first and second parts. Part II is structurally cyclic because its sonnets in the main are mimetic of the mental-emotional phases through which lust, as exposed in Sonnet 129, rotates.[19] The plan of Part I is linear, having a beginning middle, and end that trace the progress of love straight through the phases of growth, maturity, and decline. And so it is evident that Sonnet 116, with its doctrine of unalterable love, is not the index to the structure of Part I that its antithetical associate, Sonnet 129, is to that of Part II. The poet's impassioned devotion to "my lovely boy" (126.1), and while his "lips and cheeks" yet remain "rosy," undergoes a difficult, complex, but unmistakable diminution in Sonnets 100–126. This waning of love is the burden of the closing segment of Part I and the topic of the next chapter.

9

The Waning of Love

The ending of Part I, which extends from Sonnet 100 to Sonnet 126 and so consists of twenty-seven sonnets, is longer than the beginning (Sonnets 1–19) by a third, and is a third as long as the middle (Sonnets 20–99). The waning of love for the Master Mistress, the topic of the final section, is a convoluted process that may be interrupted and resisted but appears to proceed irreversibly.

A number of things signal the transition from the middle to the final section. Sonnet 99, with fifteen lines, is unique in exceeding the standard fourteen, and Sonnet 126, with twelve lines, is unique in falling short. As the irregularity of 126 clearly marks the close of Part I, so does that of 99 mark the close of its middle period. Sonnet 100, along with 101, is an invocation to the Muse—and this should betoken that something new is afoot. The Muse is dubbed "forgetful" (100.5) and "truant" (101.1) and is reproved because "thou forget'st so long" to honor the youth with love lyrics. For how long is not said, but the wording suggests a protracted interval; and the lapse of time between Sonnets 99 and 100 is also that between the two sections. Even though apologies and "amends" for "neglect" are proffered eloquently, feelingly, and repeatedly in each sonnet from 100 through 103, this admission of negligence is the first indication that the persona's response to the beloved is undergoing modification, a process that subsequent developments will verify.

Apostrophized in Sonnets 100–101 and referred to again in 103, the Muse is a leitmotif in this run of sonnets. She has "idly spent" her "fury on some worthless song" instead of celebrating him whose "ear . . . thy lays esteems" (he is the most appreciative of listeners) and who "gives thy pen both skill [in art] and argument [= subject]." Then a self-exonerating "answer" for her is invented at 101.5–8, that the friend's "truth" [= constancy, virtue] and "beauty" need no artistic embellishment; but that is unacceptable, for she has another function, which is to immortalize him. The Muse is a part of the poet; in questioning her, he is really questioning himself, exposing his own mixed feelings about continuing to compose love lyrics.

When in Sonnets 102 and 103 he makes further excuses for remissness, he does so in his own person: he would not "merchandize" his love ('treat it as vendible stuff') by publicizing it everywhere or "dull you with my song"; moreover, "your graces and your gifts," in and of themselves, far surpass anything "my verse" can "tell."

Among topics and themes anticipated in these four and the next five sonnets, through 108, are (1) various temporal concepts brought to bear on the love, (2) the immortalizing power of poetry, and (3) the monotony of continual sonnetizing.

1. Time is conceived of as literal, as metaphorical, as historical, and as stretching from the present into ages past and future. The literal time is the length of the friendship recorded in 104.3–8: "three winters cold" have undone "three summers' pride [= splendor], / Three beauteous springs to yellow autumn turn'd. . . . Since first I saw you fresh which yet are green." The seasonal cycle having turned three full times since their first meeting, the lovers would be in their fourth year together. The seasons are metaphorical in Sonnet 102, where the poet recalls the past, "when our love was new, and then but in its spring," from the vantage point of the current "summer" of love (102.5, 9). He hastens to add that this amorous "summer" is not "less pleasant now"—but he does hasten to add. Recollections of the beginnings of love, such as this one in 102.5 and the one in 104.8, discussed above, and again at 104.2, "when first your eye I eyed," and at 108.8, "when first I hallow'd thy fair name," repeatedly occur amid hints that the attachment may be entering a stage of decline.

In 107.9, "this most balmy time" refers to the historic moment in 1603 when "The mortal moon hath her eclipse endur'd." The allusion is surely the one that is widely accepted by exegetes: to the death of Elizabeth. The "moon," personified as "mortal," has a human referent; the "eclipse" she mortally suffers is 'a permanent cessation of light' (cf. OED 1b);[1] and Cynthia, the name of the mythic lunar virgin, was commonly conferred in poetry on the Virgin Queen. A period of stability and optimism, where "peace proclaims olives of endless age," has succeeded an immediate past of "incertainties," when approaching disasters were widely forecast. These "incertainties," in 107.7, "now crown themselves assur'd," that is, by their opposite, assurances; and the word "crown," though a verb which = 'bless with a fortunate outcome,' may be a play on the noun, and, if so, a secondary sense emerges, 'to gain assurances due to a royal crown,' which would be that of James I. The uncertainties about the succession would appear to be permanently settled when he, possessed of heirs, ascended the throne, so that the "sad [= gloomy, staid] augurs" might well "mock their own presage" of ca- tastrophes, and lasting "peace" might seem to be in prospect. The political events of the spring and summer of 1603 distinctly corre- spond with those adumbrated in the sonnet. Then, if this date were to be aligned with the three-year-plus span of love registered at 104.3–8, these years would seem to be the first of the new century. However, the correlation runs into bibliographical difficulties. Meres' reference in 1598 to "Shakespeare's sugred sonnets" indi- cates that at least a part of the sequence existed by then; we now learn that another part was being composed as late as 1603, some *five* years later. I cannot account for the discrepancy except to ven- ture that three may be a symbolic and indefinite rather than literal number, one that connotes, by poetic license, some few years and, feasibly, as many as five or six.

In Sonnet 106 the present is conceived of in other terms, as the fulfillment of ages past, when "descriptions of the fairest wights" in the "old rime" of chivalric romances were prefigurements of the friend's surpassing beauty. In Sonnet 107, as also in 100, 101, and 104, his present beauty will last through future ages by means of the *new* "rime" of Shakespeare's sonnets.

2. The capacity of verse to perpetuate the friend is an idea that the couplet of Sonnet 100 reintroduces, that recurs in 101.10–14 and 104.13–14, and that finds its final expression in Sonnet 107. Thus the last four of the sonnets that deal with this idea come close to- gether at the beginning of the third section of Part I (Sonnets 100– 126); the first five, Sonnets 15–19, appear at the end of the first section (Sonnets 1–19); and both clusters are equidistant from an- other five—Sonnets 54, 55, 60, 63, and 65—that occur in the middle of the second section (Sonnets 20–99) and thus occupy the center of Part I. The arrangement exhibits even more symmetry than that, as I will show later, to corroborate my division of Sonnets 1–126.

Sonnet 107 is distinctive, not only for its topical reference and as the terminal treatment of the theme of preservation through poetry, but also for working a variation on the theme: "Death to me sub- scribes, / Since spite of him I'll live in this poor rhyme." Here it is the speaker who is to gain immortal life through his art, and this notion is new to the sequence. He has occasionally before, it is true, regarded his verse as memorializing himself, but with a difference. He does so in Sonnets 32 and 74; as he puts the matter at 74.3–4, "My life hath in this line some interest / Which for memorial still [= always] with thee shall stay." He wishes simply to be thought on affectionately, after death, by the beloved, in whose memory he seeks a private vicarious existence through the agency of these love poems. In Sonnet 107 he has something else in mind for himself: a public posthumous literary existence. Shakespeare's own "prophetic soul" may be operative here, though it clearly dreams of something more modest than the bardolatry he has in fact received. He closes the sonnet on this familiar note:

> And thou in this shalt find thy monument
> When tyrants' crests and tombs of brass are spent.[2]

Two modes of conferring immortality through art are represented in Sonnet 107, as earlier. One may be called the vivifying mode; here the verse confers perpetual life on its subject (e.g., "you *live* in this" at 18.14). This mode is adduced in all of the early immortalizing sonnets (except for the discouraged Sonnet 16); in Sonnet 55 and others of the middle ones; but only exceptionally in the late ones. The second mode is the monumental; here the sonnet is conceived of as a perdurable tomb or monument. This mode is spoken of pejoratively at 83.12, and for that reason, and because the immortalizing mode is preferred in the more confident assertions of the idea, it comes through as rather inferior. The two modes coexist comfortably in Sonnet 81, the last poem on the notion in the second section, but in Sonnet 107, the last on it in the third section, they do not; for here the preeminent immortalizing mode is intended for the poet himself (107.11), while the lesser monumentalizing one is allotted to the friend (107.13). This allotment conforms to our sense of reality, for it *is* the author alone who "lives" in the Sonnets, and his thoughts and feelings alone are expressed in them; to the now unknown youth they constitute only a "monument," though one more imposing by far than any built for an unknown soldier.[3]

More to the purpose, Sonnet 107 makes notable contributions to the design of the third movement of Part I. Not only does the poet grant himself life immortal through "rhyme" and the friend but a lyric "monument"; he also gives up, at this point, his numerous efforts to poetize the friend into immortality. In Sonnet 15, the initial essay on the theme, the persona proclaimed his motive: "all in war with Time for love of you." The last campaign in that long war, where the poet's arsenal is his art, is undertaken, in modified manner, in Sonnet 107. Why the modification, which shows him less self-effacing than hitherto, and why the abandonment of the war, unless he has come to be less fully in love than before?

3. A whiff of boredom with the continual composition of love sonnets is given off by Sonnets 105 and 108. According to the former, "all alike my songs and praises be / To one, of one, still such,

and ever so"; "my verse" is "to constancy confin'd, / One thing
expressing, leaves out difference"; and "'Fair, kind, and true,'"
though "varying to other words," is "all my argument," and, even
though it "wondrous scope affords," yet does a certain tedium regis-
ter. That impression is reinforced three sonnets later, in Sonnet 108,
where the poet begins by asking "What's in the brain" concerning
"my true [= constant] spirit" that has not been penned, and "What's
new to speak," and he answers, "Nothing, sweet boy," then adds,
"but yet like prayers divine / I must each day say o'er the very
same." That his attitude was once far different can be discovered by
consulting Sonnet 38: "How can my Muse want subject to in-
vent . . . ?" One must remember, too, that Sonnets 105 and 108
closely follow the first four poems of this third movement, which
proffer various rationalizations for laxity in sonneteering.

However, the course of the love for the friend that is delineated in
the third movement is more complex than has so far been suggested.
Some of the most acclaimed of the love lyrics, such as Sonnets 115
and 116, show up in this section, and Sonnets 105 and 108 themselves, along with 106, laud the friend in religious terms of some
boldness. Sonnet 105 opens:

> Let not my love be call'd idolatry,
> Nor my beloved as an idol show,

and three reasons follow to refute the charge of "idolatry": (1) "all
alike my songs and praises be / To one, of one, still [= always] such
and ever so"—that is, idolators adore many gods, but this wor-
shiper's devotion is monotheistic; (2) "'Fair, kind, and true' is all my
argument"—that is, idolators are usually immoral, but the ethical
discriminations and values of this devotee are impeccable; and (3)
because he directs his praise to "three themes in one" ('as one' and
'in one individual'), "Which three till now never kept seat in one,"
he avoids pagan idolatry by venerating a three-in-one, a trinitarian,
god. With the next sonnet this implicit god becomes an implicit
Christ in a conceit (based, as pointed out earlier, on biblical interpretation) in which the "ladies dead and lovely knights" in romance, conceived of as an old testament, are types of the friend, and
Sonnet 106 is the gospel that announces the good news of the arrival
of the antitype, the one of beauty supreme.

In Sonnet 108 the poet, who had turned from theology to hermeneutics, now turns to Christian worship for his trope. Although
he has said everything he has to say about "my love" and "thy dear
merit . . . but yet like prayers divine" (whether in the liturgy or set
prayers memorized),

I must each day say o'er the very same,
Counting no old thing old—thou mine, I thine—
Even as when first I hallow'd thy fair name.

"Hallowed be thy name," from the Lord's Prayer, the most revered of the "prayers divine" because taught by Jesus himself, is echoed, as more than one editor has noted; but the name that is hallowed here is not Our Father's in Heaven but that of the friend, and it is "fair" because of his fairness and so is accorded amorous veneration. If Shakespeare might be thought to risk irreverence, he does so again in the suggestion of monotony in the repetition of fixed ritualistic formulas, whether they pertain to religious or to erotic devotion. The lover is no doubt tiring of his drawn-out poetic enterprise and of the love that evokes it; yet at the same time, whether in compensation or as a coverup, he extols the youth to high heaven.

Love is nowhere more eulogized than in Sonnets 115 and 116. It is conceived of in 115 on a quasi-organic model: "Love is a babe" because it constantly "doth grow" without attaining "full growth," realizing organic development without decay. In 116, the model is quasi-Platonic: love is conceived of as an abstract entity, a supernal form, an impersonal "it," unalterable and "ever-fixed," and an influence on men in time but not itself subject to time's effects. Yet the poet tenders these ringing assurances about the permanence of love when his own passion seems to be wavering.

The signs that it is wavering—and they are observable from the start of the third movement—include the lover's slackness in sonneteering, his hint that he is becoming wearied of it, his revising the theme of poetic immortalization self-beneficially and finishing it off, relinquishing the role of immortalizer, and, finally and most importantly, his turning elsewhere for sensual gratification, which he does not once but twice. Sonnets 109–12 are devoted to the first occasion, 117–20 to the second, and Sonnets 115 and 116 are sandwiched into the brief interlude between. Indeed, the very next thing we learn, after the exaltation of love in Sonnet 116, is that he has again succumbed to unfaithfulness. I do not say that he has ceased to be in love, but the dynamics of his amorous response to the youth are plainly different from what they were earlier. Impulses toward dispassion now punctuate the attachment, and promiscuous activities interfere with it. Though it at times may seem as strong and fervent as ever, it seems so only at times and for a time. The passion is in the process of winding down; the resurgences of love, most notably those in Sonnets 113–16, may interrupt the process, but they do not reverse it.

The treatment of the process entails references to an incongruity between appearance and reality, first at 102.1–2: "My love is strengthen'd, though more weak in seeming; / I love not less, though less the show appear." Although the appearances have been created by the poet's own conduct, they are to be discounted when he asserts that the love is really not diminished but greater. In Sonnet 109, where he confesses a "stain" of inconstancy, he adopts a defense along the same lines, denying that "I was false of heart," even "though absence *seem'd* my flame to qualify." Here again, while the erotic "flame" had appeared to abate, it is said to have actually remained intact. The outward symptoms of declining affection are at once admitted and dismissed.

In Sonnet 110 the poet again concedes his offenses but now discovers that "worse essays [in sexuality with someone/ones inferior] prov'd thee my best of love." Despite the happy outcome, he pledges in 110.10–11 to put a halt to such experiments. But the pledge is soon broken, for by Sonnet 117 he has repeated the offense, and in the couplet he offers the "appeal" that "I did strive to prove / The constancy and virtue of your love." This is something of a turnabout, for here he consciously imposes the trial, while in Sonnet 110 what turned out to be a test was of his own love, not the other's, and it was unpremeditated. The plea comes through as a callous rationale, for to try another's love is a dubious and forbidding way of justifying one's own inconstancy. The divided mind of the protagonist is even more strikingly dramatized in Sonnets 118 and 119. In 118 he owns up to a "policy of love," adopted because of "being full of your . . . sweetness," "sick of welfare," and having fallen "sick of you." The remedy was lechery, and, while he now views this remedy as a mistake, its failure hardly cancels out the original problem. He exclaims, "What wretched errors hath my heart committed" in Sonnet 119, but there the problem is presented even more starkly. He discovers the "benefit of ill": that "better [= love of the friend] is by evil [that of sexual infidelity] still made better," because "ruin'd love when it is built anew / Grows fairer than at first, more strong, far greater." Here we discover how far his love had deteriorated: into a ruin that had to be reconstructed. The principle of good out of evil has fortunately continued to operate, and the poet so welcomes the renewed love as to think it more secure than ever before. But this may be a momentary, euphoric, reaction.

A smooth-running course of love had never been wholly congenial to the poet; the waters that used to be disturbed by his jealous suspicions are now stirred up by his own sexual adventures; being "to constancy confined," a state that "leaves out difference" (105.7–8), alternately contents and discontents him. The end of Part I, the record of the friendship, is not far off. The groundwork of the termination is carefully, and with increasing clarity, laid in the third movement.

Until the end, at Sonnet 126, no further breaches open between the friends. Sonnets 122–25, the four sonnets that lead up to the final one, are not without difficulties and obscurities. They seem to me to vary stylistically from the others, partly in being more private of reference, with meanings less fully available than the rest. Also they offer comment, sometimes revisionary, on issues previously raised.

The circumstances underlying Sonnet 122 are plain enough in outline. The friend had made a gift of "tables," that is, a blank writing tablet, to the lover, who not only never used them—for "that idle rank" at 122.3 most likely refers to the volume of empty pages—but gave them away, to the apparent chagrin of the giver. An apology is in order, and it is undertaken in the poem; it can be paraphrased as follows: you are more fully and lastingly recorded in my mind than you could ever have been in these leaves, and here you will remain eternally, or, to be more precise, so long as my "brain and heart" are alive and functioning; the very idea that I needed that notebook to tally "thy dear love" is unacceptable, and so of course I gave it away; I wished to trust my more retentive memory of you, for to have kept the tablet as an "adjunct [= aid] to remember thee / Were to import forgetfulness in me."

But what does all this have to do, if anything, with the movement toward closure? First of all, the speaker, however ingenious his excuse, did treat the gift rather callously. Second, if the friend's motive in presenting it can be inferred from the couplet, where the "tables" appear to have been intended as "an adjunct to remember" him, he would seem to have felt some apprehension, sensing unmindfulness in his poet and lover. Finally, the sonneteer does something of an about-face in the argument of Sonnet 122: whereas "thy record" is better preserved in the persona's "brain and heart" than in writing, the poems on immortalization in verse had declared the opposite, that "The living record of your memory" (55.8) was to be preserved by "black ink" (65.14), not regarded as a "poor retention."

Sonnet 123 apostrophizes Time, at once challenging it and contemplating its subtle effects as the agent of mutability. Challenge is expressed at line 1, "No, Time, thou shalt not boast that I do change"; at line 9, "Thy registers [= records] and thee I both defy"; and in the couplet. The remaining ten verses are given over to the contemplation of time, and this subject combines less readily with the challenge than may have been expected; for what Shakespeare is pondering here is not mutability itself, so often treated before (as in Sonnets 19 or 65), but the way the mind perceives historical change, a topic touched on previously only in Sonnet 59. The octave of Sonnet 123 views time present: what may seem "novel" and "strange" now is but the reappearance of something seen before (the idea is expressed also in 59.1–2), and what is old is habitually regarded by us as newly created to suit "our desire." Hence, *plus ça change* . . . ; and there is no new thing under the sun, Ecclesiastes 1:9–10 having often been cited in connection with this passage and the one in Sonnet 59. If new forms are facsimiles of old forms, and if the old is thus misconceived, then change proves elusive. Moreover, our momentary perspective on present and past, on near and remote realities, is ever being distorted, according to the third quatrain, by the "continual rush," the relativity of Time.

The questions raised in Sonnet 59 are whether such beauty as the youth's has ever existed before and, if so, how it was written about. The issue in Sonnet 123 is firmness of amorous commitment in a mutable world. The firmness is pledged in the couplet:

> This I do vow and this shall ever be:
> I will be true despite thy scythe and thee.

"True" is to be understood as 'true in love' and 'true to the friend.' We know this from, and can know it only from, the surrounding lyrics; for neither the friend nor love is mentioned in Sonnet 123, and, if it stood alone, "true" could have an impersonal reference— for example, it could mean 'steadfast' to some principle or cause. The problem raised by the couplet, however, is how to integrate it with what goes before. Mutability in temporal-spatial phenomena is of an altogether different order from swearing, and adhering to, fidelity in love. For a partial bridging of the gap, one might regard the persona as someone exceptionally knowledgeable about time and change and as one whose defiance of time intimates a value set on permanence. Then 123.2–12 establish his character as that of a man from whom a pledge of constancy is trustworthy. Otherwise the conclusion comes across as a nonsequitur, or else lines 2–12, excepting line 9, come across as tangential to lines 1 and 13–14. Even though the poem does come to rest on the love vow, most of it is devoted to something else: to epistemological speculation. The emphasis is less on the beloved than on the speaker, who even at the end says: "*I* will be true."

The next sonnets in Q proceed along similar lines, with the poet's elaborating on the vow "I will be true" as he proclaims the constancy of "my dear love." This phrase, in 124.1, has reference not to the beloved, who again is never mentioned, but to the speaker's own prized and heartfelt devotion, the love objectified as "it" throughout the sonnet. The argument of 124.1–12, however intricate in detail, is clear in its gist, that my love is invulnerable to circumstantial mutation, and clear also in its structure, as follows: if this (line 1), then that (lines 2–4); but not this (lines 5–10), then something else (lines 11–12).

If, in the first quatrain, "my dear love were but the child of state" (= but the product of a particular set of circumstances), then might it be the "bastard" of female Fortune and without a father, paternally unprotected from the quirks of Time, which, though, may be either beneficial or inimical. In the floral metaphor of 124.4 the "weeds" correspond to love when it is subject to "Time's hate," the "flowers" to love subject to "Time's love." Both are "gather'd," but the "weeds" are presumably plucked up by the root, to be discarded, while the "flowers" are to be picked from the blossoming plant and esteemed. A love based on "state"/"Fortune"—the terms are equivalent—would not necessarily fare badly but could not be secure.

But "No," the poet's love is not of that ilk, as we learn from 124.5–10; for his love "was builded far from accident" and so is not menaced by 'chance' any more than by the accidents of "smiling pomp" and "thralled discontent." "Pomp" ('a splendid, prosperous condition') can yet make love suffer, for it is qualified by "smiling"—its favor is capricious, unreliable, of the moment. Pomp may smile and smile and turn out to be villainous. The "discontent" would be due to oppressive treatment at the hands of the loved one. While the lover may no longer fear such maltreatment, although it is all the "fashion" nowadays, he once bitterly complained of being subjected to it as "your slave" in Sonnet 58. Then in 124.9–10 his love "fears not policy"; the opposite of "accident," policy is opportunistic calculation and fearsome because egocentric and prone to craftiness; it is personified and condemned as "that heretic," one of bad faith and erroneous doctrine, who operates through short-term commitments as distinct from the timelessness of orthodox love.

That love, the persona's kind, is, in 124.11–12, "hugely politic," which denotes 'superlatively sagacious, wise in the ways of thriving,' and it is further distinct from occasional and expedient "policy" in being unalterable, for it "nor grows with heat nor drowns with showers." Those figures, as Hilton Landry remarks, "are intended to represent purely external conditions . . . and yet they may also carry hints of inner weather."[4] I agree, but view this interior dimension rather differently. The "heat" of passion and the "showers" of tears—tears of sorrow or frustration—are phenomena of the erotic climate within the lover, but even they, intimately connected with love as they are, do not cause it to increase or decay, do not affect its "ever-fixed" nature.

Then, alas, the couplet, where "fools of time," who "die for goodness" having "liv'd for crime," are called to "witness" what was said in the previous two or twelve lines. Time-servers may be criminals, but those who "die *for* goodness" are neither; nor are they deathbed repenters: they are martyrs. The dead witnesses, whose lives were bad and whose deaths are unintelligible, are hardly in a position to testify about unalterable love. I know of no one who has made sense of the couplet.

Sonnet 125, the penultimate poem in Part I, touches on themes that enter into the immediately preceding poems as well as on themes of longer standing. The sentence in each of the first two quatrains is interrogative; in the first, it is subjunctive as well. The speaker asks at the start, "Were it aught to me [that] I bore the canopy . . . Or [that I] laid great bases for eternity," that is, 'Would it have been anything of consequence to me that I did these things?' The "canopy," the portable kind, carried over the king or some other dignitary in ceremonies as a mark of honor, is figurative, and it was borne in celebrating the friend, "With my extern the outward honoring." "My extern," or 'exterior,' is also figurative and is rightly taken by I/R to denote "my public tributes," which are those in verse; "the outward" alludes to the physical beauty that is primarily and consistently acclaimed in sonnets to the youth. Then the "great bases of eternity" would be, from the earlier context, the eternalizing sonnets. The former confidence has eroded, however, for "eternity" in 125.4 "proves more short [of duration] than [ever prevalent and irresistible] waste or ruining." Does the poet no longer believe that poetry is indestructible? That inference, I believe, can be drawn from the evidence, which has been mainly negative since Sonnet 107, the last sonnet to affirm the perdurability of verbal art, but is now positive in Sonnet 125, where the "great bases of eternity," referring to the "powerful rhyme" of the lyric immortalizations, are regarded as having been "laid" in vain. What does it matter, the poet asks at this late stage, that I did these things?

In Sonnet 125's second quatrain he turns the spotlight on contrasting types—on others who, like him, have loved but, unlike him, have lost. They are the "dwellers on [admirers smitten with] form [shape] and favor [beauty or face]," who "Lose all and more [everything and then some] by paying too much rent." The figurative "rent" stands for the passionate investment they make, what it costs them emotionally to hang about a beauty who magnetizes them but affords them nothing in return. They prefer, in the metaphorical shift of 125.7, some exotic concoction of sweetmeats to the pure, natural taste of ordinary, and implicitly more wholesome, nutriment. As so often in the Sonnets, food stands for sexual gratification, and they forgo the "simple savor" of someone less glamorous but sexually available for the "compound sweet" of someone out of reach. These frustrated suitors are, indeed, "Pitiful thrivers," an oxymoron that = 'pathetic succeeders' and ironically denotes 'failures.' They are "in their gazing spent," exhausting themselves and their resources, which are paid out "too much" in merely "gazing" upon, but never getting to taste, the delicious morsel whom they crave.[5]

"No" at 125.9 denotes 'not that'—not the fate of spent gazers—and also 'but rather.' The speaker would be "obsequious in thy heart" not as the "thrivers" are, in 'fawning,' but in the sense of 'dutiful, devoted.' Not until the third quatrain are we made aware that the poem addresses the friend. "My oblation" ('offering'), if "poor," is yet "free" ('spontaneous and unreserved'), unadulterated with "seconds" ('low-grade matter'), and it "knows no art" except that which is the 'practice' (Schmidt) of "mutual render." The phrase would suggest a 'reciprocal rendering-up or surrender' were it not qualified by "only me for thee," which can be construed as 'simply me for you,' and, secondarily, as 'me *alone* and no one else for you,' but in both cases the flow of the rendering goes from "me" to "you" without the counterflow of you for me. The mutuality seems to consist of one's giving and the other's accepting, as in 125.9, "let me be . . . in thy heart," and in 125.10, "take thou my oblation." The lover, close now to the end, plays down his reception of love from the other, a marked change from Sonnets 117–20. However, with "mutual render" at 125.12 he does contrast himself with gazers on the "outward," who fail to find inward acceptance, as also with his former self, ambitious to build for eternity; for he now settles for something more humble. And he does not close on that note.

Once again, and for the third time in a row, the couplet is problematic.[6] On this occasion it erupts into aggression: "Hence [= away] thou suborn'd informer [= bribed accuser]!" Who on earth is this obtrusive villain? Has he been addressed all along? But that cannot be, since the friend has been clearly established as the recipient, and he is the emphatic "thee" at the end of 125.12. The point of view of the poem is saved from incongruity if this 'false witness' is taken to be apostrophized as a rankling presence in the persona's mind throughout the discourse and against whose censures it is largely directed. From the discourse one might infer that snide remarks had been uttered, such as that the poet has made quite a public spectacle of himself in adulating that beautiful boy (cf. 125.1–2), and with all that nonsense about eternal lines, which are already out of fashion (cf. 125.3–4); and questions would have been raised about what the poet is getting and what he expects to get out of it all. He then defends himself before the friend, and in the course of doing so finally bursts out in angry invective against his detractor. The last statement is aimed at him: "a true soul [a person true in love and to principle, such as I am] / When most impeach'd [= reproached] stands least in thy control," for the reason that you have done your utmost by making false accusations, and so there is nothing further that one with a clear conscience need fear from you.

Sonnets 122 to 125 so interrelate with one another as to constitute a distinct group, one with affinities to Sonnet 121, and these five poems, which follow hard upon the obviously grouped Sonnets 117–20, about the poet's second fall into sexual infidelity, treat of his devotion in a special way, with attention focused more on the loving subject, less on the beloved. The latter remains a highly significant figure, but the impression is given that he is a less vivid and compelling presence than earlier. Only two of the five, Sonnets 122 and 125, address him, and not until its third quatrain does the latter advert to him. Sonnet 121 is not about him and is not a love lyric. Never before has an *assemblage* of sonnets been so abstracted from his person, though an isolated one, such as Sonnet 62, may have been. In both Sonnets 121 and 125 the speaker assumes a self-defensive posture. He justifies the homoerotic component of his bisexual orientation against adverse critics in Sonnet 121 ("I am that I am"), and in 125 he defends the genuineness of his dedication to the beloved, which has been called into doubt by the "informer." Sonnets 123–25 are each marked (marred?) by ill-fitting couplets, and the three couplets have an interesting common denominator, as a juxtaposition of the initial clauses of each will demonstrate: "This [what follows] do I vow . . ."; "To this [what I say above] I witness call . . ."; and "Hence, thou suborn'd informer. . . ." The word "suborn" in Shakespeare 'is applied especially to false witnesses' (Schmidt), so that witnesses are summoned at 124.13, presumably somehow supportive ones, and, at 125.13, a false one, to be refuted and then dismissed. Either way, the testimony bears on the soundness of the avowed love and, consequently, on the validity of the "vow" sworn at 123.13.

Yet the protagonist's love, however attenuated, endures, though it is now more humble, defensive, and possibly self-absorbed. The profession of devotion in Sonnet 125, as in 123, is convincing; and if a diminution of ardor and idealization is perceivable, as I believe it is, it can be perceived only relative to the more impassioned responses to the beloved expressed earlier in the sequence. The most telling evidence that love is expiring, though, is imminent. Part I, devoted to the friend, is very near its finish, having only one sonnet to go.

Sonnet 126, consisting of six couplets, is unique in both rhyme scheme and length. In one sense it is not a sonnet, and in another it is. It is insofar as it is an amatory lyric, for to Elizabethans the term could signify that without reference to stanzaic pattern, and the word is so used in Donne's title *Songs and Sonnets*, though in his designation *Holy Sonnets* it denotes the unvaried—and there Italian—sonnet form. In Shakespeare's sequence Sonnet 126 is one of only three sonnets that do not fully conform to his standard English form, the others being Sonnets 99, where an extra verse is added to the normal fourteen, and 145, where tetrameters replace the normal pentameters. While Sonnet 126 varies from the norm in two respects, it is internally organized in sonnet-like fashion, in that an octave is followed by a volta at line 9, but the "sestet" is aborted to four lines. However, after line 12 Q has two pairs of parentheses, one beneath the other, to indicate "missing verses."

> O thou my lovely Boy, who in thy power
> Dost hold time's fickle glass, his sickle, hour,
> Who hath by waning grown, and therein show'st
> Thy lover's withering as thy sweet self grow'st,
> If Nature (sovereign mistress over wrack),
> As thou goest onwards still will pluck thee back,
> She keeps thee to this purpose, that her skill
> May time disgrace and wretched minutes kill.
> Yet fear her, O thou minion of her pleasure,
> She may detain but not still keep her treasure!
> Her audit (though delay'd) answer'd must be,
> And her quietus is to render thee.
> (   )
> (   )

The four parentheses are omitted by virtually all editors on the grounds that the poem is complete as it stands and that these parentheses represent a mistaken assumption by the printer (or whoever) that, fourteen lines being normal, two must be lost. The editorial consensus may well be correct, but I prefer to take up the matter as one of a number of exegetical problems to be found in the text.

The first of these problems arises in 126.2 and concerns the identity and even the number of "time's" possessions. His "fickle glass" would seem to be a looking glass, "fickle" in reflecting the ever-aging face of the beholder (cf. 77.1, 5–6); possibly 'hourglass' is denoted, but I think that that is less aptly described as "fickle," and often in the sonnets "glass" imports 'mirror,' never 'hourglass.' The "sickle"—with a comma after the word in Q—is the conventional tool of Time the mower; he wields it also at 116.10. Then what is the "hour"? Tucker Brooke glosses it as 'hourglass,' which then becomes, along with the 'mirror' and the "sickle," the third concrete and symbolic item appertaining to Time. This makes good sense, and the gloss has since been widely accepted by editors. The main difficulty with it is that I am unable to locate another instance of "hour" with this meaning. Possibly after "hour," which is "time's," the term 'glass' is to be understood or to resound from its usage just three words before. An alternative interpretation, in which "sickle hour" = 'the moment when the sickle strikes' (Tyler et al.), requires that Q's comma after "sickle" be removed and that the ostensible noun be construed as an adjective. The internal rhyme "fickle"/"sickle" is, admittedly, neater if both words are adjectives; this reading also does away with the need for 'his' or 'and' before "hour," the absence of which is otherwise bothersome. Neither solution is satisfactory; my own inclination is to go along, hesitantly, with the former (Brooke's).

Another problem arises in 126.4, with Q's word "lovers." In the possessive case, it may be singular—in modernized form "lover's," referring to the poet alone, or plural, "lovers'," referring to him and others. Most commentators prefer the latter alternative, thinking, I suspect, to make the poem morally a bit more palatable. To my mind the former alternative, "lover's," alone is plausible, for it alone is consistent with the context of the preceding sonnets and of Part I generally. The best evidence in support of this reading is furnished by the text itself. It begins, "O thou *my* lovely [also = 'lovable'] boy." If, then, he is mine, it follows logically that it is I, not I and some vague, unspecified others, who would be "Thy lover."

This "lovely boy" is the object of address and the focus of attention throughout the poem. His initially tender and admiring but increasingly stern and admonitory lover views the two personified figures, Nature his patroness and Time his implacable destroyer, as engaged in conflict over him. In the first quatrain, "power" over Time, control of its emblems and implements, is imputed to him because he, paradoxically, "hast by waning grown," that is, he has become simultaneously older and fairer and has thereby accented the more normal "withering" of the speaker. Then, in the second quatrain, the poet evokes Nature to account for the youth's miraculous growth in beauty. She, the "sovereign mistress over wrack [= ruin], / As thou goest onwards" temporally will constantly "pluck thee back" from deterioration, preserving "thee to this purpose," namely, to "disgrace" Time and his "wretched minutes kill" by canceling out their destructive function. A dramatic turn occurs at 126.9: "Yet fear her," because, though you are "her treasure," she cannot succeed in safeguarding you from mightier Time. The word "treasure" introduces the financial metaphors of the last two lines, where her "audit [= account]" may be postponed but must be settled, and "her quietus [= quittance, discharge of debt] is to render [= surrender] thee." Being given over to Time means your subjection to decay and ultimately to death. And on this chilling prophetic note the sonneteer makes a valediction to the still "lovely" boy.

The argument seems straightforward and clear enough until a closer look uncovers some internal inconsistencies. To Dame Nature two distinct motives are ascribed: (a) antagonism toward Time, whom she challenges, using the youth as her pawn, in 126.5–8, and (b) that of favoritism toward the youth, whom she shields as the "minion [= darling and creature] of her pleasure," in 126.9–10. The motives may not be strictly incompatible, but they are separately adduced and are kept disjoined. In 126.1–3 the "boy" himself holds "power" over Time's instruments and thereby saves himself from its ravages, but in 126.5 it is Nature who, as "sovereign mistress over wrack," keeps him unblemished; yet, as it turns out, she must surrender him to Time, so it is Time, instead of her, who is the true sovereign over "wrack." Read by itself, the poem may be seen as substandard, with its execution unusually flawed. There are, besides the inconsistencies and the semantic opacity of 126.2, dictional infelicities, which include the internal rhyme of "fickle" with "sickle," particularly if one is an adjective, the other a noun, and the repetition of the verb "hast . . . grown" in one line by "grow'st" in the next (126.3 and 4). Signs of hasty or careless composition abound, so much so that the couplet form and the abbreviated length, to which Q's vacant parentheses call attention, might be symptomatic of authorial nonchalance. One might entertain the possibility that the shortcomings, whether on purpose or by inadvertence, contribute to the terminative process by evincing the persona's fading interest in the love-sonnet project.

And yet, from another perspective, Sonnet 126 gives the impression of painstaking design. Editorial and critical expositors have frequently remarked, usually without elaboration but justly, that the poem serves as an envoy to the sonnets devoted to the friend, and, as such, it possesses dimensions hidden unless the finality of its position in Part I is taken into account. Not only do its unique features, of rhyme and relative brevity, serve to set it apart, thereby marking its conclusive function, but the text has various affinities with sonnets both near and remote. The phrase of 126.4, "thy sweet self," had occurred in 1.8 and again at 4.10; in each case the affectionate phrase is set in an admonitory address that dwells on the inevitable passing of beauty and of life, though Sonnets 1 and 4 posit a remedy, that of begetting offspring, unlike Sonnet 126, which posits none. Sonnet 4 also has other elements in common with 126; those include conceits of financial reckoning—the word "audit" appears in both (4.12, 126.11)—and the presence of Nature personified. She is represented as the bountiful benefactor of the youth; she is his guardian spirit always—in Sonnets 4, 11, and 126; and in Sonnet 20 she is also depicted as his creatrix and he as her artistic subject, on whom she "fell a-doting." He is, as well, the artistic subject of the poet, who also "fell a-doting" on him. The lover projects his own passion for the Master Mistress onto Nature in Sonnet 20, and in 126 he follows the same practice of identifying himself with her, again ascribing to her his own attitudes toward the "lovely boy." In both texts the "pleasure"/"treasure" rhyme appears. If Nature is foreseen in Sonnet 126 as surrendering the youth, that is because the persona, whose alter ego she is, is now prepared to surrender him, not only to the processes of mortality but emotionally as well. The efforts, motivated by love, to perpetuate the beloved are given up, and both his end and the end of love are sighted at the end of Part I.

The last poem of Part I, Sonnet 126, points back through related phrases, images, and concepts to the earliest poems, especially to Sonnet 4 but also to Sonnet 1 and others, such as 2 and 6, that contain financial tropes, and to 20, *the opening sonnet of the middle movement*, where carnal passion is initially declared, and to subsequent sonnets as well. For example, "my lovely boy" of 126.1 echoes the vocative "sweet boy" at 108.5. (Incidentally, in neither instance does "boy" mean 'prepubescent male'; it is rather the affectionate term for a young man that one older than he may adopt.) Then, "Thy lover's withering" in 126.4 recalls "I am . . . With Time's injurious hand crush'd and o'erworn" at 63.1–2. Finally, in Sonnet 104 the beauty of the friend appears not to have declined, to be "yet . . . green," despite the three-year span "Since first I saw you fresh," and though the poet can suspect a subjective distortion due to partiality—"mine eye may be deceiv'd"—he finds there, just as in Sonnet 126, the beauty unmarred by the passage of time.

Sonnet 126 also stands related, by contrast and continuities, to its immediate predecessors. It addresses the youth, as Sonnets 121, 123, and 124 do not, and, of greater moment, it keeps him at the center of attention, whereas Sonnets 123–25 and 121 had focused more directly on the feelings and responses of the poet-lover. Thus he returns, at last, to his erstwhile habit of concentrating on the person of the other. The verb "render" at 126.12, denoting Nature's act of relinquishing the youth, picks up the noun from "mutual render" at 125.12, which had denoted, conversely, the giving of the lover's self to the beloved. In other thematic respects, however, Sonnet 126 accords with the immediately antecedent sonnets, and particularly with 125, where the enterprise of transcending time by verse is expressly waived, the erotic pressure to keep something of the friend forever intact now having subsided; for the poet can assent, in Sonnet 126, to the inevitable fact of mutability. He closes by recognizing that everything sublunary is subject to time, that time, whose devastations are a salient and recurrent topic throughout Part I, is dominant, and that any apparent exemption from its vicissitudes must be, if not illusory (Sonnet 104), then transitory (126.9–12). Nature is the surrogate of the persona, and what she must do—"render" the "minion of her pleasure" to Time—he does, or anticipates doing, in Sonnet 126, whereupon all the lyrical expressions of attachment to the youth cease.

Part I of the Quarto does not end with 126.12 but, as I have said, with two sets of parentheses, indented just as the closing couplet is in every other sonnet. That they are superfluous, as scholars contend, cannot be disallowed; and they might be stricken, for, yes, the text is complete without them. Still, a further hypothesis is inviting: that these parentheses might have been added by Shakespeare himself. This is pure speculation, which does not entail postulating canceled verses, much less guessing what they might have said. Instead, one might ponder the import of the parentheses as they are presented in Q: as terminal and empty.

To begin with, it must be recalled that each closing couplet from Sonnets 123 through 125 is problematic and tenuously attached to the forerunning discourse. The effect, or the strategy, might be to set up an expectation of some sort of peculiarity at the close of Sonnet 126, and the parentheses would certainly satisfy such an expectation. Moreover, when the question of the friend's decay and demise had come up before in Part I, a solution was provided: he might procreate; but that solution was abandoned long ago, by Sonnet 17. He might be granted immortality by "powerful rhyme," but not after Sonnet 107. It is noteworthy that quite often the final couplets are utilized to make these themes overt or else to encapsulate them.

But neither "breed," nor poetry, nor unalterable commitment is advanced to solace or save the friend—Nature herself cannot save him—when he is foreseen, in Sonnet 126, to be doomed to ruination by Time. The remedies normally proposed (Sonnet 64 being exceptional in this regard) are missing, and the two blanks can serve to call attention to the omission. A change of heart in the poet would be evident anyway, but the parenthetical muteness underscores it.

More immediate indications of his change of heart are furnished by the sonnets lying just ahead of 126. At 123.13–14, a vow of fidelity was made; at 124.13–14 and 125.13–14, testifiers were evoked to validate the lover's constancy. While affection may still exist between "my lovely boy" and "thy lover" in Sonnet 126, no promise is now made of continuing devotion. The time-ridden future holds decline and extinction in store for the youth, and the poet is not horrified by that prospect, as he had so often been before (notably at 64.12–14). The blanks appear where the three preceding sonnets encourage us to look for some kind of avowal of love. Why is none forthcoming? It would be nice to suppose that the lover is so upset by the thought of Nature's delivery of the youth to Time that he cannot go on writing. The inference, however, does not quite accord with the rather severe tone taken in 126.9–12 or with the fact that this is the last of the poems composed for the Master Mistress. The final, pregnant void between the parentheses, if they are Shakespeare's, could conceivably support the verbal context by intimating that the poet is entering upon a course of gradual detachment or of falling out of love. The parenthetical message might then be translated, "the rest is silence."

The drift under way since Sonnet 100—that is, throughout the third and closing section of Part I—has been toward that silence. It is a trend that, while proceeding unevenly, by fits and starts, entails a moderating of passion on the part of the lover and, concomitantly, a lessening of his interest in sonneteering. The principal incidents of the section may be summed up as follows: the poet's admission of having neglected to present love lyrics (Sonnets 100–103); his two confessed lapses into sexual infidelity; his elimination of the themes of poetic immortalization after Sonnet 107; his more self-defensive and relatively more self-regarding attitudes in Sonnets 121 to 125; and his unprotesting relegation of the "lovely boy" to Time's relentlessness in Sonnet 126, with which the sonnets to and for him come to a halt. Unless the various actions and reactions of the persona, his omissions and commissions, are closely examined in their sequentiality and interrelationship, the full design and effect cannot be apprehended. Those who start with the assumption, or even the

suspicion, that the arrangement of the sonnets in the Quarto is de-
fective forfeit in advance that apprehension.

In the Quarto, Sonnet 126 is not the last poem, since the twenty-
eight sonnets of Part II, 127–54, ensue. But I have argued that Sonnet 126 is *chronologically* last and that the affair with the mistress,
which was brief, occurred concurrently with Sonnets 40–42.[7] I cannot conceive of a better arrangement than that of Q, which presents
the second sequence as intact and separate, even at the price of
chronological dislocation.

My position is not modified but complemented by new glimmer-
ings of a further relationship between Parts I and II. We can ascertain
very little about those with whom the lover had the sexual liaisons
confessed in Sonnets 109–12 and 117–20. However, the "limbecks
foul as hell within" at 119.2 do suggest female partners, as might
also the word "nothing" (as 'pudenda') at 109.12. It would be under-
standable that the heterosexual impulses of the bisexual protagonist, after what seems to be lengthy dormancy, might begin to
reassert themselves. That would help account for the waning of his
impassioned preoccupation with the Master Mistress. The lover
may well be ripe for another amour with a woman—for a repetition
of the kind of lustful intrigue he formerly enjoyed with a lady outwardly and inwardly "black." If so, Part II would not only treat in
flashback of an actual past experience but would also preview the
type of experience that the end of Part I suggests he is ready to venture upon once again. In that case, the placement of Sonnets 127–54
in the Quarto would add a further dimension to the overall pattern
of the Sonnets and make it yet more cogent and complex. This design is far beyond the capacities of a Thorpe and calls, along with
everything else organizational, for recognition as Shakespeare's.

10

Arrangement and the
Poetic Genre

The old question of the Quarto's disposition of the Sonnets has finally to be settled. The commentary is of many minds on the
subject, published opinion running the following gamut: the poems
are in hopeless disarray, their original order irrecoverably lost; the
authorial order, however much disturbed in Q, not only can be recovered but has been, in fact, by the scholarly rearranger of the moment; some of the poems may be out of place, but there is no
feasible alternative to the received order; this order on the whole
seems passable and is likely to be the writer's. The last position, not
widely taken, is the closest to my own. Only I argue that the position can be verified, and I proceed by discovering previously un-
detected modes of integration, organizational principles, and other
aspects of the grand design and then utilizing these discoveries to
demonstrate that the arrangement of the Sonnets in Q is so intelligible, coherent, and aesthetically satisfying as to be indubitably and
conclusively that of Shakespeare himself.

This thesis, which has already received extensive if intermittent
support in these pages, will find further corroboration in this final
chapter. Evidence will be drawn from two separate sources, the first
of which is textual. I will recapitulate the evidence I have already
drawn from the text and add some more. The second source is
largely extratextual and consists of the Renaissance love-sonnet sequence as a poetic genre. Questions to be considered are the extent
to which other cycles are unified and whether they are more or less
highly structured than Shakespeare's. This inquiry into genre will
lead, as a matter of course, into a related subject: whether the
thought, attitudes, and experiences of the Shakespearean persona
may or may not be construed as Shakespeare's own.

I

The one hundred twenty-six poems of Part I of the sequence fall, as I
have said, into three subdivisions, as follows:

1. The "beginning" comprises the first nineteen sonnets (some 15

percent of the total number), in which the persona, while urging the youth to preserve his rare beauty by propagation, falls in love with him, and, as a result, the means for immortalizing the youth changes, in the last five sonnets, from "breed" to verse. This section was surveyed in full in chapter 2.

2. The "middle" comprises the next eighty sonnets (approximately 63 percent of the total), beginning with Sonnet 20, in which the poet reveals his erotic passion for the Master Mistress, and ending with Sonnet 99, the only poem of fifteen lines, an anomaly that serves to mark the terminus of this section. The passion, which finds fruition in sexual acts, can be affected by changing moods and circumstances, but it remains full-fledged. I have discussed this section, necessarily in a more selective and fragmentary way than the other two, in chapters 3, 4, and 6, in much of 5, and in the latter part of 8.

3. The "end" comprises the last twenty-seven sonnets (some 21 percent), those numbered 100 through 126, with the final poem consisting of six couplets and so, again, anomalous. This section, which delineates the ebbing of the passion, was surveyed in chapter 9.

The twenty-eight sonnets of Part II extend from a brief "beginning" in Sonnets 127–28 to a close in 153(4), and here the terminal anomaly is stylistic rather than formal. The structure is for the most part based on and determined by the cyclic character of the protagonist's lust for the "dark" mistress. This second part, which is less than a quarter the length of the first, I considered principally in chapters 7 and 8. In the latter part of chapter 8 I explored the chief contrasts—thematic, emotional, attitudinal, organizational, and durational—between Parts I and II, while in chapter 7 I examined their episodal and chronological intersections.

Each of the four sections—three in Part I, one in Part II—into which I have divided the Sonnets has proved to have its component poems intelligibly arranged, and the sections have proved, moreover, to be coordinated with one another.

The numerous sonnets that have to do with jealousy, which appear in the second and third sections of Part I and again in Part II, cohere impressively, as I showed in chapters 5 and 6. The disposition of these sonnets makes sound psychological sense in terms of Freud's exposition of the mechanism of jealousy, and it makes aesthetic sense when the final sonnet about infidelity, where it is the poet's, harks back to the first episode that deals with infidelity, where it is the youth's. It makes sense in other ways as well; for example, the jealousy toward the friend occurs only in the "middle" phase, not in the final one, when passion declines and the formerly jealous lover is himself the one who strays.

As compared with the sonnets devoted to jealousy, those collectively devoted to another major theme exhibit an arrangement that differs in principle and effect but is no less remarkable. I refer to the sonnets about versifying the friend into immortality. The first of these is Sonnet 15, the last is 107. There are some fifteen of them, and they occur in all three subdivisions of Part I, where they compose a strikingly symmetrical pattern. They tend to be clustered together: the first five, Sonnets 15–19, are successive and come at the end of the opening movement (1–19); the next five, more loosely grouped, are Sonnets 54, 55, 60, 63, and 65, and they come at the center of the central movement (20–99); and the last four—Sonnets 100, 101, 104, and 107—come at the beginning of the closing movement (100–126). Another treatment of this subject, Sonnet 81, stands in relative isolation, nearly midway between the second cluster and the third, the sixteenth sonnet after 65 and the nineteenth before 100. An additional sonnet that might be included in this category is Sonnet 38. It may not quite promise the friend immortality; but in praising him as the "sweet argument" that alone yields worth to the poetry and praising him, too, for "thyself" giving "invention light," it appoints him to be "the tenth Muse," superior to the "old nine," and it goes on to say: "he that calls on thee, let him bring forth / Eternal numbers to outlive long date." Here it is the friend who makes the verses eternal rather than the other way around, and he will do so by being their eternalized "argument." In the arrangement of Part I, Sonnet 38 balances 81, holding an exactly corresponding position, in relative isolation from the other clusters and standing nearly midway between the first and second of them: *it is the sixteenth sonnet before 54 and the nineteenth after 19*. And there is yet more to ponder for those who are skeptical about Thorpe's ordering. In the division of Part I—a division originally perceived by me on wholly other grounds—Sonnets 54–65 appear in the middle of the second section (20–99), which has thirty-four sonnets before 54 and another thirty-four after 65. Again, the first sonnet on the topic is Sonnet 15, and the last, Sonnet 107, is the nineteenth from the end of Part I, while another, Sonnet 63, appears at the center (1/2 × 126). If, more strictly, Sonnets 63 and 64 share the midpoint, it does not much matter; for 64 proceeds, through lines 1–12, as if it were on the same topic as the sonnets adjacent and akin to it. But the couplet of Sonnet 64 surprises; for instead of alluding to "black lines" (63.13) or "black ink" (65.14), it expresses the poet's

strong emotions, of shock and sorrow, on contemplating the loss of
the youth to Time, and these are the very emotions that give rise to
the treatments of the theme of eternalizing rhyme.

The sonnets on that theme are italicized in the following outline
of the design that is described above:

First movement (1–19)	{	(Fourteen sonnets, 1–14)
		First cluster: 15, 16, 17, 18, 19 (five)
Second movement (20–99)	{	(Eighteen sonnets, 20–37) ⎫
		Sonnet 38 ⎬ (34 sonnets)
		(Fifteen sonnets, 39–53) ⎭
		Central cluster: 54, 55, 60, 63, 65 (five)
		(Fifteen sonnets, 66–80) ⎫
		Sonnet 81 ⎬ (34 sonnets)
		(Eighteen sonnets, 82–99) ⎭
Third movement (100–126)	{	*Third cluster: 100, 101, 104, 107* (four)
		(Nineteen sonnets, 108–26)

Even apart from the segmentation into the three movements, the
arrangement of the sonnets on immortalization through verse exhibits a clear-cut symmetry, apparent if one simply counts back and
forward from the central cluster. This is a symmetry that those who
disparage the Quarto's arrangement have failed to catch.

There is a wealth of internal textual evidence to show that the
Sonnets themselves insist on their own integration and, throughout,
provide detail that bespeaks their incorporation into a holistic literary work. This proposition is so amply substantiated by the data
that I have assembled and reviewed in this book that I feel justified
in claiming that the case has been made that the Quarto's organization is in fact Shakespeare's own.

It is a claim that runs counter to the currents of scholarly opinion.
"The traditional order" of the Sonnets, "that of the first edition," to
repeat Hubler's dogmatic pronouncement, "is highly imperfect, as
everyone knows."[1] This statement simply assumes that the question has long been settled by the authoritative opinion of "experts"
and, implicitly, that the burden of proof now devolves on the misguided defenders of the first edition. Those who do attempt to rationalize their skepticism about the Quarto (though the reasons
they advance are never sufficient or persuasive) may do so, as Brents
Sterling and J. W. Lever do, to justify their rearrangement of the
Sonnets. In Lever's judgment, "Thorpe's quarto was of the order of
'stolen and surreptitious copies,' neither supervised nor approved by
Shakespeare," and he does devote a page or so to arguing that they
are in disarray.[2] The arguments are all answerable, and virtually all

of them have been countered in the course of this study, as any reader who cares to take the trouble may verify for himself. Having upheld his view, Lever feels free to reshuffle the poems as he sees fit.

Hubler's "everybody" is, however, an exaggeration, for some expositors do accept the Q arrangement. A. L. Rowse does so because he sees the work as a historical document, a faithful record of Shakespeare's friendship with the earl of Southampton and his affair with one Emilia Lenier, née Bessano.[3] A number of others are willing, with varying degrees of confidence, to go along with the "traditional order" simply in lieu of anything better. They reject rearrangement for the unsatisfactory game that it is, a kind of solitaire in which each player makes up his own rules and none accedes to those of another. The trouble with their position is that it relegates to the limbo of conjecture a question that not only is of central and crucial importance but admits of a validated and definitive answer.[4] The lack of such an answer has tended, on the one hand, to inhibit serious study of the Sonnets as a unified sequence, while, on the other hand, the answer cannot be authenticated unless such a study is undertaken. I hope finally to have broken that vicious circle.

2

Having used textual analysis to demonstrate that the Sonnets in Q are unimpeachably ordered, I shall now approach the issue from another angle, that of genre, and shall do so by inquiring into the nature of Ranaissance, and particularly Elizabethan, love-sonnet sequences. One of my aims will be to find out whether there are any norms by which the arrangement of the component poems can be judged.

David Kalstone remarks that

> the term "sonnet sequence" is as bedeviling as the designation "novel". . . . Renaissance sonneteers did not know their collections as "sequences," and the word must apply to the very different achievements of Sidney, Shakespeare, and Spenser. So, rather than giving a clue to the poet's intention, "sonnet sequence" depends for its definition upon the practice of individual poets, upon the advantages poets may find in setting sonnets in tandem.[5]

The achievements of the three foremost practitioners of love-sonnet sequences in English certainly do exhibit pronounced differences. Sidney depicts a course of erotic experience that leads to catastrophe for Astrophel, whose loss of Stella, because of her chastity, leaves him bitterly disappointed and woebegone. Spenser's *Amoretti*, by contrast, depicts a course of love that might be deemed comic, for the lover proceeds, through courtship and betrothal, to the marriage with his lady, Elizabeth, that is celebrated in *Epithalamion*. Shakespeare's Sonnets are manifestly and manifoldly different from the other two sequences: the poet has not one but "two loves," male and female; chastity is not an issue, nor is marriage (at least in the ordinary sense, though he does at times conceive of the connection with the youth in marital terms); in neither of the two parts does the course of passion take a comic or a tragic turn, for the persona's love in Part I follows a curve of growth, maturity, and decline and, in Part II, his lust follows a psychological pattern of circularity; if the demise of his love for the youth and the attenuation of his desire for the mistress are foreshadowed at the close of Parts I and II, respectively, he does not lament these outcomes but appears to determine them himself; and he, in contrast to Astrophel and the *Amoretti* persona, actually engages in sexual relations, and with the idolized male beloved as well as with the contemned but seductive paramour. Further variations might be enumerated even in these three sonnet sequences, and they would be vastly multiplied by bringing other Renaissance cycles, both English and Continental, into consideration. Undeniably, the sonneteers realize different intentions in their sequences; even so, it is possible to discern certain features that they have in common.

The *sonnet sequence* as a Renaissance genre may be described as follows: it is a work in verse, composed, usually, of autonomous fourteen-line poems that collectively render, in a form lyrical rather than narrative, and often lyrically dramatic, a prolonged experience of love on the part of the poet-persona, whose successive reactions to a beloved are disclosed solely from his point of view; the primary function of the beloved, who is never directly or independently characterized and so remains rather shadowy, is to elicit erotic responses. Beyond this, generalization hardly dares venture, though some of the definitive elements may be further elucidated.

The poems that the Elizabethans called *sonnets* on account of both their amorous subject and their versification can vary as to rhyme scheme, Spenser employing the Spenserian, which he devised, Shakespeare the English or Shakespearean, which Surrey devised, and Sidney a number of schemes, but mostly the Italian or Petrarchan, which was modified, after Wyatt, with a final couplet. The component sonnets are ordinarily autonomous, each having its own beginning, middle, and end, so that the sequence is a whole made up of wholes in their own right. This peculiar feature of the genre not only presents the sonneteer with the problem of unifying unities but invites anthologists to select favorite lyrics and ignore the rest and tempts Shakespearean critics either to rearrange the Sonnets or else to suspect the validity of the given arrangement. The lyric discourse can take diverse forms: it may be epistolary (Shakespeare's Sonnet 26) or verse calling attention to itself as such (Sonnet 55); it may be an address to the beloved, which can be either written or spoken (it is impossible to distinguish between these modes in the majority of Shakespeare's sonnets), or an address to someone other than the beloved (this is virtually nonexistent in Shakespeare, unless the couplet of Sonnet 125 qualifies); it may address a personification (e.g., the apostrophe to Time in Sonnet 19) or an unspecified audience or the reader directly (as, at least apart from context, in Sonnets 116 and 121); finally, it may take the form of a soliloquy (Sonnets 56, 129, 144).

The poems constituting a Renaissance cycle are never organically synthesized in the manner of the incidents of a complete and unified plot—never, that is, according to Aristotle's criterion, by which probability or necessity so conjoin them as to preclude the removal or transposition of any one of them. Whatever there is in the way of plot is more implicit than explicit; it is fragmented and is of subordinate interest to the sonneteer's perceptions and emotions. Sonnet sequences cannot be classed as narratives. They take on dramatic coloration insofar as they can be conceived of as scenes from a romance, but even that must be heavily qualified; for the romance may be a one-sided entanglement, and the scenes, which may present but one character, whose utterance may be written rather than spoken, are commonly disjunctive. Often a major event occurs in the silent interval between two sonnets and must be inferred from the second. The amorous experience may be of indefinite or of some fixed duration, may remain static or undergo distinguishable stages, and may or may not come to some resolution. Even when a story line can be abstracted, it is, as such, fairly uninteresting and uneventful. The writers of *Tales from Shakespeare* may recount the plots of his dramas or even those of his narrative poems, but they would never include the Sonnets.

It is generally agreed that *Astrophel and Stella* is plotted to an unusual degree, being, in the judgment of Ringler, "more dramatic and highly ordered than any other [sequence] in the renaissance."[6] That impression is due in no small measure to the eleven interspersed "songs," for these, as Kalstone remarks, "carry a heavy narrative burden," with the result that this work "comes closer than most groups of sonnets to telling a story."[7] Nevertheless, Ringler makes the observation that "some of the sonnets could with more appropriateness occupy different positions."[8] Even in Sidney's special case, then, the underlying plan is not found to come through as inexorable. The two major divisions of *Amoretti* (the first, comprising the sonnets through 60 or 61 and dealing with courtship; the second, from 61 on, dealing with betrothal—the lovers becoming betrothed between 62 and 63) are so loosely organized, though by the author, that a considerable amount of transposition might be tolerated with relatively little disturbance to the overall effect. And that is true of most Renaissance sequences. If "everybody knows" that the "traditional order" of Shakespeare's Sonnets is "highly imperfect," then everybody ought to have in mind a perfect order by which to gauge the imperfections. Nobody does, and standards of judgment will be looked for in the commentary in vain.

Lever sees the genre as both "heavily indebted to convention" and "the most personal of poetic forms."[9] While the love-sonnet sequence accommodates such diversity and flexibility as to allow each practitioner to reinvent in it his own way, certain conventions can be deduced. These may multiply where adherence to the Petrarchan stance is more strict, but the essential literary conventions are few. The main one is the sonnet itself as the formal unit of expression; others include the invariable viewpoint, that of the textual "I," his amorous preoccupation with another, and the role of the other as mover and object of the poet's passions. That other need not be female and is not in many of Michelangelo's poems or in Richard Barnfield's *Certain Sonnets*, to cite instances aside from Shakespeare. The "personal" aspect is to be viewed not as distinct from the conventional but, rather, as another convention of the "poetic form."

If a Renaissance poet was in love and felt impelled to express his feelings imaginatively, the sonnet sequence not only was accessible but was the obvious genre for him to adopt, since it was better suited to his purpose than any other that was available to him. Apropos of *Astrophel and Stella*, Kalstone remarks that "while Sidney can point up inadequacies in the Petrarchan mode, he has no private mode to substitute for it."[10] "But the experience of love and the writing of love poetry do not necessarily have any direct connection," Northrop Frye writes, since "one is experience and the other craftsmanship."[11] "Necessarily" is evasive, but in any case the connection between the poet's experience and his craftsmanship in the Renaissance sequence cannot be so simply dissevered. The one may be transparent to or through the other, and Lever's sense of Part II of Shakespeare's Sonnets strikes me as just: "No ordinarily sensitive reader can doubt that these sonnets have roots in real and painful experience."[12] As Ringler points out with regard to Sidney, he "took considerable pains" in *Astrophel and Stella* "to indicate that the . . . poems were based upon personal experience," that of his passion for Lady Penelope Rich.[13] These pains include his quibbles on "Rich" and on his own name of *Phil*ip with Astro*phil*—the alternative spelling that Ringler adopts in his edition. Spenser in the seventy-fourth of the *Amoretti* identifies his lady as Elizabeth and as one of three important Elizabeths in his life—Boyle, Spenser, and Tudor, his fiancée, mother, and sovereign. In the *Rime* Petrarch never tires of wordplay on the name Laura. The *Vita Nuova* records Dante's love for Beatrice. Ronsard names himself in his best-known poem, "Quand vous serez bien vieille . . . ," one of the *Sonnets pour Hélène*, who was the historical Hélène de Surgères. When these sonneteers name themselves, the beloved, or both, they not only signify an autobiographical factor inherent in and common to their works; they call attention to it. Shakespeare does likewise.

As Sidney has a "-phil," so William Shakespeare has, as a namesake-persona in Sonnets 57, 135, and 136, a "Will," the familiar form that would be used by intimates, certainly by a close friend or a mistress. The device serves to associate and even to equate the author with the "I" who bears both his nickname and his authorial function. Which one says, at the close of Sonnet 136, "my name is *Will*"? With this clause the distance between the two seems virtually to vanish. Spenser has his three Elizabeths, and the dark lady has her three Wills in Sonnet 135: the poet, her husband, and the youth. The latter ("Mr. W. H." of Thorpe's dedication?) is denominated "Will" again at 143.13. Though all three of Spenser's Elizabeths are historically identifiable, only one Will is—Shakespeare; but that is no reason to deny the historicity of the other two or that of the anonymous mistress. An aesthetic response that is disregardful of the author when he deliberately introduces himself and his acquaintance into the text, and when, moreover, its organization can to some extent be accounted for by the course of his own erotic experience, would seem to me arbitrary and willfully constrictive.

These observations on genre—that of the Renaissance love-sonnet sequences, with the Elizabethan cycles being stressed because of their more immediate relevance to Shakespeare's work—furnish a basis for handling some of the questions often raised about the Sonnets, such as whether or not they treat of Renaissance friendship, whether or not persons other than the friend are addressed in Part I, and whether or not the author recreates experiences of his personal life.

What I have been calling a love-sonnet sequence might more aptly be termed an erotic-love-sonnet sequence, for amorous desire is the uniform and principal attribute of the poet-lover, and the Shakespearean persona is no exception to the rule, however exceptional he may be in depicting his passion as indulged rather than frustrated. The province of this literary form is, then, sexuality (even if it is restricted to yearning, as of course it is not in either division of the Sonnets), including "Renaissance" homosexuality. Hence its province is not the nonsexual "Renaissance friendship" presupposed by a long line of regnant expositors. Although I refuted their position earlier, I recall it here in order to bring the genre and its conventions to witness against it.

In discussions of the derangement of the Quarto, the following observations often appear: that a male is referred to in those sonnets of Part I where the gender of the beloved is discernible, but these are few in number; that most, with second-person address, give no express indication of gender; and that whenever the language in Part II reveals the gender of the sexual partner, it is feminine. Well and good, when the proper corollaries are drawn: that Sonnets 1–126 concern the poet's love for a particular man, while Sonnets 127–54 concern his affair with a particular woman. Often enough, however, other conjectures are entertained with respect to Part I: that its sonnets may be intended for different men, not just one, or that, where gender is not specified, the recipient may in some instances be a woman—the mistress or another. These conjectures cannot be absolutely disproved, any more than the supposition that certain of the *Amoretti*—for example, where second-person discourse is employed—are possibly amorous addresses to some unknown man or that Petrarch here and there might have an unspecified lady other than Laura in mind. Such suggestions would be patently absurd, of course, but hardly more so than that certain poems in Shakespeare's Part I are directed to anyone else than the friend. Never does or can the sonneteer stipulate the sex of the beloved in every lyric, nor would it have occurred to him to do so, for he could not have anticipated such a finical expectation. It is true that Shakespeare has peculiarly created a bipartite sequence, but the parts are carefully demarcated, and neither should be confused with the other. Hardly any sonnet to the mistress could have been written to the youth, and hardly any to him could have been written to her, for the themes, attitudes, and emotions presented in the two parts are kept sharply distinct. By a rule—one of the few of the genre—the poet-lover keeps his attention fixed on the beloved, and if, occasionally, he directs his words to another, he gives clear indications that he is doing so. The idea that he might secretly insert amatory lyrics to an undesignated second individual is outlandish; it is without precedent in other cycles and would, if applied to them, introduce only chaos.

It may safely be said that a vast majority of readers, no matter how variously they otherwise construe the Sonnets, have regarded both those to the young man and those to the dark lady as vehicles of the author's experiences of love and lust—as "the eloquence" of Shakespeare's own "speaking breast" (23.9–10). That he did what Astrophel's muse counseled—looked into his heart and wrote—is a conviction they share, and share with Wordsworth, who, in "Scorn Not the Sonnet" says, "with this key / Shakespeare unlocked his heart." Wordsworth clearly viewed the lyric form as not only congenial but essential to self-revelation and even to self-knowledge. On "the biographical or autobiographical question" Denis Donoghue has remarked, "I wouldn't mind excluding the question if I knew what I was excluding."[14] One of the things excluded is a prominent convention of the Renaissance sequences, which encouraged the translation of the poet's love experiences into art.

The Sonnets produce a paradoxical impression. On the one hand, as I have amply demonstrated, they can be perceived, by criteria both formal and psychological, as highly organized. On the other hand, one's impression, as one reads along, is that the successions of feelings within the poet—the prime subject matter—follow, rather than a preconceived plan, the unpredictable course of passionate love or lustful passion. This course is rendered with a remarkable comprehensiveness, embracing joys, desires, revulsions, hurts, suspicions, jealousies, contentment, hopes, fears, depression, elation, tenderness, devotion, enthrallment by beauty, self-doubts, anger, recriminations, disgust, conflicts, reconciliations, courtings, yearnings in absence, generosities, selfishness, dependence, dread of rejection, offenses, remorse, shame, obsession, dreams of the beloved, sleeplessness, aggression, idealizations, contempt, disappointments, confessions, and concealments. The intimacies in the Sonnets are explored in greater range and depth than can be managed in the plays, on account of the plot demands made on the latter in relation to their length, and this exploration exhibits a psychological realism that I believe is unexampled in earlier poetry and perhaps unexcelled in later.

If the Sonnets create the dual impression of a rich flow of spontaneous feeling and thought *and* of imaginative design, the effect may well derive from Shakespeare's rendering of his own life-experiences under the shaping power of art. His artistic shaping need not distort or obscure the contours of the experiential love and lust that might lie behind the work. That he is very likely to have personally known love in the stages of becoming, being, and subsiding depicted in Part I and to have known lust in the compulsive and repetitive cycles reproduced in Part II is a hypothesis supported by textual evidence, genre convention, and the sense of readers.

Shakespeare admits nothing into the Sonnets that is not germane to the topic, but he does scant some vital information and withholds some major occurrences from explicit treatment. Both procedures have precedents in other Renaissance sequences, where they produce the same effect as in Shakespeare's: they let us know that the amorous experiences included are not exhaustive but partial and selective. The Shakespearean persona takes several journeys, but we are informed of neither their destination nor their purpose. Undisclosed business, independent of his affectionate attachment, draws him away, and so there are facets of his life, a career of some kind, about which nothing is said, and we learn only of his impassioned reactions to the distant youth. Sonnet 111 makes reference to "my life" as cursed by "public means which public manners breeds." Annotators who find the author here alluding to his theatrical profession introduce biographical information that lies outside the scope of the text; within it "public means" is an obscure detail.[15] Gaps in the action include the following: the departure of the rival poet (between Sonnets 86 and 87), the first instance of copulation with the mistress (between Sonnets 128 and 129), the first instance of sexual intimacy with the youth (prior to Sonnet 33), and some reconciliations between the friends (such as the one that occurred between Sonnets 58 and 59). These incidents are silently passed over and must be inferred; even so crucial a matter, which reaches a head in Sonnet 144, as to whether or not the youth and the mistress make love is not expressly resolved. Never does Shakespeare leave out so much, and so much of significance, in a play, where different conventions rule, where the structure of events must realize a predetermined plot, and where the subject dramatized is not drawn from his own experience.

Reasons to suppose that Shakespeare sonnetized his own amorous experiences go beyond the self-references (to "Will") and other features of the genre. What is the likelihood that a writer of strictly heterosexual orientation would choose for the principal subject of his cycle the impassioned liaison of a pair of male lovers? Shakespeare not only does so but, in assigning the poet-lover his own name and authorship, he minimizes the disguise of a fictional mask. Is it conceivable that a Sidney or a Spenser would ever consider homosexual love as a subject? And if, against all odds, either did, would he have been able to achieve the penetrating insight into the dynamics of homoerotic relations that the Sonnets exhibit? The most feasible source of this insight, centuries before it was authenticated by psychoanalytic inquiry, was the author's insight into himself.

Northrop Frye, as might be expected, dissents. For him "the 'homosexual view' of the sonnets disappears at once as soon as we stop reading them as bad allegory." Then does the "heterosexual view" of, say, *Astrophel and Stella* or, for that matter, of Shakespeare's Part II, likewise entail our reading them as "bad allegory"? This is a peculiar use of the term "allegory," and yet, come to think of it, "bad allegory" might well serve to label certain interpretations, Frye's to begin with.

Frye calls Sonnets 1–16 the "prelude," and he titles it "The Awakening of Narcissus." But from what sleep and into what state is the youth in this mythic guise awakened? He is certainly *not* awakened into procreation, the act to which the sonneteer repeatedly calls him. Nor does Frye tell us when or how Narcissus evolves into one who "incarnates divine beauty, and so is a kind of manifestation of Eros."[16] Myths are protean, no doubt, but this conception of Eros cuts sharply against the one that Socrates tells in the *Symposium*, where Eros is the offspring of Poverty and Plenty and seeks the beauty that is lacking in himself. Frye then finds that the poet worships the manifestation of Eros nonerotically. He offers all this as model archetypal criticism as opposed to "bad allegory," a term he reserves for the "homosexual view" of the Sonnets.

"Bad allegory" better describes the "heterosexual view" of Part I. Exegetes who adopt this view are wont to impose gratuitous and fanciful meanings quite at odds with the literal import of the words. That is what I would call bad allegory.

The protagonist whose discourse fills each and every one of the one hundred fifty-four Shakespearean sonnets affords us a wealth of insight into his private self, including insight into his personal morality and religion. His mores significantly deviate from those thought to be generally accepted at the time. He does entertain severe qualms about his heterosexual attachment, which is compulsively, wastefully, and unlovingly lustful. Even so, it is never disapproved on the basis of the scriptural injunction against adultery. Never does he judge his sexually activated passion for the Master Mistress to be sinful. On the contrary, this homoerotic love is the poet's primary commitment and supreme felicity.

The ethical values are heterodox, and so, correspondingly, are the religious attitudes. The sonneteer is much concerned in Part I with transcending the limits of mortality. He proposes procreation and verse as the two modes of doing so, and both serve only to preserve the friend's surpassing and passing beauty in this world. What he does not propose is an otherworldly afterlife for the disembodied soul. Such an afterlife is, in fact, implicitly negated time and again in the poet's conceptions of death, expressed, for example, in the phrase "barren rage of death's eternal cold" at 13.12, or in the clause "when I [i.e., my total self] in earth am rotten" at 81.2, or in Sonnets 71–74 in their entirety. The grave is ultimate for more than the corpse if "My name be buried where my body is" (72.11). To die means to depart "this vile world" but only "with vildest worms to dwell" and to be "compounded . . . with clay" (71.4, 10). The winter, night, and ashes that tacitly stand for death in Sonnet 73 are final, not to be followed by a spring, dawn, or blaze of rebirth. Since the body, the "dregs of life," is made of "earth," its "due" is then the earth, where it will be interred to become "the prey of worms," and it is "too base" a thing to be remembered. But, also in Sonnet 74, a higher, noncorporal element of human nature is posited; this is the "spirit" that is "the better part of me," and it may live on, but under specific conditions: verse alone will serve for the "memorial" that "still [= ever] with thee will stay." The only immortality the poet has in mind here consists of vicarious existence in the mind of the beloved. On the further question of whether or not he might also achieve public immortality through his lyric art, the answers are mixed—"no" at 81.4, "yes" at 107.10–12.

These conceptions of death and its aftermath are not Christian, and neither, to judge by his ethics and beliefs, is the protagonist. Sonnet 146, "Poor soul," need not, when viewed in context, contradict this judgment, as my reading of the poem in chapter 7 demonstrates. Affinities between Sonnet 146 and the set of Sonnets 71–74 are noteworthy: graveworms are alluded to at 71.4, 74.10, and 146.7–8; the body is "earth" at 74.7 and 146.1; the "better part of me" is the "spirit" that will remain with the friend by means of verse in Sonnet 74, while the better part in Sonnet 146 is the "soul" that should quell fleshly lust and should go about its own proper business in this life, such as poetic composition. The conflict is similar to the one faced by the pastoral singer in *Lycidas*: whether "To scorn delights, and live laborious days" in meditation of the muse, the duty of the soul, or "To sport with Amaryllis in the shade, / Or with the tangles of Neaera's hair," where the sport is paralleled in the sonnet by the carnal "hours of dross" spent with the mistress at the behest of the body.[17] In the couplet of 146 only the soul can "feed on death," and it would do so with the keen sense of mortal finitude that can prompt its time-redeeming intellectual and imaginative endeavors.[18] Then, once "death" is "dead" (= annihilated) for the defunct individual, the fear and process of "dying" are over and done with for him. The alternative reading of the sonnet—that the soul is to "feed on death" by mortifying the flesh in order to enjoy, after its demise, a sempiternal hereafter—is supported neither by the text (where death is said to "feed on *men*," not merely on their bodies) nor by the broader frames of reference of Part II or of the Sonnets in their totality.

As the views they take of death and homoerotic love indicate, the Sonnets are secularistic. Christian doctrines are brought in, though not as truths of faith but rather as figures of speech. "Hell" is metaphorical in Sonnet 144, standing for the female organ at 144.12 and at 144.5 for a psychological state, as it also does, along with "heaven," at 129.14. And "heaven" at 110.13 refers to the "breast" of the beloved, "a god in love." "God" appears twice: as the friend at 110.12, as Cupid at 58.1. Theological tropes attach to the youth: he is trinitarian in Sonnet 105, a messiah prophetically prefigured in Sonnet 106, and a redeemer whose tears can "ransom all ill deeds" in 34.13–14. With fine discernment Paul Ramsey sees the "analogy to Christian typology" in Sonnet 106, "the doctrine of the Atonement" as relevant to Sonnet 34, and, at 105.12, "the clear reference to the Trinity," which is "a denial of the Trinity in the young man's favor"; Ramsey further states that "this identification of the loved one with the divine . . . takes specifically Christian forms, which is to say anti-Christian forms, since love is a competing religion."[19]

I contend that this competing religion entails—and here Ramsey and I part company—a competing ethics, one that sanctions the passionately homoerotic love for the fair friend that Shakespeare makes his dominant subject. Since by the criteria of neither faith nor morals can the protagonist be thought Christian, might the same judgment then be made of the author?

Shakespeare himself may have been, even though characterizing his persona otherwise, a believing, practicing Christian at the time he wrote the Sonnets, but I regard such a discrepancy as neither likely nor explicable. If, as I have shown, the data furnished both by the Sonnets and by the poetic genre give evidence that the persona's experiences of love and lust are probably those, or close to those, of William Shakespeare, it follows that the intellectual and moral dimensions of those experiences, no less than the sexual and emotional dimensions, should likewise coincide with his own.

Shakespeare's Christianity, I might add, would be extremely difficult to establish on the basis of his writings. Santayana finds

"Shakespeare . . . remarkable among the greater poets for being without a philosophy and without a religion." Of the Sonnets—the only work we have that could possibly be autobiographical and the only one in which the pronoun "I" could refer to the author (and where the "I" is named Will to boot)—Santayana justly observes: "with the *doubtful* exception of [Sonnet 146], they are not Christian."[20]

One way to appraise and appreciate Shakespeare's stunning achievement as a writer of love sonnets in sequence is to consider, with the poetic genre as a criterion, how he now follows, now diverges from, and now transcends the practices of his sonneteering precursors. The conventional aspects include the component lyrics in sonnet form, the single voice, and the treatment of erotic experience, which most likely reflects that of the author, the persona being created in his image and likeness. Shakespeare's innovations include the bipartite division of the cycle, the bisexual protagonist, the ambivalence toward a mistress desired and contemned, the sexual consummation, not only with her but with the Master Mistress, and, finally, the waning of the love for him. The Sonnets transcend other sequences in depth of perception, in the range and complexity of feelings and the sense of experiential authenticity they convey, and in their exemplary arrangement. A secret of their power lies in their remarkable insights into the psychologies of love, lust, jealousy, and homoeroticism and into the bisexual self who is the subject of these and other emotional responses and mental states—insights articulated in the consummate language and art of the greatest poetic genius. Shakespeare's genius is also structural. In creating this masterwork of sonneteering organization, he set, certainly in English, the highest standard for ordering a sequence—a standard that Sidney alone approximates.

Notes

NOTES TO CHAPTER ONE

1. Sonnets 138 and 144 would have survived, for they had been printed ten years earlier in *The Passionate Pilgrim*, by W. Shakespeare (few of the poems in the collection were actually his), published by William Jaggard in 1599, with another edition in 1612.

2. Josephine Waters Bennett defends Benson against the charge of piracy in "Benson's Alleged Piracy of *Shake-speares Sonnets* and of Some of Jonson's Works" (*Studies in Bibliography* 21 [1968]: 235–48). According to her, Benson simply sought to rescue the Sonnets from oblivion, which he did, and to make some money (p. 248).

3. Hyder Rollins, ed., *The Sonnets* (Philadelphia: Lippincott, 1944), 2:39, in *A New Variorum Edition of Shakespeare*, vol. 25. Hereafter this edition will be cited as Rollins, with 1 and 2 used to refer to the first and second volumes of *The Sonnets*, which are also numbered 24 and 25 in the *New Variorum*.

4. The identity of the sonnet personages, while still of primary concern to some expositors, is generally no longer the dominant issue it used to be.

5. Or she did until a well-publicized recent "discovery" by A. L. Rowse, that she was the wife of a Will Lenier, born Emilia Bessano (Rowse, *Shakespeare's Sonnets: The Problems Solved* [New York: Harper and Row, 1973], pp. xxxiv–xliii). The identification has not found wide acceptance.

6. Richard P. Blackmore, introduction to *The Art of the Novel: Critical Prefaces by Henry James* (New York: Scribner's, 1947), p. xix.

7. W. C. Ingram and Theodore Redpath, in "A Note on the Dedication" (pp. 3–5 in their edition of the Sonnets, documented below), provide a judicious and helpful analysis. On the question of whether or not Mr. W. H., regardless of whose initials these may be, is the subject of the poems, much depends on whether the word "begetter" means 'inspirer' or 'procurer' (of the manuscript for "T. T."). If it means 'inspirer' of "these insuing sonnets," he must be the friend; if not, he would have to be the 'procurer' of the copy from which the sonnets were printed. (There is another, but I think negligible, possibility: that Thorpe erroneously thought Mr. W. H. to be the friend.) Ingram and Redpath, by arguing on linguistic grounds—and very convincingly, I think—that "begetter" could not signify 'procurer' in 1609, undercut all surmises based on that definition and establish the strong possibility that W. H. is none other than the youth addressed in Sonnets 1–126.

They refuse, wisely, to speculate on his historical identity; neither do they consider his title. But a nobleman is not addressed as "Mr.," and by 1609 both Southampton (in 1581) and Pembroke (in 1601) had long succeeded to their earldoms. The difficulty has been circumvented in a number of ways—too many to be surveyed here, but surveyed by Rollins (2:166–76)—and often in ways that require "begetter" to mean 'procurer.' I construe the Dedication in its plainest sense: as Thorpe's witness that W. H. is the "onlie" male "begetter" (= 'agent . . . that occasions,' OED 2) of "these insuing sonnets," the one "promised" poetic "eternitie" in them (this could never be said of a procurer), and that he is a "Mr." rather than a lord.

8. *Shakespeare's Sonnets*, ed. W. C. Ingram and Theodore Redpath (1964; rpt., New York: Barnes and Noble, 1968). (This edition will hereafter be referred to by the editors' names, sometimes abbreviated to I/R.)

9. The text of the Quarto that I quote from or consult is that edited by Rollins.

10. E. A. M. Colman,*The Dramatic Use of Bawdy in Shakespeare* (London: Longman, 1974); Eric Partridge, *Shakespeare's Bawdy: A Literary and Psychological Essay and a Comprehensive Glossary* (New York: Dutton, 1969). These books will be cited, respectively, as Coleman (sometimes C) and Partridge (sometimes P).

NOTES TO CHAPTER TWO

1. The changes made in the text given by Ingram and Redpath are the following. At 1.2, where they have "beauty's rose," I retain the capitalization and italics of the Quarto's "beauties *Rose*." At 1.6 they give "light's flame" (as do all modernized texts that I know of) for Q's "lights flames"; but I take "lights" to be a possessive plural and to = 'eyes' (OED 4). Then the phrase "lights' flame" is equivalent to "bright eyes" in the previous line, and the idea is close to that of "the fire" that "Thine eye darts forth" at line 196 of *Venus and Adonis*. Only rarely from here on will such editorial modification be noted.

2. The phrase "thy sweet self" crops up at 1.8 and 126.4, in the first and last sonnets to the friend—a touch that is surely the product of design rather than chance.

3. Edward Hubler, *The Sense of Shakespeare's Sonnets* (1952; rpt., New York: Hill and Wang, 1962), pp. 68–69.

4. Stephen Booth annotates 8.11 as follows: "This trio suggests the paradox of the Holy Trinity and multiplies our sense of paradox by also and simultaneously suggesting the Holy Family—Jesus, his mother Mary, and his foster father Joseph." Jesus, Mary, and Joseph! The Trinity is a mystery, which is very different from a paradox. For more of the same see the note on 7.5 in his edition, "with analytic commentary," of *Shakespeare's Sonnets* (New Haven and London: Yale University Press, 1977), pp. 146, 143 (hereafter cited as Booth).

5. Spenser's composite sequence—or so I regard *Amoretti-Epithalamion*—moves toward, and ends with, the subject of propagation that Shakespeare's Sonnets begin with and move away from.

6. *Spenser's Minor Poems*, ed. Ernest de Sélincourt (Oxford: Clarendon Press, 1910), p. 433. Spenser will be quoted from this edition.

7. "Pupil" in the phrase "my pupil pen" is usually taken to mean 'inexperienced,' and it may; but the adjective may rather mean 'studious'—of the subject you. An essential meaning of "this time's pencil" is something like 'the brush of the present-day artist.'

8. Ingram and Redpath list ten separate meanings attributed to "lines of life" by nine interpreters, with William Empson adopting eight of them in his explication of the phrase (see his reading of Sonnet 16 in chapter 2 of *Seven Types of Ambiguity*). Booth goes over much of the same ground but, typically, makes no semantic discriminations (preface, p. xiii). I/R do, assigning "highest priority" to 'children (as "living pictures")' and 'lineage, descendants,' and an order of "lower priority" to three additional senses (pp. 38–39). But the sense of the phrase that I take to be primary does not appear in their list.

9. Under the entry "garden," John S. Farmer and W. E. Henley give the following: '(venery) the female pudendum,' and cite Sonnet 16. See their *Slang and Its Analogues, Past and Present* (7 vols., 1890–1904; rpt., New York: Kraus Reprint Corporation, 1965). Eric Partridge gives that definition too, dating the usage from the sixteenth to the present century, in *The Macmillan Dictionary of Historical Slang* (New York: Macmillan, 1974). According to Freud, "*gardens* are common symbols of the female genitals" in dreams ("Symbolism in Dreams," *Introductory Lectures on Psychoanalysis*, in *The Standard Edition of the Complete Psychological Works*, ed. James Strachey [London: Hogarth Press, 1965], 15:158). (The *Standard Edition* of Freud's *Works* will hereafter be cited as *SE*.)

10. Among the enclosed hollow spaces that represent the female genitals in dreams are *rooms* and *bottles*, and this psychoanalytic observation coincides with the conceit of 5.9–6.4, where "walls of glass" that contain the "liquid" of "summer's distillation" become "some vial" and "some place," that is, 'a womb' as repository of sperm. Freud remarks, "There is scarcely one of the symbolic representations of the male genitals [and surely of the female too] which does not recur in 'joking' and in 'vulgar or poetic usage' " (*Introductory Lectures, SE*, 15:156, 163).

11. Shakespeare is not the first sonneteer to introduce this subject into an English cycle if Sidney's Tenth Song is composed of the erotic fantasies of a frustrated, rejected Astrophel and culminates in his solitary orgasm. That implication in the last stanza is made clearer in a version of the stanza given by Max Putzel in his edition of *Astrophel and Stella* (Garden City, N.Y.: Anchor Books, 1967), p. 201.

12. *Shakespeare's Sonnets: The Problems Solved* (New York: Harper and Row, 1973), p. xlv.

13. Onan's sin is coitus interruptus, but the OED defines onanism only as 'self-abuse, masturbation,' with the earliest use recorded as mid-eighteenth century.

14. Plato, *Symposium* 204d–205d, from the third edition of the Jowett translation (New York: Modern Library, 1928), pp. 371–73.

15. Baldassare Castiglione, *The Courtier* (the Hoby translation, 1561), in *Three Renaissance Classics,* ed. Burton A. Milligan (New York: Scribner's, 1953), p. 592. For the Renaissance psychology of love, see also Clay Hunt, *Donne's Poetry* (New Haven: Yale University Press, 1954), pp. 62–63.

16. *The Poems of Sir Philip Sidney,* ed. William A. Ringler, Jr. (Oxford: Clarendon Press, 1962), pp. 165–66. Sidney will be cited from this edition.

17. The poet's increasing attachment to his friend has not quite been lost on some few expositors. Brief observations on the matter can be found in the introductions to their editions of the Sonnets by Tucker Brooke (New York: Oxford University Press, 1936), pp. 34–35, and Martin Seymour-Smith (London: Heinemann, 1963), pp. 45–46, as also in Kenneth Muir, *Shakespeare's Sonnets* (London: Allen and Unwin, 1979), pp. 45–46, and Northrop Frye, "How True a Twain," in *Fables of Identity* (New York: Harcourt Brace and World, 1963), p. 97. Anton M. Pinkhofer notes the "absence of 'I' from Sonnets 1–9," in "The Dramatic Character of Shakespeare's Sonnets," *New Essays on Shakespeare's Sonnets,* ed. Hilton Landry (New York: AMS Press, 1976), p. 121.

18. I do not mean to imply that the sonneteer ascends Plato's ladder of love. He hovers always about the lowest rungs, those where physical beauty attracts. He may even be said to descend, in Sonnet 1, from a concern with fair creatures in general to a concentration on one particular beautiful form. If he becomes aware of a beauty of soul in the friend, he appreciates this "inward worth" along with, and as a result of, appreciating the "outward fair." But those who do make the ascent to absolute Beauty in Plato begin where the sonneteer begins, by responding to the beauty discovered in the body of one youth.

Notes to Chapter Three

1. *The Plays and Poems of William Shakespeare,* ed. Edmond Malone (London, 1821), 20:241. The edition includes "the Corrections and Illustrations of Various Commentators," of whom Steevens is one, and his annotation was published in Malone's edition of 1780. Malone's reply first appeared in his edition of 1790. See Rollins, 1:xi, 55.

2. J. Dover Wilson considers Malone's comment "the final (if almost the earliest) word" on "this much-debated because much misunderstood sonnet" (*The Sonnets* [Cambridge, Eng.: Cambridge University Press, 1966], p. 117; hereafter cited as Wilson). And Rollins writes of Malone: "few have surpassed him as an annotator, and dozens have taken credit for details borrowed from him without acknowledgement" (2:39).

3. Alexander Schmidt, *Shakespeare-Lexicon: A Complete Dictionary of All English Words, Phrases and Constructions in the Works of the Poet* (London and Berlin, 1874–75), 2:842. (Hereafter cited as Schmidt.) His glosses on 20.2 are very much out of the ordinary.

4. T. G. Tucker, ed., *The Sonnets of Shakespeare* (Cambridge, Eng.: Cambridge University Press, 1924), p. 96. (Hereafter cited as Tucker.)

5. C. S. Lewis, *English Literature in the Sixteenth Century* (Oxford: Clarendon Press, 1954), p. 503.

6. Wilson glosses "passion" quite simply: "Almost certainly = love-po-etry." Booth glosses the word as follows: "(1) emotion; (2) love; (3) poem," adding that "poems and speeches that expressed strong feelings were often called passions." That poems were *often* so-called is unsubstantiated. The omission of 'sexual passion' is glaring, for Booth habitually adduces any and every meaning a term might possibly bear, with little concern about con-gruity or textual cohesion. In his preface Booth writes that "an editor . . . who presents only the gloss demanded by the author's clear intent and the ongoing logic of a poem will not be incorrect but incomplete" (p. xii), but when it comes to annotating "passion" at 20.2, he sets aside this principle of editorial completeness.

7. Tucker, p. 97. In the note on "Steals men's eyes" he cites line 1651 of *The Rape of Lucrece*: "That my poor beauty had purloined his eyes." Just what is this parallel supposed to elucidate? True, eyes are stolen by beauty in both instances; but in *Lucrece* the beauty belongs to a woman and the eyes to a man who is aroused by it to a pitch of sensual desire. Tucker assumes that the linguistic similarity goes along with a semantic contrast. The opposite assumption would appear more logical, that both expressions refer to carnal arousal.

8. *Three Essays on the Theory of Sexuality: I. The Sexual Aberrations*, *SE*, 7:144.

NOTES TO CHAPTER FOUR

1. *Shakespeare's Bawdy*, p. 23.

2. *Introductory Lectures on Psycho-analysis*, *SE*, 15:153, 158.

3. *The Interpretation of Dreams*, *SE*, 5:354; *Introductory Lectures*, *SE*, 15:158.

4. "Peace" is probably not a quibble on "piece" in the sense of "a girl (or a woman) regarded sexually" (Partridge), not because it is applied at 75.3 to a man but because, in the plays, the term is "applied pejoratively" (Coleman). However, when the Capulet servant Samson says, " 'tis known I am a pretty piece of flesh" (*Romeo and Juliet*, 1.1.28), the self-reference is nonpejorative and is to a *male* sex object.

5. It may be worth noting that Shakespeare rhymes "treasure" with "pleasure" four times, all in Part I of the Sonnets (at 20, 52, 75, and 126), and, at least in the first three instances (already discussed), the words bring sexual senses into play.

6. Paul Ramsey, *The Fickle Glass: A Study of Shakespeare's Sonnets* (New York: AMS Press, 1979), p. 31.

7. John Wilmot, second earl of Rochester, *Complete Poems*, ed. David M. Vieth (New Haven: Yale University Press, 1968), p. 117.

8. Perhaps only the recipient could know with certainty whether there is bawdy wordplay in the couplet of Sonnet 50. The word "behind" is an ad-verb rather than a noun—and in any case the noun is unrecorded in its anatomical sense before the 1780s. The "groan" is from a horse into whose "hide" a "spur" had been angrily "thrust." The "groan" reminds the poet

not only of his "grief," understandably, but also of his "joy," and that is a noteworthy association, particularly when "my joy" is that got from the beloved. Now "groan" as glossed by Coleman can = 'an orgasmic exclamation, whether of pleasure or pain.' I think 'orgasmic' may be too specific, on the basis of his citations, to the groaning of women during intercourse. But here groaning is connected with pain/pleasure, and on a sexual basis. Then when a "groan" from his mount makes the lover think of "my joy behind," the link is also likely to be sexual, and the link is reinforced two sonnets later, in 52, by the phallic figure of the "key" to "my sweet up-locked treasure."

9. *Shakespeare's Sonnets: The Problems Solved* (New York: Harper and Row, 1973), p. 109.

10. Apropos of 53.14 Rollins remarks, "Many commentators have been struck by the inapplicability of this tribute to the personage addressed in 35, 40–42, and others." It is true that the poet doubts his friend's faithfulness in those and other sonnets, doing so out of habitual jealousy, a subject that I will examine in a later chapter. But that the lover now, at 53.14, as at 20.3–5 and in Sonnet 54, feels confident of the other's fidelity but elsewhere is plagued by jealous fears, in the course of a long-enduring and passionate association, need not be puzzling, and it certainly provides no reasonable basis for positing a second male object of address.

11. The editorial emendation of "by" to "my" alters the sense of 54.14 so that "your truth" is the product only of "verse" distillation and evident only when the young man will have grown old; the implied other means of distillation, erotic and occurring during his period of youth, is eliminated, and that makes for a more "decent" poem.

12. Shakespeare has Enobarbus similarly analogize the activities of eating and lovemaking during his famous encomium of Cleopatra: "other women cloy [satiate] the [sexual] appetites they feed [coitally], but she makes hungry [sexually avid] where most she satisfies" (*Antony and Cleopatra*, 2.2.236–38). Can one suppose that the language of the sonneteer can be so closely allied to that of Enobarbus and yet be devoid of erotic content?

13. Sandor Ferenczi (*Sex in Psycho-Analysis* [New York: Dover, 1956], pp. 232–33) states that in the "work of repression the eyes have proved to be specially adapted to receive the affects displaced from the genital region, on account of their shape and changeable size, their movability, their high value, and their sensitiveness"—and, it might be added from Sonnet 56, on account of their appetitive course of drooping with satiety.

Freud speaks of the "release of the sexual tension" in copulation "and a temporary extinction of the sexual instinct—a satisfaction analogous to the sating of hunger" (*SE*, 7:149). Drowsiness might follow a sexual climax as well as a large meal, and a falling, of penis or eyelids, respectively, follows both.

14. Coleman on "expense of spirit" (129.1): "Pouring-forth of (primarily) vital energy, but with a suggestion of seminal fluid also." See also Patrick Cruttwell, *The Shakespearean Moment* (New York: Random House, 1960), p. 14, and Partridge's entry on "spirit."

The annotations are all based on Sonnet 129, where the "spirit" is expended on a woman, and none cites 56.8, because it is taken for granted that the attachment to the Master Mistress is devoid of sexuality.

15. See Herbert A. Ellis, *Shakespeare's Lusty Punning in "Love's Labor's Lost"* (The Hague: Mouton, 1973), p. 95. (Hereafter cited as Ellis.)

16. The "with" in 56.8 may change somewhat from one to the other reading, in A signifying 'by means of' and in B possibly signifying 'having, as a result' (OED 31), to make the "perpetual dulness" an attribute of the defunct "spirit of love"; the retention of Q's comma after "love" is necessary to preserve this sense.

17. *Three Essays on Sexuality, SE*, 7:209.

18. Ibid., p. 156.

19. "Being in Love and Hypnosis," *SE*, 18:111–12.

20. In his notes on 56.9–12, Rollins quotes, last, J. Q. Adams, whose reading of the passage (in *A Life of William Shakespeare* [Boston, 1923]) is the one I consider valid; but it seems to have had little impact, annotators persisting in positing, untenably, an allusion to Hero and Leander. They did dwell on opposite shores, but otherwise their story bears little resemblance to the situation in the third quatrain.

21. Malone is quoted at the beginning of chapter 3, where see also note 2.

22. Introduction to *Shakespeare's Sonnets*, ed. Douglas Bush (Baltimore: Penguin Books, 1961), pp. 14–15.

23. *The Fickle Glass*, p. 30.

24. *Nicomachean Ethics* 1156b, 1158b, and *passim* in Book 8; *De Amicitia* 5.18, 6.20–21, 8.27–28, and elsewhere.

25. "Of Friendship," *Essayes*, trans. John Florio (London: Dent, 1910), 1:199–200.

26. Objections were raised to this poem, at the time it was written, on the grounds of homosexuality, as we learn from Barnfield himself: "Some there were, that did interpret *The affectionate Shepherd*, otherwise then (in truth) I meant, touching the subject thereof, to wit, the love of a Shepheard to a boy; a fault, the which I will not excuse, because I never made." He does offer the excuse, though, of classical precedent: "Onely this, I will unshaddow my conceit: being nothing else, but an imitation of *Virgill*, in the second Eglogue of *Alexis*" (*Poems 1594–1598*, ed. Edward Arber [Westminster, Eng. 1896], p. 44). Barnfield not only failed to consider Virgil's theme but went on to write "Certaine Sonnets," on the same love of the shepherd for the boy. The defense is curious and perfunctory.

27. Rollins, 1:79.

28. Rollins, 2:233.

29. Edward Hubler, *The Sense of Shakespeare's Sonnets* (1952; rpt., New York: Hill and Wang, 1962), p. 14.

30. Rowse, *The Problems Solved*, p. 89. Useful to each other, patron and client engage in Aristotle's friendship of utility, which in Book 8 of the *Ethics* is the lowest of the three types of friendship he discerns.

31. Wilson, p. li.

32. C. S. Lewis, *English Literature in the Sixteenth Century* (Oxford: Clarendon Press, 1954), p. 505.

33. C. S. Lewis, *The Allegory of Love* (1936; rpt., New York: Oxford University Press, 1958), p. 2.

34. Leslie Fiedler, *The Stranger in Shakespeare* (New York: Stein and Day, 1972), pp. 34–35.

35. There is not much kissing in Petrarchan sequences; usually the lover doesn't get that near the lady, nor is she so compliant. A kiss does, however, play a prominent part in *Astrophel and Stella*—the one he steals from her when she is asleep, in the Second Song.

36. See J. B. Leishman, *Themes and Variations in Shakespeare's Sonnets* (New York: Hillary House, 1963), pp. 62, 75.

37. Hubler, *The Sense*, p. 153.

38. Wilson, pp. xliii, lvii.

39. Ingram and Redpath, p. xi.

40. Booth, pp. 548–49. On the nature of the relations between the persona and the friend, Booth has little to say, and that little is far from definitive, as is evident in his note on 126.4, which is a hazy discussion of the textual use of the word "lover."

41. Booth does now and again consider the bawdy language, but he does so curiously, as his inconclusive ruminations on "all" (to mean male or female genitalia) in the note on 26.1–14 can demonstrate, as can also his explications of "the *con-*, *cun*-jokes" on "female organs" (pp. 526, 548). The prefixes are alleged to have "a potential for suggesting 'vulva' . . . that *Shakespeare was ready to hear in any word containing* con, *or* cun, *or a similar sound*" (p. 231; my italics), and apparently Shakespeare was ready to hear this in the most inappropriate contexts, where female organs are quite remote from the topic, or even where females are remote—56.10, 53.5, 58.3, and 26.7 being cited in this connection. The effect is to undermine serious investigation of the bawdy element in Shakespeare's diction and to throw up a smoke screen to obscure the real signification of that element in the Sonnets.

42. G. Wilson Knight, *The Mutual Flame* (London: Methuen, 1955), pp. 24–25. Knight seems to conflate, on p. 24, Renaissance friendship with Renaissance homosexuality.

43. Lewis, *English Literature in the Sixteenth Century*, p. 503.

44. Kenneth Muir, *Shakespeare's Sonnets* (London: Allen and Unwin, 1979), p. 54; italics added.

45. Ramsey, *The Fickle Glass*, pp. 29–32. Such an "ideal of chastity" in the light of the dark-woman sonnets, 127–54?

46. Fiedler (*The Stranger*, pp. 34–36) makes much of the fact that the diction of courtly love is found in poetry concerned with "a male beloved." That he finds the fact "a little disturbing" foreshadows his conclusion: "The point is that the poet confesses to sleeping with women and considering it filthy, while chastely (but passionately) embracing an ideal male." "Embracing" is ambiguous, but "chastely," even in this charged context, is not. We are also told that the youth is "loved purely." Despite Fiedler's early flourishes, the poet and male beloved turn out not to engage in "physical relations"—as usual.

47. In his edition of the Sonnets (London: Heinemann, 1963), Seymour-Smith held that "on at least one occasion," in Sonnets 33–36, "Shakespeare did have some kind of physical relationship with the Friend" (pp. 34–35, 128–30); but thirteen years later he retreated from that position, holding in a 1976 article that Shakespeare "did 'fall in love with' the Friend" yet "did not experience homosexual emotions or desires" ("Shakespeare's Sonnets 1–42: A Psychological Reading," in Hilton Landry, ed., *New Essays on Shakespeare's Sonnets* [New York: AMS Press, 1976], p. 38).

48. Martin writes that "with Shakespeare one senses the presence" of "sexual desire" but "for temperamental as well as moral reasons its consummation is . . . out of the question" (*Shakespeare's Sonnets: Self, Love and Art* [Cambridge, Eng.: Cambridge University Press, 1972], p. 84.

49. The text cited is in *The Riddle of Shakespeare's Sonnets*, ed. Edward Hubler (New York: Basic Books, 1962), p. 209.

50. W. H. Auden, introduction to *The Sonnets*, ed. William Burto (New York: New American Library, 1964), pp. xxix–xxxiii.

51. Robert Craft, *Stravinsky: Chronicle of a Friendship, 1948–1971* (New York: Knopf, 1972), p. 257.

NOTES TO CHAPTER FIVE

1. *Three Essays on the Theory of Sexuality*, SE, 7:136–37.

2. Ibid., p. 146.

3. "A Special Type of Choice of Object Made by Men," *SE*, 11:165.

4. "Some Neurotic Mechanisms in Jealousy, Paranoia, and Homosexuality," *SE*, 18:230–31.

5. *Three Essays*, *SE*, 7:144–45. The passage from Freud is quoted more fully above, in chapter 3.

6. "On the Sexual Theories of Children," *SE*, 9:215–16.

7. "Some Neurotic Mechanisms," *SE*, 18:230.

8. "On Narcissism: An Introduction," *SE*, 14:88–90, 101.

9. "Some Neurotic Mechanisms," *SE*, 18:230.

10. "The Relique," line 25.

11. "The Canonization," line 24.

12. Lines 45–48, 51–52, 55. Helen Gardner, "on internal evidence" (p. xlvi), questions Donne's authorship; Grierson does not. Donne's verse throughout is quoted from Gardner's editions, here, and usually, from *The Elegies and the Songs and Sonnets* (Oxford: Clarendon Press, 1965).

13. James Winny, too, finds it "nowhere clearly stated . . . that the friend was of noble blood" (*The Master-Mistress: A Study of Shakespeare's Sonnets* [London: Chatto and Windus, 1968], p. 78). Oscar Wilde and Samuel Butler concur. In *The Portrait of Mr. W. H.* Wilde sees the friend as a boy actor named Will Hughes, and Butler thinks him likely to be one William Hughes or Hewes, who was in the Navy, where he ultimately became a cook (Samuel Butler, *Shakespeare's Sonnets Reconsidered* [1899; rept., London: Jonathan Cape, 1927], p. 150). (The surname derives from "*Hews*" at 20.7 in Q, where "hues" is so spelled and capitalized and italicized, and the first name, Will, comes from 135.1–2 and 143.13.) G. Wilson Knight re-

marks, "It is perhaps natural that academic enquirers have tended to read the Sonnets in terms of patronage and advancement," while "creative writers have concentrated rather on art and erotics" (*The Mutual Flame* [London: Methuen, 1955], p. 8).

14. "Some Neurotic Mechanisms," *SE*, 18:230.

15. "On Narcissism," *SE*, 14:87–88; cf. *SE*, 7:145 and 11:100.

16. And the Shakespearean persona presents himself as a father without spousal connection with a woman, and the father-child relationship is descriptive of a homoerotic relationship. If Freudian theory does strictly and validly require an unconsciously maternal identification for all such cases, the persona may transform this *consciously* into a paternal identification more acceptable to his masculine self-image. True, as nurse he allows himself a female role, but nowhere else does he do so. At 93.2 he figures himself as a husband, for example, but in an implicitly male marriage.

17. "A Special Type of Choice of Object," *SE*, 11:165.

18. "On Narcissism," *SE*, 14:87.

19. *Leonardo da Vinci and a Memory of His Childhood, SE*, 11:99.

20. See, for example, Ernest Jones, "The Madonna's Conception through the Ear," *Essays in Applied Psycho-Analysis* (New York: International University Press, 1964), 2:327; Emil A. Gutheil, *The Language of the Dream* (New York: Macmillan, 1939), p. 53.

21. "Some Neurotic Mechanisms," *SE*, 18:231–32. A complete clinical picture of the "new mechanism" could hardly be expected in the Sonnet cycle.

22. Ibid., pp. 230–31.

23. Ibid.

24. Ibid.

25. *Lear*, 4.6.127–31. Lear's mad diatribe stems from an obsession with his daughters' ingratitude, though why he should proceed from that to this horror of pudenda is somewhat problematic.

26. *Three Essays, SE*, 7:144–46, note 1.

27. Ibid.

28. *Leonardo, SE*, 9:99.

29. *Three Essays, SE*, 7:145, note 1.

30. *Leonardo, SE*, 9:101.

31. Jacques Lacan, "Desire and the Interpretation of Desire in *Hamlet*," in Shoshana Felman, ed., *Literature and Psychoanalysis: The Question of Reading: Otherwise* (Baltimore: Johns Hopkins University Press, 1982), p. 11.

32. Wilson, p. xliii.

33. *Three Essays, SE*, 7:161. Freud cautions, on the previous page, against "the use of the word perversion as a term of reproach."

34. J. Laplanche and J.-B. Pontalis, "Perversion," *The Language of Psycho-Analysis*, trans. Donald Nicholson-Smith (New York: Norton, 1973), pp. 306–9.

35. *Three Essays, SE*, 7:138–39.

36. Ernest Jones, *The Life and Work of Sigmund Freud*, edited and

abridged by Lionel Trilling and Steven Marcus (New York: Basic Books, 1961), p. 502.

37. The couplet does offer the reprovers a face-saving out: if "this general evil they maintain," that "All men are bad," that is, totally depraved, then they would indiscriminately disallow goodness to any and every human action, and "rank thoughts" like theirs would truly represent *all* deeds. This closing proviso is tongue-in-cheek.

NOTES TO CHAPTER SIX

1. On "ride," see also Coleman's gloss and the entry in Farmer and Henley, *Slang and Its Analogues* (see Chap. 2, n. 9). That riding regularly represents sexual intercourse in dreams is well known from the Freudians.

2. Hilda M. Hulme writes that "'green' had underlying sexual connotations to an Elizabethan audience" (*Explorations in Shakespeare's Language* [New York: Barnes and Noble, 1963], p. 135). Herbert Ellis, in his entry under "Green (verdant/libidinous)," says, "The association of *green* with love and lovesickness, both chaste and 'luxurious,' has for centuries been commonplace" (*Shakespeare's Lusty Punning in "Love's Labour's Lost"* [The Hague: Mouton, 1973], p. 53). Ellis instances Chaucer's reeve, who, though past his "gras tyme," ascribes to himself "an hoor head and a *greene* tayl, / As hath a leek." Ellis also cites Farmer and Henely; see their entry "*Greens* 'chlorosis,'" where "To have, get, or give one's greens" = 'to enjoy, procure, or confer the sexual favour,' and is 'said indifferently of both sexes.'

3. "Loss" is emended to "cross," always and ever since Malone in the eighteenth century, in order to "normalize" the quatrain, "losse" terminating both 34.10 and 12 in Q. The emendation is unwarranted. "Loss," it seems to me, can be justified on a number of counts: (1) the speaker shows up as distraught in failing to come up with the anticipated rhyme; (2) the symmetry of sounds between the first four words of 34.11 ("The offender's sorrow lends") and the last four of 34.12 ("the strong offence's loss") ought not to be disturbed; (3) a theological oddity results when it is the one offended who bears the cross in 34.12, but it is the offender's tears that do the ransoming of "all ill deeds" in 34.14.

4. Martin Seymour-Smith, *Shakespeare's Sonnets* (London: Heinemann, 1963), pp. 34–35, 129–30.

5. Martin Seymour-Smith, "Shakespeare's Sonnets 1–42: A Psychological Reading," in Hilton Landry, ed., *New Essays on Shakespeare's Sonnets* (New York: AMS Press, 1976), p. 38.

6. One of the ways this departs from the standard reading is in finding no allusion to the mistress in these lines. Ingram and Redpath gloss "my love receivest" as "'you "receive" my mistress'—a masterly understatement." I follow them only insofar as they affirm the erotic import of "receive." When expositors thus take "my love" to indicate 'my mistress' here, their reading is not without a certain plausibility, but they (1) read back into Sonnet 40 information gleaned from Sonnets 41–42, and (2) have no alternative, since they disallow passionate transactions between the two men.

7. J. W. Lever, seeing "the Friend" here as "the ocean itself, with the Rival 'riding' on its 'soundless deep,'" goes on to comment: "For all the apparent dignity of the metaphor [!], it is basically the same as that applied to the Mistress, 'the bay where all men ride.' If she was physically accessible to all, the Friend by his acceptance of flattery was spiritually just as promiscuous" (*The Elizabethan Love Sonnet* [London: Methuen, 1966], p. 230). The very same language that has physical reference when spoken of a woman is supposed automatically to take on spiritual reference when spoken of a man. This is a fine illustration of a habit of mind, already noted, among commentators.

8. "To the Memory of My Beloved Author Mr William Shakespeare: And What He Hath Left Us," line 31. This poem was printed in the First Folio.

9. "Some Neurotic Mechanisms," *SE*, 18:223–25. Later citations from this paper are from these same pages.

10. The reiteration of the couplet is undoubtedly intentional and not a mistake of the printer or author, as is often thought (see Rollins, 1:238). Spenser provided something of a precedent, for he repeated, as LXXXIII of *Amoretti*, an entire sonnet, XXXV—also to fine effect, and also to the puzzlement of expositors.

11. See Martin Waugh, "*Othello*: The Tragedy of Iago," *Psychoanalytic Quarterly* 29 (1950): 202–12; see also Gordon Ross Smith, "Iago the Paranoiac," *American Imago* 14 (1959): 155–67. The former article, the better one, is seminal; and while the textual analysis might be extended and in some details revised, the thesis, that Iago exemplifies Freud's idea of "delusional jealousy," is persuasive.

NOTES TO CHAPTER EIGHT

1. Tucker glosses the noun "blood," at 109.10 and 121.6, as 'sensual passion,' and Partridge does the same, though with citations from the plays.

2. Q has "mad" at the end of line 8, "Made" at the start of line 9. Most editors emend "Made" to "Mad," but the past participle (of "make" in line 8) yields perfectly good sense. Yet Shakespeare did sometimes write "mad" for "made" and vice versa and sometimes punned on the two words (see Helge Kökeritz, *Shakespeare's Pronunciation* [New Haven: Yale University Press, 1953], pp. 126, 164). The pun, then, seemingly homonymic, probably does occur here.

3. Patrick Cruttwell, *The Shakespearean Moment and Its Place in the Poetry of the 17th Century* (New York: Random House, 1960), p. 14. He writes: "'The expense of spirit,' for the modern reader, has only emotional force; it is in fact a piece of contemporary sexual physiology. From the heart to the sexual organs, was believed to go a vein, bearing in it the 'spirit generative.' 'Expense' means 'expenditure': what the phrase refers to is the loss of the 'spirit generative' in the act of sex." See, also, Donne's "First Anniversary," lines 105–10. Clay Hunt, in *Donne's Poetry* (New Haven: Yale University Press, 1954), annotates "rob" in "The Indifferent" as "probably"

alluding to "the Renaissance medical theory that each indulgence in the sexual act shortened a man's life by a day" (pp. 205–6).

4. Richard Levin, "Sonnet CXXIX as a 'Dramatic' Poem," *Shakespeare Quarterly* 16 (1965): 179.

5. Helen Vendler, "Jakobson, Richards, and Shakespeare's Sonnet CXXIX," in *I. A. Richards: Essays in His Honor*, ed. Reuben Brower, Helen Vendler, and John Hollander (New York: Oxford University Press, 1973), p. 193. Vendler's searching critique of the analysis of Sonnet 129 by Roman Jakobson and Lawrence G. Jones, *Shakespeare's Verbal Art in "Th' expense of Spirit"* (The Hague: Mouton, 1970), makes further consideration of their monograph unnecessary.

6. *SE*, 18:111–12, 115.

7. Ibid., p. 112.

8. Andrew Gurr argues persuasively for wordplay on the surname Hathaway at 145.13, "'I hate' from *hate away* she threw" ("Shakespeare's First Poem: Sonnet 145," *Essays in Criticism* 21 [1971]: 221–26). Booth adds that the "And" of 145.14, "And sav'd my life . . . ," may be a pun on Anne. These attractive suggestions carry the further implication of early composition, before Shakespeare's marriage at eighteen to Anne Hathaway, as Gurr points out, and with this he accounts for the flaws he observes: the repetition of "gentle" at 145.7–10 and the "padding" of 145.10–12. The octosyllabic measure would also indicate an imperfect grasp, as yet, of the sonnet form. If Shakespeare did write this poem long before, and for another occasion, the question arises of why and how it came to be inserted in his sequence and, particularly, between Sonnets 144 and 146. It serves an important thematic and structural function in that position, as I have shown, and its removal would drastically alter the relationship of Sonnets 144 and 146. Lines 10–12 may not be felicitious, but they do offer images that tie in with those of Sonnet 144. However inferior as a poetic performance, Sonnet 145 does do the job required of it in its place. As to how it got there, who more feasibly could have put it there than its own author (its authorship being further confirmed by Gurr's discovery), Shakespeare himself, when he later was at work on the Sonnets?

9. "Array" can hardly denote 'attire'; for while the flesh is sometimes said to clothe the soul, the idea of armed forces as a garment for their object of attack would be an awkward, wrenching mixed metaphor.

10. Ingram and Redpath list some ninety-seven possible emendations for the first foot of 146.2, their criteria being "two syllables" and words that make "good sense" in this context and that are "used elsewhere by Shakespeare in the sense required here" (pp. 358–59, 336). Of my suggested emendations, only "Slav'd by" is missing from their list; their own choice is "foil'd by."

11. The pagan belief in the soul's afterlife was well known—by Dante of course, and universally. Shakespeare makes his own awareness of that belief evident in *Antony and Cleopatra* 4.14.50–54; 5.2.279–89.

12. John Crowe Ransom and Elizabeth Drew have voiced the following

impressions of Sonnet 146. Ransom: "I am struck by the fact that the divine terms which the soul buys are not particularly Christian: there are few words in the poem that would directly indicate conventional dogma." Drew: "I would agree that the poem is not essentially Christian. . . ." These remarks are reported by Donald Stauffer in "Critical Principles and a Sonnet," *American Scholar* 12 (1943): 61.

13. "Poetic intuition," writes Jacques Maritain, "is both creative and cognitive" and "can be considered especially either as creative, and, therefore, with respect to the engendering of the work, or as cognitive, and therefore with respect to *what is grasped* by it" (*Creative Intuition in Art and Poetry* [New York: Pantheon Books, 1953], p. 125; Maritain's italics).

Thomas Tyler, in his edition of the Sonnets (London: David Nutt, 1890), annotates 146.11: "To be understood most probably of immortal renown, which is to be purchased by sacrificing a few years to intent study and enthusiastic literary work" (p. 308).

14. James Hutton, "Analogues of Shakespeare's Sonnets 153–154: Contributions to the History of a Theme," *Modern Philology* 38 (1940): 401.

15. Ibid., p. 400.

16. As long ago as the late eighteenth century Edmund Malone astutely recognized Sonnets 153 and 154 as alternative "essays" of the poet, "who perhaps had not determined which he should prefer" but who "hardly could have intended to send them both out into the world" (*Plays and Poems of William Shakespeare*, edited by the late Edmund Malone [London, 1821], 20:356, note 8.

17. It is interesting that two "earlier" sonnets got into Part II: Sonnet 145 is earlier in one sense, as being apparently written long before the rest (see note 8, above), and Sonnet 154 in another sense, as being an early draft of 153. The former, I believe, was intentionally assigned its place in Q by Shakespeare, while the latter was included by inadvertence.

18. *SE*, 18:111–13.

19. Michael J. B. Allen apprehends Part II as a structure of interrelated parts and upholds "the appropriateness of the Quarto's ordering" on page 137 of his "Shakespeare's Man Descending a Staircase: Sonnets 126–154," *Shakespeare Survey* 31 (1978): 127–38. He arrives at a conclusion like mine but from another approach.

NOTES TO CHAPTER NINE

1. The Egyptian queen is "our terrene moon" in *Antony and Cleopatra* 3.13.153–54); she is also "eclips'd" but in the sense of 'tarnished' rather than 'expired.'

2. These "tyrants" are nonspecific; the word cannot refer to Elizabeth or James, since the attitudes taken toward the "mortal moon" and toward the implicit bringer of "this" peaceful and "balmy time" are clearly not hostile.

3. That the youth's name is omitted from a work so pledged to preserve it is continually astonishing. Was the name once there but then for some reason eliminated before publication, either to protect the privacy and repu-

tation of the subject or because Shakespeare by then had lost all interest in honoring him? I do believe that there was a specific name, now missing, and I think that those who feel they know the name and those who evoke "fiction" and "convention" to deny that it ever existed both miss the mark.

4. Hilton Landry, *Interpretations in Shakespeare's Sonnets* (Los Angeles and Berkeley: University of California Press, 1963), p. 119. Landry views the poet's love at 124.12 as exempt both from growing "under the influence of lust or desire" (= "heat") and from "death . . . to the accompaniment of weeping" (= "showers").

5. I/R remark on 125.5–8 that "the image is of court life." The image might in some vaguely figurative way weave in and out. Courtiers may bear a canopy, but they do not lay "bases for eternity"; they may be "dwellers on form and favor" *if* these are redefined as 'ceremony' and 'favoritism'; and do courtiers "pay rent" and spend themselves in simply "gazing"? Often the commentary stems from a presupposition of the friend's noble rank.

6. In his comment on 125.13–14 Stephen Booth acutely remarks that "this is the third of three successive couplets that pertain to solemn oaths and do not immediately pertain to the sonnets they conclude." His notes on all three couplets well substantiate the observation, which seems to be original with him.

7. Paul Ramsey's view of the arrangement of the Sonnets has much in common with my own. He takes Sonnets 127–52, although they "have comparatively little order, whether in chronological sequence or rearranged," to be "overlapping Sonnets 40–42 in time" and "extending an indefinite length of time before and after those poems." He takes Sonnets 1–126 to be in "Shakespeare's order and essentially chronological." But more original and to me most interesting is Ramsey's perception that "in the poems to the young man *from Sonnet 100 on* . . . the relation is nearing its end" (*The Fickle Glass* [New York: AMS Press, 1979], pp. 8, 150; italics added).

NOTES TO CHAPTER TEN

1. Edward Hubler, *The Sense of Shakespeare's Sonnets* (1952; rpt., New York: Hill and Wang, 1962), p. 5.

2. J. W. Lever, *The Elizabethan Love Sonnet* (London: Methuen, 1956; rpt., 1966), pp. 170–71. Brents Stirling's theory and practice of rearrangement are found in his *The Shakespeare Sonnet Order: Poems and Groups* (Berkeley and Los Angeles: University of California Press, 1968).

3. Other scholars may both see the author's friendship with a specific young nobleman documented in the Sonnets *and* opt for rearrangement, as do Tucker Brooke and J. Dover Wilson.

4. Gerald Hammond, in *The Reader and Shakespeare's Young Man Sonnets* (Totowa, N.J.: Barnes and Noble, 1981), says that one of his "purposes is to argue that the order of the sonnets" in Q is "substantially right." But that purpose soon changes into something else, namely into one of several "assumptions which need the reader's assent" (pp. 2, 3). Hence, the ques-

tion whether Thorpe's disputed arrangement is to be proved or assumed correct is left hanging, and the study hardly provides what I would call proof. As the title indicates, Part II of the Sonnets is left out entirely. I discuss this book in a review in *Renaissance Quarterly* 25 (1982): 119–21.

Northrop Frye, in his essay "How True a Twain," thinks "it is a reasonable assumption that Sonnets 1 through 126 are in sequence" and that "there is a logic and rightness in their order which is greatly superior to any proposed rearrangement." Fine, except that, two pages later, he entertains doubt, and not once but twice, as to "whether the sonnets are in sequence or not." Then he finds Part II "a unity" that "can hardly be a sequence"! He manages to come down on both sides of another principal question as well, that of erotic relations between the male friends. He says that "the poet . . . falls in love with the youth" but that "neither the youth nor the poet has any sexual interest except in women" (*Fables of Identity: Studies in Poetic Mythology* [New York: Harcourt, Brace and World, 1963], pp. 97, 99, 104, 89, 96).

5. David Kalstone, *Sidney's Poetry: Contexts and Interpretations* (1965; New York: Norton, 1970), p. 133.

6. William A. Ringler, Jr., ed., *The Poems of Sir Philip Sidney* (Oxford: Clarendon Press, 1962), p. lix.

7. Kalstone, *Sidney's Poetry*, pp. 175, 133.

8. Ringler, ed., *Poems of . . . Sidney*, p. xlix.

9. Lever, *Elizabethan Love Sonnet*, p. 56.

10. Kalstone, *Sidney's Poetry*, p. 180.

11. Frye, *Fables of Identity*, p. 92. He ridicules reading the Sonnets as "a transcript of experience," and yet he also discovers a vertical scheme that consists of "three main levels of experience," the lowest being the "world of ordinary experience," which is "associated with winter and absence," where the poet operates as a "busy actor-dramatist" (ibid., pp. 90, 101). Nothing is said in the sequence about the sonneteer as either actor or dramatist, and so a "transcript of experience" is here smuggled in.

12. Lever, *Elizabethan Love Sonnet*, p. 181.

13. Ringler, ed., *Poems of . . . Sidney*, p. 440.

14. Denis Donoghue, "Shakespeare at Sonnets," *Sewanee Review* 88 (1980): 463.

15. As James Winny rightly recognizes, nowhere does "the speaker describe himself as a dramatist or associate himself with the stage" but, rather, "presents himself as a poet whose writing is confined to lyrical and complimentary verses" (*The Master-Mistress: A Study of Shakespeare's Sonnets* [London: Chatto and Windus, 1968], p. 81).

16. Frye, *Fables of Identity*, pp. 96, 99.

17. *Lycidas*, with, *inter alia*, its allusion to Christ in line 173 and its vision of Lycidas among the saints in heaven, is indisputably Christian; but the ideas that render it so are not to be found in Sonnet 146.

18. Giorgio Melchiori finds the Pauline "doctrine of the resurrection of the body of man" missing from Sonnet 146 and writes: "the Soul postulated by Shakespeare debars the Body and man as such from any hope of a new life

after death. What is missing in the sonnet is the specifically *Christian* idea of redemption." Melchiori does think, however, that Shakespeare "accepts the idea of a world of immortal souls" (*Shakespeare's Dramatic Meditations* [Oxford: Clarendon Press, 1976], pp. 190–91, 182–83).

19. Paul Ramsey, *The Fickle Glass*, 152–56.

20. George Santayana, *Interpretations of Poetry and Religion* (New York: Scribner's, 1900), pp. 163, 152. Emphasis added.

Index to the Sonnets

Individual Sonnets

Groups of Sonnets

General Index

Adams, J. Q., 231 n.20
Alchemist, The, 108
Allen, Michael J. B., 238 n.19
Amoretti, Epithalamion, 7, 218; and the
 anacreontics after the sonnets, 180;
 comic course of love in, 213–14; the
 kiss in, 72; organization of, 216; procreation in, 13, 226 n.5; repeated
 sonnet in, 236 n.10; ship conceits in,
 120; the three Elizabeths in, 217
Antithetical sonnets, 180–86
Aristotle, 215; on friendship, 65, 231
 n.30
Arrangement of the Sonnets. *See* Order
 of the Sonnets
Astrophel and Stella, 7, 214, 221; catastrophe at the end of, 213; the kiss in,
 232 n.35; organization of, 215–16;
 and the Petrarchan mode, 215–16;
 Sidney's personal experience reflected
 in, 216–17; on sleep and dreams, 67;
 Sonnets 2, 23; Tenth Song, 227, n.11
Auden, W. H., 79–80

Barnfield, Richard: *Certain Sonnets,* 65,
 75, 216; *The Tears of an Affectionate
 Shepherd,* 65–66, 75, 231 n.26
Bawdy: as glossed with regard to the
 Sonnets, 49–50, 232 n.41; homoerotic
 import of, suppressed, 49–52; interest
 in, since Partridge, 49; texts dense in,
 43–49, 52–53, 106–8, 119–20
Beauty: associated in the friend with
 sexuality, 13–14, 19, 41; as basis of
 persuasions to breed, 10–11; as cause
 of love in Renaissance psychology,
 22–23, 67–68, 182; of the friend, 7,
 55, 65, 68; a key concept of Part I, 9;
 of mistress and of friend, compared;

186–87; poet feels deficient in, 47,
 85–86; poet's reactions to the youth's,
 28, 80; theme of, yoked with theme of
 love, 21; in two types of young men,
 56. *See also* Friend; Love
Bennett, Josephine Waters, 225 n.2
Benson, John, 2–3
Bible, 184; Genesis 1:28, 2:18, and 2:24,
 12; Gen. 3:6, 129; Gen. 38:9–10, 17,
 227 n.13; Gen. 2:7, 169; Jeremiah 5:8,
 53
Bisexuality: Freud on, 81, 82; of the persona, 81–82, 91, 92, 96, 142, 151, 154,
 208. *See also* Homoeroticism
Blackmore, Richard B., 5
Booth, Stephen, 138, 237 n.8, 239 n.6;
 on bawdy, 232 n.41; on Christian allusions, 226 n.4; on homosexuality,
 77; on masturbation, 17; on "passion"
 at Sonnet 20.2, 229 n.6; on poet-friend
 relationship, 232 n.40
Brooke, Tucker, 203, 228 n.17, 239 n.3
Bush, Douglas, 64–65, 76
Butler, Samuel, 233 n.13

Castiglione, Baldassare, *The Courtier,*
 22
Chapman, George, 3–4
Cicero, 65
Coleman, E. A. M., 6, 50, 104, 120, 230
 nn.8,14
Craft, Robert, 79–80
Cruttwell, Patrick, 159, 230 n.14, 236
 n.3

Dante, 174, 217, 237 n.11
Donne, John, 124; *Anniversaries,* 64,
 236 n.3; "The Canonization," 74, 85;
 "The Good-morrow," 74; *Holy Son-*